Recipes: Classic Fren

D0326187

Contents

Foods of the World

TIME-LIFE BOOKS, ALEXANDRIA, VIRGINIA

Stocks & Sauces

STOCKS: Fine French cooking owes much of its distinction to the stocks used in its preparation. These stocks are called "fonds de cuisine"—foundations of cooking—and no classic French cook would be without them. Stocks are easily made from various kinds of meat, fowl, or fish trimmings, vegetables, herbs and water—simmered slowly together to concentrate their flavors.

Though their cooking often takes many hours, the process requires little supervision. The completed stocks may be refrigerated for days or frozen for weeks or even months. (For freezing, divide a stock into small quantities that can be thawed or melted quickly.) With the exception of chicken stock, canned broths cannot be considered an acceptable substitute for the homemade varieties.

The recipes below and on the following pages describe the most frequently used chicken, beef, veal and fish stocks as well as the techniques for clarifying them, making aspic and reducing meat stock to the essence known as "glace de viande."

Fond blanc de boeuf et fond brun de boeuf
WHITE AND BROWN BEEF STOCK

To make about 2 quarts

3 pounds beef shin bones, sawed into 2-inch lengths

3 pounds beef marrow bones, sawed into 2-inch lengths

2 pounds beef short ribs, sawed into 2-inch lengths

2 pounds veal shank, sawed into 2-inch lengths

1 pound chicken parts: wings, necks and backs

5 to 6 quarts cold water

2 medium-sized onions, peeled

2 medium-sized leeks, including the green tops, trimmed and thoroughly washed to rid them of sand

2 medium-sized carrots, scraped and cut into 1-inch lengths

5 fresh parsley sprigs

2 fresh thyme sprigs or ½ teaspoon crumbled dried thyme

1 unpeeled garlic clove, crushed with the side of a cleaver or heavy knife

1 medium-sized bay leaf

½ teaspoon whole black peppercorns

1 teaspoon salt

FOND BLANC DE BOEUF (WHITE BEEF STOCK): Combine the shin and marrow bones, short ribs, veal, chicken and 5 quarts of water in a 12-quart stock pot. The water should cover the meat and bones by at least 2 inches; if necessary add up to 1 quart more. Bring to a simmer slowly over moderate heat, skimming off and discarding the foam and scum as they rise to the surface. Then reduce the heat and simmer undisturbed and uncovered for about 30 minutes. (Do not let the liquid come to a boil at any point, or the finished stock will be cloudy.)

Add the onions, leeks, carrots, parsley, thyme, garlic, bay leaf, peppercorns and salt. Stir, partially cover and simmer for 7 to 8 hours.

With a slotted spoon, pick out and discard the meat, bones and chicken. Strain the stock into a large bowl through a fine sieve lined with a double thickness of dampened cheesecloth. Discard the vegetables.

Let the stock cool to room temperature; then refrigerate uncovered until it is thoroughly chilled and the surface is covered with a layer of solidified fat. Sealed with its fat, the stock may be kept safely in the refrigerator for 3 or 4 days. Before using it, carefully lift off and discard the fat. If you prefer to freeze the stock (it can be kept frozen for several months), remove the layer of fat as soon as it has solidified and cover the bowl or other container tightly with foil or plastic wrap.

ADDITIONAL INGREDIENT FOR FOND
  BRUN DE BOEUF
2 tablespoons clarified butter *(page 13)*

FOND BRUN DE BOEUF (BROWN BEEF STOCK): In a heavy 12-inch skillet, preferably a sauté pan, heat 2 tablespoons of clarified butter over moderate heat for 10 seconds. Brown the shin and marrow bones, short ribs, veal and chicken in separate batches, taking care not to crowd the pan. Turn the pieces frequently with tongs so that they color richly and evenly, and regulate the heat to prevent the meat or bones from burning. As they brown, transfer the pieces to a 12-quart stock pot.

Add the onions and carrots to the fat remaining in the skillet and, stirring from time to time, brown them lightly on all sides. With a slotted spoon transfer the onions and carrots to the stock pot. Pour 1 quart of the water into the skillet and bring to a boil over high heat, stirring constantly and scraping in the brown particles that cling to the bottom and sides of the pan. Pour the entire contents of the skillet into the stock pot and add the remaining 4 to 5 quarts of cold water (or as much as you need to cover the meat and bones). Following the recipe above, bring to a simmer slowly over moderate heat, skimming off and discarding the foam and scum as they rise to the surface. Then simmer the brown stock for 7 to 8 hours and follow the straining, cooling and storing procedures described above for the white stock.

Fond blanc de veau et fond brun de veau
WHITE AND BROWN VEAL STOCK

To make about 2 quarts

5 pounds meaty veal shank, sawed into 2-inch lengths
2 pounds meaty veal shin bones, sawed into 2-inch lengths
1 pound veal marrow bones
2 pounds chicken parts: wings, necks and backs
5 to 6 quarts cold water
2 medium-sized onions, peeled and cut into quarters
2 medium-sized carrots, scraped and cut into 1-inch-thick rounds
2 medium-sized celery stalks, including the green leaves, cut into 1-inch lengths
2 medium-sized leeks, including 2 inches of the green tops, trimmed, cut lengthwise into quarters and washed thoroughly to remove any hidden pockets of sand
1 large unpeeled garlic clove, crushed with the side of a cleaver or heavy knife
10 fresh parsley sprigs
2 fresh thyme sprigs or ½ teaspoon crumbled dried thyme
1 large bay leaf
½ teaspoon whole black peppercorns
1 teaspoon salt

FOND BLANC DE VEAU (WHITE VEAL STOCK): Combine the shank, shin, marrow bones, chicken and 5 quarts of water in a 12-quart stock pot. The water should cover the meat and bones by at least 2 inches; if necessary add up to 1 quart more. Bring to a simmer slowly over moderate heat, skimming off the foam and scum as they rise to the surface. Reduce the heat and simmer undisturbed and uncovered for 30 minutes. (Do not let the liquid boil at any point, or the stock will be cloudy.)

Add the onions, carrots, celery, leeks, garlic, parsley, thyme, bay leaf, peppercorns and salt. Stir, partially cover and simmer for 7 to 8 hours.

With a slotted spoon, pick out and discard the meat, bones and chicken. Strain the stock into a large bowl through a fine sieve lined with a double thickness of dampened cheesecloth. Discard the vegetables.

Let the stock cool to room temperature, stirring it from time to time; then refrigerate uncovered until it is thoroughly chilled and the surface is covered with a layer of solidified fat. Sealed with its fat, the stock may be kept safely in the refrigerator for 3 or 4 days. Before using it, carefully lift off and discard the fat. If you prefer to freeze the stock (it can be kept frozen for several months), remove the layer of fat as soon as it has solidified and cover the container tightly with foil or plastic wrap.

ADDITIONAL INGREDIENTS FOR FOND BRUN DE VEAU
2 tablespoons clarified butter (page 13)
2 medium-sized firm ripe tomatoes, quartered
½ cup canned unflavored tomato purée

FOND BRUN DE VEAU (BROWN VEAL STOCK): In a heavy 12-inch skillet, preferably a sauté pan, heat 2 tablespoons of clarified butter over moderate heat for about 10 seconds. Brown the veal shank, shin, marrow bones and chicken in batches, taking care not to crowd the pan. Turn the pieces frequently with tongs so that they color richly and evenly, and regulate the heat to prevent the meat or bones from burning. As they brown, transfer the pieces to a 12-quart stock pot.

Add the onions and carrots to the skillet and, stirring from time to time, brown them lightly on all sides. With a slotted spoon, transfer the onions and carrots to the stock pot. Pour 1 quart of the water into the skillet and bring to a boil over high heat, scraping in the brown particles that cling to the bottom and sides of the pan. Pour the contents of the skillet into the stock pot and add the remaining 4 to 5 quarts of cold water (or as much as you need to cover the meat and bones). Following the recipe above, bring to a simmer slowly over moderate heat, skimming off and discarding the foam and scum. Add the tomatoes and tomato purée. Then simmer the brown stock for about 7 hours and follow the straining, cooling and storing procedures described above for the white stock.

Fumet de poisson
FISH STOCK

To make about 2 quarts

3 pounds fish trimmings: the heads, tails and bones of any firm white fish, preferably flounder, whiting or halibut
2 quarts cold water
1 cup coarsely chopped onions
¾ cup coarsely chopped celery with the leaves

⅓ cup coarsely chopped leek tops, thoroughly washed
1 medium-sized bay leaf
2 fresh thyme sprigs or ½ teaspoon crumbled dried thyme
1 teaspoon salt
5 whole black peppercorns

ADDITIONAL INGREDIENT FOR
FUMET DE POISSON WITH WINE
1 cup dry white wine

Wash the fish trimmings in a deep bowl set under cold running water. Drain, then mash the pieces of fish with the back of a large spoon.

Place the mashed fish in a 6- to 8-quart enameled or stainless-steel saucepan or casserole, and pour in the water and the wine, if you are using it. Bring slowly to a simmer over moderate heat and cook uncovered for 5 minutes, skimming off the foam and scum as they rise to the surface. Add the onions, celery, leek, bay leaf, thyme, salt and peppercorns, and reduce the heat to low. Partially cover the pan and simmer for 30 minutes, skimming the surface every 10 minutes or so.

Remove the pan from the heat and, with a slotted spoon, lift out and discard the fish and vegetables. Strain the stock into a deep bowl through a fine sieve lined with a double thickness of dampened cheesecloth. The stock will keep refrigerated for 2 or 3 days or it can be cooled to room temperature, covered tightly and frozen.

Fond blanc de volaille
WHITE CHICKEN STOCK

To make about 5 quarts

A 6-pound stewing fowl, cut into 6 or 8 pieces, plus 2 pounds of chicken wings, necks and backs, or a 3-pound chicken, cut into quarters, plus 5 pounds of chicken wings, necks and backs
5 to 6 quarts cold water
3 medium-sized carrots, scraped and coarsely chopped
2 medium-sized leeks, including 2 inches of the green tops, trimmed, cut lengthwise into quarters and washed thoroughly to remove any hidden pockets of sand
2 celery stalks with the leaves
1 medium-sized onion, peeled and pierced with 1 whole clove
⅓ cup coarsely chopped parsley
1 medium-sized unpeeled garlic clove, crushed with the side of a cleaver or heavy knife
1 medium-sized bay leaf
2 fresh thyme sprigs or ½ teaspoon crumbled dried thyme
1 teaspoon salt
10 whole black peppercorns

Combine the fowl or the chicken and chicken parts with 5 quarts of the water in a 10- to 12-quart stock pot or casserole. If the water does not cover the chicken by at least 2 inches, add up to 1 quart more.

Bring the liquid to a simmer slowly over moderate heat, skimming off and discarding the foam and scum with a large spoon as they rise to the surface. Reduce the heat and simmer undisturbed and uncovered for 30 to 45 minutes. (Do not let the liquid come to a boil at any point, or the finished stock will be cloudy.)

Then add the carrots, leeks, celery, onion, parsley, garlic, bay leaf, thyme, salt and black peppercorns. Partially cover the pot and continue to simmer over low heat for 2½ hours longer, or until the stock has acquired an intense and definite flavor.

Turn off the heat. With tongs or a slotted spoon, pick out and discard the chicken or fowl, and the vegetables. Strain the stock into a large deep bowl through a fine sieve lined with a double thickness of dampened cheesecloth. Do not add salt or season the stock further. Set the bowl aside uncovered and, stirring the stock from time to time, let it cool to room temperature.

Refrigerate the stock uncovered until it is thoroughly chilled and the surface is covered with a layer of solidified fat.

Sealed with its fat, the stock may be safely kept in the refrigerator for 3 or 4 days. Before using it, carefully lift off and discard the fat. If you prefer to freeze the stock (it can be kept frozen for several months), remove the layer of fat as soon as it has solidified and cover the bowl or other container tightly with foil or plastic wrap.

Glace de viande
MEAT GLAZE

To make about ½ cup

2 quarts *fond brun de veau (page*	4), strained and thoroughly degreased

Pour the *fond brun de veau* into a heavy 12-inch enameled-iron or copper skillet and bring it to a simmer over moderate heat. Reduce the heat to low and let the stock cook until it has reduced to 2 cups.

Transfer the stock to a small, heavy copper or enameled-iron pan and cook over the lowest possible heat, stirring occasionally, until it is reduced to ½ cup of thick syrupy glaze.

Strain the glaze into a small bowl or jar through a fine sieve lined with dampened cheesecloth. The glaze, tightly covered, can safely be kept in the refrigerator for several months. If any mold should form on the top, simply scrape it off with a spoon.

SAUCES: Sauces are the hallmark and the glory of classic French cooking. At first glance, they seem to be innumerable. In fact, however, there are about a dozen basic formulations and the myriads of recipes in a "saucier's" repertory are usually made by simply amplifying them with other ingredients. Thus "sauce velouptée" with cream added to it becomes "sauce suprême"; "sauce béchamel" with grated cheese and sometimes with egg yolks, is "sauce Mornay." Most sauces are best prepared shortly before serving, but the three basic sauces that follow—"fond lié," "béchamel" and "veloutée"—may be prepared at your leisure and stored in the refrigerator for days, or in the freezer for months. (For freezing, divide a sauce into small quantities that can be thawed or melted quickly.) These sauces should not be reheated more than once or twice; after that they may thin out and separate. "Fond lié," which is a sauce of brown stock thickened with arrowroot, has taken the place of the more complicated "sauce espagnole" in most contemporary French kitchens. For traditionalists, there is a recipe for "sauce espagnole" in the Recipe Booklet.

Caramel
CARAMEL FOOD COLORING

To make about 1½ cups

1 medium-sized onion, peeled and	cut into ¼-inch-thick slices 1 cup water 1½ cups sugar

In a heavy 6- to 8-cup enameled-iron saucepan, cook the onion slices over

Continued on next page

moderate heat. Do not use butter or oil and stir until the onions are an almost black mahogany color on both sides. Stirring constantly, add ½ cup of the water and the sugar and continue to cook until the mixture foams up and rises in the pan. Stir in the remaining ½ cup of water. (Do not be alarmed if the caramel hardens at this point.) Still stirring, continue to cook until the hardened caramel melts and the syrup is smooth. Strain the caramel through a fine sieve into a heatproof jar. Cool to room temperature, then cover with a lid. The caramel may be kept at room temperature indefinitely. Caramel is used to color such sauces as *fond lié* (*page 10*).

Sauce Mornay
BÉCHAMEL SAUCE WITH EGG YOLKS, CREAM AND GRATED CHEESE

To make about 2 cups

1½ cups *sauce béchamel (opposite)*
¼ cup heavy cream, plus ¼ cup
   heavy cream, whipped into soft
   peaks
2 egg yolks

Salt
Freshly ground white pepper
¼ cup finely grated imported
   Parmesan combined with ¼ cup
   finely grated imported Gruyère
   cheese

In a heavy 8- to 10-inch skillet, combine the *sauce béchamel* and ¼ cup of heavy cream. Stirring constantly with a wire whisk, cook over low heat until it is heated through, but do not let it come to a boil. Whisk in the egg yolks, one at a time, add a little salt and pepper, bring the sauce to a simmer and cook for about a minute longer, stirring constantly. Taste for seasoning. Remove the skillet from the heat and stir in half of the grated cheese. At this point you may dot the sauce with butter to prevent a skin from forming on the top, then cover it and set it aside for 2 or 3 hours before finishing. Just before using, fold in the whipped cream. Spread the sauce over the dish you are serving, sprinkle the top with the remaining cheese and place the dish under a broiler for a minute or so until the top is golden brown. Serve at once.

    NOTE: Sauce Mornay is used with meat, fish and such vegetables as string beans and broccoli. It can also be used with pasta.

Sauce veloutée
VELOUTÉ SAUCE

To make about 2 cups

2 cups white stock: *fond blanc de
   volaille, fond blanc de veau* or
   fumet de poisson (pages 6, 4

and 5)
4 tablespoons unsalted butter,
   preferably clarified butter *(page 13)*
6 tablespoons flour

Bring the stock to a simmer over moderate heat. Meanwhile, in a heavy 1½- to 2-quart saucepan, melt the butter over low heat. Remove the pan from the heat and stir in the flour with a wire whisk. Then return to low heat and, stirring constantly, cook for about 2 minutes, or until the roux foams.

Pour in the heated stock and beat vigorously with a whisk until the roux and liquid are thoroughly blended. Scrape the sides of the pan to ensure that all of the roux is incorporated into the sauce. Increase the heat to moderate and, still stirring, cook until the sauce comes to a boil and thickens enough to coat the wires of the whisk heavily.

Reduce the heat to the lowest possible point and simmer the sauce gently for 15 minutes, whisking it every few minutes to prevent the bottom from scorching. Then strain the sauce through a fine sieve set over a bowl. If you do not plan to use the sauce immediately, cool it to room temperature, stirring occasionally. Tightly covered, the velouté may safely be kept in the refrigerator for 10 days, or in the freezer up to three months.

Sauce béchamel
BÉCHAMEL SAUCE

To make about 2 cups

2 cups milk
1 tablespoon finely chopped onions
⅛ teaspoon ground nutmeg, preferably freshly grated

1 sprig fresh thyme or ⅛ teaspoon crumbled dried thyme
⅛ teaspoon ground white pepper
4 tablespoons unsalted butter, preferably clarified butter (page 13)
6 tablespoons flour

Combine the milk, onions, nutmeg, thyme and pepper in a small saucepan and bring to a boil over moderate heat. Immediately remove the pan from the heat, cover tightly and set aside for about 10 minutes.

In a heavy 1- to 2-quart enameled-iron or copper saucepan, melt the butter over low heat. Remove the pan from the heat and stir in the flour with a wire whisk to make a smooth roux. Then return to low heat and, stirring constantly, cook for about 2 minutes, or until the roux foams.

Pour in the milk mixture and beat vigorously with a whisk until the roux and liquid are thoroughly blended. Scrape the sides of the pan to ensure that all of the roux is incorporated into the sauce. Increase the heat to moderate and, still stirring constantly, cook until the béchamel comes to a boil and thickens enough to coat the wires of the whisk heavily.

Reduce the heat to the lowest possible point and, stirring occasionally, simmer the sauce gently for about 15 minutes to remove any taste of raw flour. Then strain the sauce through a fine sieve set over a bowl, pressing down gently on the onions with the back of a spoon to extract all their moisture before throwing them away. If you do not plan to use the sauce immediately, cool it to room temperature, stirring occasionally. Tightly covered, the béchamel may safely be kept in the refrigerator for 10 days, or in the freezer up to three months.

Fond lié

BROWN SAUCE WITH ARROWROOT

To make about 1 quart

1 quart *fond brun de veau (page 4)*
½ cup coarsely chopped fresh
   mushrooms

3 sprigs fresh parsley
5 tablespoons arrowroot
⅓ cup cold water
Caramel *(page 7)*

In a heavy 2-quart saucepan, bring the *fond brun de veau,* mushrooms and parsley to a simmer over moderate heat. Reduce the heat to low and cook uncovered for about 15 minutes. Combine the arrowroot and water in a bowl and stir until the arrowroot has dissolved. Stirring with a wire whisk, gradually pour the mixture into the stock. Add the caramel a few drops at a time until the sauce is a rich brown color, ¼ teaspoon will probably be enough. Simmer the sauce for 8 to 10 minutes, stirring occasionally. The sauce is ready when it thickens lightly. Pour the contents of the pan through a fine sieve set over a bowl, pressing down gently on the mushrooms with the back of a spoon.

If you are not using the *fond lié* at once and plan to set it aside, dot the top with 1 tablespoon unsalted butter cut into ¼-inch bits. Tip the pan from side to side until the butter melts and coats the entire surface of the sauce. When cooled to room temperature the sauce may be covered and refrigerated up to a week, or kept in the freezer up to three months.

Sauce espagnole

BROWN SAUCE WITH FLOUR

To make 5 to 6 cups

4 ounces fresh beef suet, cut into
   ¼-inch bits
1 cup flour
2 quarts *fond brun de boeuf (page 2)*
3 tablespoons clarified butter *(page 13)*
1 cup finely chopped onions

⅔ cup finely chopped celery
⅓ cup finely chopped scraped
   carrots
1 large bay leaf
2 sprigs fresh thyme or ½ teaspoon
   crumbled dried thyme
1 teaspoon tomato paste
3 fresh parsley sprigs

In a heavy 8-inch skillet, cook the suet over low heat, stirring frequently with a wooden spoon until the bits are crisp but not brown and have rendered all their fat. Strain the fat through a fine sieve into a heatproof measuring cup. There should be about ½ cup; if there is less, add enough vegetable oil to make the required amount.

Pour the fat into a heavy 4- to 5-quart casserole and, with the wooden spoon, mix in the flour to make a roux. Stirring constantly, cook over moderate heat until the roux turns a nutlike brown. Watch carefully for any sign of burning and regulate the heat accordingly. Pour in the stock in a thin stream and continue to stir (now with a whisk) until the roux dissolves. When the mixture comes to a boil and thickens heavily, reduce the heat to the lowest possible point and let the sauce simmer uncovered and undisturbed while you proceed with the next step.

In the skillet, melt the butter over moderate heat but do not let it brown. Add the onions, celery, carrots, bay leaf and thyme (this mixture is called a *mirepoix*). Stirring frequently, cook for 5 to 8 minutes, or until the vegetables are soft and a delicate golden color.

Add the *mirepoix,* tomato paste and parsley to the simmering sauce and continue to cook over the lowest possible heat for 4½ to 5 hours. Check from time to time and as fat and scum accumulate on the surface, skim off and discard them. The sauce when done should have a glistening sheen and be entirely free of fat.

Strain the sauce through a fine sieve set over a bowl. Use at once, or cool the sauce to room temperature. Then cover the bowl tightly with foil or plastic wrap and refrigerate until ready to use. *Sauce espagnole* can safely be kept, tightly covered, in the refrigerator for 2 weeks or in the freezer for several months. In cooking, it may be substituted for *fond lié*.

Sauce bordelaise
RED WINE SAUCE WITH SHALLOTS AND BEEF MARROW

To make about 1 cup

2 ounces beef marrow
1½ cups dry red Bordeaux wine
⅓ cup finely chopped shallots
1 small bay leaf

⅛ teaspoon crumbled dried thyme
⅛ teaspoon freshly ground black
  pepper
½ cup *fond lié (opposite)*
¼ teaspoon strained fresh lemon juice
½ teaspoon salt

Place the beef marrow in a small bowl and pour in enough cold water to cover it completely. Refrigerate for at least 30 minutes to remove any traces of blood and to firm the marrow for dicing.

Meanwhile, combine the wine, shallots, bay leaf, thyme and pepper in a small, heavy enameled-iron or copper saucepan. Bring to a boil over high heat and cook briskly, stirring occasionally, until the mixture has reduced to about ½ cup.

Add the *fond lié* and, stirring from time to time, simmer uncovered over low heat for 20 minutes. Then strain the sauce through a fine sieve set over a bowl, pressing down gently on the shallots with the back of a spoon to extract their juice before discarding them.

Drain the marrow, pat it completely dry with paper towels, and cut it into ¼-inch dice. Return the sauce to the saucepan. Over low heat, stir in the marrow, lemon juice and salt. Taste for seasoning. Serve at once or cool to room temperature and refrigerate until ready to use. Then reheat briefly but do not let the sauce come to a boil.

Sauce bordelaise may be served with a beef fillet cooked following the directions for *filet de boeuf Richelieu (page 88)* or with large steaks.

Beurre moussant
FOAMING BUTTER

To make about ¾ cup

¼ cup water
2 tablespoons strained fresh lemon
  juice

⅛ teaspoon salt
8 tablespoons unsalted butter (1
  quarter-pound stick), cut into
  1½-inch bits

In a heavy 1-quart saucepan, bring the water, lemon juice and salt to a boil over high heat. Sliding the pan back and forth over the heat, drop in the butter a few pieces at a time. Still moving the pan gently back and forth, cook over high heat until the butter melts, foams and rises about 3 inches in the pan. Pour the foaming butter into a sauceboat and serve with such vegetables as asparagus, artichokes, broccoli and boiled potatoes, or with poached fish.

Sauce Nantua
BÉCHAMEL SAUCE WITH CRAYFISH BUTTER

To make about 2 cups

BEURRE D'ÉCREVISSES
¼ pound live fresh-water crayfish,
  or substitute ¼ pound uncooked
  shrimp in their shells
8 tablespoons unsalted butter (1
  quarter-pound stick), melted but
  not browned
2 tablespoons hot water

2 cups *sauce béchamel (page 9)*
⅓ cup heavy cream
½ cup *fumet de poisson (page
  5)*
½ teaspoon salt
⅛ teaspoon freshly ground white
  pepper
1 teaspoon canned tomato paste

BEURRE D'ÉCREVISSES (CRAYFISH BUTTER): Drop the crayfish (or shrimp) into enough boiling water to cover them by at least 1 inch and cook briskly, uncovered, for 4 minutes. Drain the crayfish (or shrimp) in a sieve or colander and chop them coarsely. Then put the crayfish (or shrimp), shells and all, through the coarsest blade of a food grinder. Transfer the ground mixture to the jar of an electric blender, pour in the melted butter and hot water and blend at high speed for 30 seconds. Turn off the machine, scrape down the sides of the jar with a rubber spatula, and blend again until the mixture is a smooth purée.

With a spatula, scrape the purée into a small saucepan and, stirring constantly, simmer over moderate heat for 5 minutes. Force the purée through the finest disc of a food mill or rub it through a fine sieve with the back of a spoon, pressing down hard on the shells to extract all their juices before discarding them. Cover the crayfish butter with foil or plastic wrap and refrigerate until ready to use.

To prepare the *sauce Nantua,* bring the *sauce béchamel* to a simmer in a heavy 1- to 1½-quart saucepan over moderate heat. Pour in the cream and, stirring frequently, simmer until the mixture is reduced to about 1½ cups. Add the *fumet de poisson,* salt and pepper, and stir until the sauce is smooth. Remove the pan from the heat and whisk in the *beurre d'écrevisses* a tablespoonful at a time. Add the tomato paste and taste for seasoning. The *sauce Nantua* may be served at once or tightly covered and refrigerated, then warmed briefly over low heat before serving. The sauce may be served with *turban de sole, quenelles de brochet* and *mousse de sole (Recipe Index).*

Sauce mayonnaise
MAYONNAISE

To make about 2 cups

4 large egg yolks, at room
  temperature
2 to 3 teaspoons strained fresh

lemon juice or 2 to 3 teaspoons
  wine vinegar
1 teaspoon salt
⅛ teaspoon freshly ground white
  pepper
2 cups vegetable oil

In a deep mixing bowl, beat the egg yolks, lemon juice or vinegar, salt and pepper vigorously for about 2 minutes until they thicken and cling to the beater. Then beat in ½ cup of the oil, ½ teaspoon at a time; make sure each addition is absorbed before adding more. By the time ½ cup of the oil has been beaten in, the sauce should be the consistency of very thick cream. Pour in the remaining oil in a slow, thin stream, beating constantly. Taste for seasoning.

NOTE: Although it is not strictly classic, you may wish to flavor the mayonnaise more highly by adding 2 teaspoons of Dijon-style prepared mustard to the egg-yolk mixture before beating in the oil.

Beurre clarifié
CLARIFIED BUTTER

To make 10 or 12 tablespoons

½ pound unsalted butter, cut into
  ¼-inch bits

In a small, heavy saucepan, heat the butter over low heat, turning it about to melt it slowly and completely without letting it brown. Remove the pan from the heat and let the butter rest for a minute or so. Then skim off the foam and discard it. Tipping the pan slightly, spoon the clear butter into a bowl. Discard the milky solids that will settle at the bottom of the pan. If you are not using the butter immediately, refrigerate it in a tightly covered container. Clarified butter can safely be kept for a month.

Sauce vin blanc
FISH VELOUTÉ WITH WHITE WINE AND EGG YOLKS

To make about 2 cups

2 cups *sauce veloutée (page 8)*
  made with *fumet de poisson* with
  wine *(page 5)*
½ cup *fumet de poisson* with wine
2 egg yolks, lightly beaten

8 tablespoons (1 quarter-pound
  stick) unsalted butter, chilled and
  cut into ¼-inch bits
1 tablespoon strained fresh lemon
  juice
Salt
Freshly ground white pepper

In a heavy 1- to 1½-quart saucepan, bring the *sauce veloutée* to a simmer over moderate heat. Whisking constantly, pour in the *fumet de poisson* and the egg yolks. Stirring frequently with a whisk, simmer until the sauce is reduced to about 1¾ cups. Do not let the sauce come to a boil or it may curdle. Remove the pan from the heat and whisk in the butter bits, a tablespoon at a time. Add the lemon juice and season to taste with salt and white pepper. Serve at once or refrigerate tightly covered and warm briefly over low heat before serving.

Sauce hollandaise et sauce mousseline
HOLLANDAISE SAUCE AND HOLLANDAISE SAUCE WITH WHIPPED CREAM

To make about 2 cups

1 pound butter, clarified *(page 13)*
6 egg yolks
¼ cup cold water
⅓ cup strained fresh lemon juice

1 teaspoon salt
A pinch of ground hot red pepper
  (cayenne)

ADDITIONAL INGREDIENT FOR SAUCE
  MOUSSELINE
1 cup heavy cream, chilled

Warm and melt the clarified butter in a small, heavy saucepan over low heat. Meanwhile, in a heavy 2- to 2½-quart enameled-iron or copper saucepan, beat the egg yolks and water vigorously together with a wire whisk until they are foamy. Place the egg mixture over the lowest possible heat and continue whisking until it thickens and almost doubles in volume. Do not let the eggs come anywhere near a boil or they will curdle; if necessary, lift the pan off the heat from time to time to cool it.

Still whisking constantly, pour in the hot butter as slowly as possible, and continue to beat until the sauce thickens heavily. Beat in the lemon juice, salt and red pepper and taste for seasoning. Serve at once or set the pan in a bowl of hot water and keep the sauce warm for up to 30 minutes before serving.

SAUCE MOUSSELINE: Prepare the hollandaise sauce exactly as described above and set it aside to cool to room temperature. As soon as it is cool, whip the cream in a chilled bowl with a wire whisk, or a rotary or electric beater. When the cream is stiff enough to stand in unwavering peaks on the beater, fold it gently but thoroughly into the *sauce hollandaise* and serve at once.

Soups

Consommé de volaille royale
CHICKEN CONSOMMÉ WITH CUSTARD GARNISH

To serve 8

1 teaspoon butter, softened
1 whole egg
2 egg yolks
¼ cup heavy cream
¼ cup *fond blanc de volaille (page 6)*, or substitute ¼ cup canned chicken stock, chilled, then

degreased
A pinch of ground nutmeg, preferably freshly grated
A pinch of freshly ground white pepper
⅛ teaspoon salt
Consommé de fond blanc de volaille (page 24)

Preheat the oven to 300°. With a pastry brush, spread the softened butter over the bottom and sides of an 8-inch-square glass baking dish.

With a whisk or a rotary or electric beater, beat the egg and egg yolks together in a deep bowl. Beat in the cream, chicken stock, nutmeg, pepper and salt and pour into the buttered dish. Place the dish in a roasting pan set in the middle of the oven. Add enough boiling water to the pan to reach about halfway up the sides of the dish. Bake for 20 minutes, or until a knife inserted in the center comes out clean. Cool to room temperature, then refrigerate until the custard *(royale)* is thoroughly chilled.

To unmold the *royale,* run a spatula around the sides of the dish and dip the bottom in hot water for a few seconds. Place an inverted plate on top of the dish and, grasping plate and dish together firmly, turn them over. Rap the plate on a table and the *royale* should slide out easily.

Bring the consommé to a simmer. With a truffle cutter or a knife, cut the *royale* into decorative shapes. Place the *royale* garnish in a heated tureen or individual soup plates and pour in a little consommé. Let the garnish heat for a minute, then add the remaining consommé and serve.

Petite marmite
BEEF CONSOMMÉ WITH FINELY CUT CHICKEN, BEEF AND VEGETABLES

To serve 6

A 2-pound white cabbage
1 teaspoon salt
6 ounces fresh beef marrow, in the
    largest pieces possible
4 to 6 tablespoons clarified butter
    (page 13)
3 slices homemade-type white bread,
    each about ½-inch thick, squared
    and trimmed of all crusts,
    and cut diagonally into 4 triangles
A 6- to 8-ounce chicken breast,
    skinned, boned and cut into
    ½-inch cubes
2 chicken thighs, skinned, boned
    and cut into ½-inch cubes
1 pound lean boneless beef,
    preferably top round, trimmed
    of excess fat and cut into
    ½-inch cubes

2 quarts consommé *(page 24)*
    made with *fond blanc de boeuf*
3 medium-sized carrots, scraped and
    cut into 12 olivelike shapes each
    about 1 inch long
3 medium-sized white turnips,
    peeled and cut into 12 olivelike
    shapes each about 1 inch long
1 large leek, white part only,
    trimmed, cut lengthwise into
    quarters, washed thoroughly to
    remove any hidden pockets of
    sand, and cut lengthwise into
    strips ⅛ inch wide and 1 to
    1½ inches long
1 celery heart, all ribs removed and
    the base cut into strips about
    ⅛ inch wide and 1 inch long
1 cup freshly grated imported
    Parmesan cheese

Trim off and discard any discolored or badly bruised outer leaves of the cabbage and wash it under cold running water. Place it in enough boiling water to cover it completely and cook briskly for about 5 minutes. Lift it out of the pot but keep the water at a boil. Carefully peel off as many of the outside leaves as you can without tearing them. When the leaves become difficult to separate, return the cabbage to the pot and boil it for a few minutes longer. Repeat until you have peeled off 6 perfect leaves.

Spread the 6 leaves on a flat surface and one by one, with a small, sharp knife, trim off the tough rib end at the base of each. Cut each leaf into quarters and return to the boiling water for 5 minutes. Drain and pat the pieces dry with paper towels. Roll each piece into a ball and set it in the middle of a 10-inch square of doubled cheesecloth. Bring the corners of the cheesecloth together and twist them until you form a tight ball of cabbage in the center. Each cabbage ball with be about 1 inch in diameter. Set the cabbage balls in a pan just large enough to hold them, and pour in enough water to barely cover them. Add ½ teaspoon of the salt and bring to a boil over high heat. Reduce the heat to low and poach uncovered for 20 minutes. Set the cabbage balls aside at room temperature in the poaching liquid.

To prepare the beef marrow, refrigerate it in a bowl of cold water for about 15 to 20 minutes to remove all traces of blood. Pat the marrow dry with paper towels and cut it into ¼-inch-thick rounds with a sharp knife that has been dipped into hot water. Set aside.

In a heavy 8-inch skillet warm 4 tablespoons of the butter over moderate heat for 10 seconds. Add the bread triangles 5 or 6 at a time and, turning them frequently with a slotted spatula, fry until they are crisp and golden brown on both sides, adding more butter to the pan if necessary. Arrange the croutons side by side on paper towels and let them drain while you are preparing the other ingredients.

In a 2- to 3-quart saucepan, bring 1 quart of water to a boil over moderate heat. To blanch the chicken pieces, drop them into the water, return the water to a boil, reduce the heat and simmer the chicken for about 1 minute. Drain the chicken in a sieve or colander and, tossing the pieces about with a spoon, run cold water over them to remove all traces of foam or scum. Drain once more and set the blanched chicken aside. Wash the saucepan and in it bring another quart of water to a simmer over moderate heat. Drop in the beef, return the water to a boil, reduce the heat and simmer for 2 minutes. Drain the beef in a sieve or colander, rinse it under cold water, then drain it again.

Combine the blanched beef, the beef consommé and the remaining ½ teaspoon of salt in a heavy 4- to 5-quart *marmite* or casserole. Bring to a simmer slowly over moderate heat, reduce the heat to low and cook partially covered for 15 minutes. Add the carrots and simmer 10 minutes; then add the blanched chicken and the turnips and cook 10 minutes more. Drop in the leek and celery strips and continue cooking for about 5 minutes, or until the meat and vegetables are tender. Taste for seasoning.

Meanwhile, bring 2 cups of lightly salted water to a simmer over moderate heat and drop in the reserved marrow. Immediately remove the pan from the heat and let the marrow poach for 3 or 4 minutes. With a slotted spoon transfer the rounds to a small serving dish.

Serve the consommé directly from the *marmite* or ladle it into a heated tureen or individual bowls. Present the cabbage balls, croutons, and grated cheese along with the marrow, in separate serving dishes. Just before serving, pour about ½ cup of the hot consommé over the marrow.

Consommé Célestine

CHICKEN CONSOMMÉ GARNISHED WITH HERB-SEASONED CRÊPES

"Fines herbes" literally means small savory herbs—and the term is often confused with finely chopped fresh parsley. More precisely, "fines herbes" is a mixture of fresh parsley, tarragon, chervil and chives, all finely chopped (or cut). The proportions used may be varied to suit your taste, and one or more of the herbs may be omitted if unavailable. One half teaspoon of dried tarragon can be substituted for 1 teaspoon of fresh tarragon if necessary, but the other herbs must always be fresh.

Continued on next page

To serve 8

CRÊPES AUX FINES HERBES
½ cup plus 2 tablespoons all-
   purpose flour
2 eggs
½ cup milk
½ cup plus 2 tablespoons cold
   water
1½ tablespoons unsalted

butter, melted and cooled
plus 3 tablespoons melted
clarified butter *(page 13)*
¼ teaspoon salt
¼ cup *fines herbes*

*Consommé de fond blanc de
   volaille (chicken consommé,
   page 24)*

Prepare the crêpe batter with the ingredients listed and fry them, following the technique described in the recipe for *coulibiac (page 40)*.
Covered with plastic wrap, the crêpes may safely be kept at room temperature for 2 to 3 hours before they are used.

   Just before serving, bring the consommé to a simmer over moderate
heat. Stack 3 or 4 crêpes on top of each other and roll them into a cylinder. With a sharp knife, slice it crosswise into fine strips. Place the
crêpe strips in a heated tureen or in eight heated individual soup plates.
Pour in the consommé and serve at once.

Potage Germiny
CREAM OF SORREL SOUP

To serve 4 to 6

1 pound fresh sorrel
2 to 6 tablespoons unsalted butter
4 cups *fond blanc de volaille (page
   6)*, or substitute 4 cups

canned chicken stock, chilled, then
   degreased
6 egg yolks
1 cup heavy cream
Salt
1 teaspoon finely chopped fresh chervil

Wash the sorrel under cold running water. With a sharp knife, trim
away any bruised or blemished spots and cut off and discard the white
stems. Stack the leaves together a handful at a time, roll them lengthwise
into a tight cylinder and cut it crosswise as fine as possible.

   In a heavy 8- to 10-inch skillet set over moderate heat, melt 2 tablespoons of butter without letting it brown. Add the sorrel and, stirring
constantly, cook for 3 or 4 minutes until the shreds have wilted slightly.
Set the skillet aside off the heat.

   In a heavy 3- to 4-quart saucepan, bring the chicken stock to a simmer
over moderate heat, regulating the heat so that only the smallest bubbles
form at the edges of the pan. Beat the egg yolks and cream together with
a wire whisk. Then, whisking constantly and gently, pour the mixture
into the stock in a slow thin stream. Reduce the heat and simmer, stirring
constantly, until the soup is thick enough to cling lightly to the wires of

the whisk. (Do not allow the soup to come anywhere near the boil or it will curdle.) Strain the soup through a fine sieve into another saucepan and stir in the sorrel.

If you plan to serve the soup hot, immediately swirl in 4 tablespoons of chilled butter. Taste for seasoning and pour the soup into a heated tureen or individual soup plates. Sprinkle with the chervil. If you plan to serve the soup cold, do not add the butter enrichment. Pour the soup into a large bowl; let it cool to room temperature, then refrigerate for at least 4 hours, or until thoroughly chilled. Taste for seasoning and sprinkle with chervil just before serving. The soup may need more salt.

Potage crème de laitue
CREAM OF LETTUCE SOUP

To serve 6

4 firm 6-inch heads Boston or Bibb
    lettuce (about 4 pounds)
5 tablespoons unsalted butter plus 4
    tablespoons unsalted butter,
    chilled and cut into ½-inch bits

3 cups *sauce béchamel (page 9)*
5 cups *fond blanc de volaille (page*
    6), or substitute 5 cups canned
    chicken stock, chilled, then
    degreased
¼ teaspoon sugar
½ cup heavy cream

Remove the wilted outer leaves of the lettuce and rinse the heads in cold water, spreading the leaves gently to remove any sand. With a large, sharp knife, cut the heads into quarters and remove the cores. Slice each quarter crosswise into the finest possible chiffonade strips and set 1 cup of the chiffonade aside.

In a heavy 4-quart casserole, melt 4 tablespoons of the butter over moderate heat. Add all but the reserved cup of chiffonade and toss with a spoon to coat it evenly with butter. Reduce the heat to low, cover and cook for 3 minutes, or until the lettuce wilts.

Combine the béchamel, stock and sugar in a bowl and whisk until they are thoroughly blended. Stirring constantly, pour the mixture over the lettuce and bring to a simmer over moderate heat. Cook uncovered for about 10 minutes, whisking occasionally. Purée the soup through the finest disc of a food mill, or rub it through a fine-meshed sieve. Return the soup to the casserole and whisk in the cream. Warm the soup over moderate heat, stirring from time to time, but do not let it boil.

Meanwhile, melt 1 tablespoon of butter in a small skillet over moderate heat. Add the reserved cup of chiffonade and, stirring constantly, cook for 1 or 2 minutes. Set aside off the heat.

Remove the casserole from the stove and swirl in the butter bits. Taste for seasoning and pour the soup into a heated tureen or individual soup plates. Sprinkle the reserved chiffonade on top and serve.

Potage Bagration
CREAM OF VEAL SOUP WITH MACARONI AND CHEESE

To serve 6 to 8

SAUCE VELOUTÉE
1 quart *fond blanc de veau* or *fond blanc de volaille (pages 4 and 6)*, or substitute 1 quart canned

chicken stock, chilled, then degreased
8 tablespoons clarified butter *(page 13)*
¾ cup flour

Prepare the velouté, following the directions on page 8 but using a 2- to 3-quart saucepan to hold the doubled quantity of ingredients.

SOUPE
3 tablespoons unsalted butter plus 2 tablespoons unsalted butter, chilled and cut into ½- inch bits
2 pounds lean boneless veal, preferably shoulder, trimmed of fat and cut into ½-inch cubes
1 quart *fond blanc de veau* or *fond blanc de volaille (pages 4 and 6)*, or substitute 1 quart canned

chicken stock, chilled, then degreased
½ teaspoon salt
3 egg yolks
½ cup heavy cream
1 cup cooked macaroni, cut into ¼-inch lengths (½ cup uncooked)
1 cup freshly grated imported Parmesan cheese

In a heavy 12-inch skillet, melt 3 tablespoons of butter over moderate heat. When the foam subsides add the veal and, turning it frequently, sauté for 5 minutes, or until it is lightly colored, but not brown. Remove the veal with a slotted spoon, chop coarsely and return to the pan.

Stirring constantly with a wire whisk, gradually add the velouté, the quart of *fond blanc* and salt, and bring to a simmer over moderate heat. Reduce the heat to the lowest possible point and cook uncovered for 30 minutes, whisking the soup occasionally to keep it smooth.

Strain the contents of the skillet through a fine sieve set over a heavy 3- to 4-quart saucepan, pressing down hard on the pieces of veal with the back of a spoon to extract all their juice before discarding them. Combine the egg yolks and cream in a bowl and beat them together with the whisk.

Whisking the soup constantly, pour in the egg-yolk-and-cream mixture in a slow, thin stream. Stir over low heat for 2 or 3 minutes until the soup thickens lightly, but do not let it come to a boil. Add the macaroni and continue to simmer, still stirring until the pasta is heated through. Remove the pan from the heat and swirl in the 2 tablespoons of butter bits. Taste for seasoning. Pour the soup into a heated tureen or individual soup plates. Serve the cheese separately.

POTAGE CRÈME DE VOLAILLE (CREAM OF CHICKEN SOUP) : Substitute chicken meat and stock for veal and veal stock, and follow the recipe exactly but omit the macaroni and the cheese.

Potage crème cressonière
WATERCRESS SOUP

To serve 8

2 bunches fresh watercress (about 6 ounces each)
4 tablespoons clarified butter *(page 13)*, plus 1 tablespoon unsalted butter, chilled
1 medium-sized onion, peeled and thinly sliced
2 medium-sized leeks, including 2 inches of the green tops, trimmed, cut into quarters lengthwise and thoroughly washed to remove any hidden pockets of sand
3 large boiling potatoes (about 1 pound), peeled and thinly sliced
6 cups *fond blanc de volaille (page 6)*, or substitute 6 cups canned chicken stock, chilled, then degreased
1 cup milk
½ teaspoon salt
Freshly ground black pepper
2 egg yolks
½ cup heavy cream

Separate the bunches of watercress and wash under cold running water. Pat dry with paper towels, then cut off about ½ cup of the most perfect leaves with scissors and set them aside. Chop the remaining leaves and all the stems coarsely with a sharp knife.

In a heavy 3- to 4-quart casserole, heat the 4 tablespoons of clarified butter over moderate heat for about 10 seconds. Drop in the onion and leeks and, stirring frequently, cook for about 5 minutes until they are soft but not brown. Add the potatoes and turn them with a spoon until they glisten with butter. Then pour in 2 cups of the stock and cook partially covered over moderate heat until the potatoes are tender and show no resistance when pierced with the point of a small, sharp knife.

Pour in the remaining 4 cups of stock and the milk, and add the chopped watercress, salt and pepper. Stirring occasionally, bring to a simmer over moderate heat and cook uncovered for 15 minutes. Purée the contents of the saucepan through the medium disc of a food mill set over a deep bowl, or rub through a medium-meshed sieve with the back of a spoon. Return the purée to the saucepan and bring it to a simmer over low heat. Combine the egg yolks and cream in a small bowl and beat them lightly with a wire whisk. Then, whisking the soup constantly, pour in the egg yolks and cream in a slow stream. Stir over low heat for 2 or 3 minutes to heat the soup through. Do not let the soup come near the boil or it will curdle.

Remove the pan from the heat and swirl in the tablespoon of butter. Taste for seasoning. Stir the reserved watercress leaves into the soup and serve at once from a heated tureen or individual soup plates.

Bisque de homard

LOBSTER BISQUE

To serve 6

3 live 1- to 1½-pound lobsters
4 tablespoons unsalted clarified
  butter *(page 13)*
¾ cup finely chopped celery
¼ cup finely chopped scraped
  carrots
¼ cup finely chopped onions
⅛ teaspoon crumbled dried thyme
½ small bay leaf, crumbled
⅛ teaspoon ground hot red pepper
  (cayenne)
⅛ teaspoon ground white pepper
⅛ teaspoon salt

½ cup plus 3 tablespoons cognac
1 cup dry white wine
7 cups *fond blanc de volaille (page
  6)*, or substitute 7 cups canned
  chicken stock, chilled, then
  degreased
¼ cup long grain white rice, not
  the converted or precooked type
2 medium-sized firm ripe tomatoes,
  cut into quarters
1 tablespoon tomato paste
3 tablespoons unsalted butter,
  softened
½ cup heavy cream

With a cleaver or large, heavy chef's knife, chop off the tail section of each lobster at the point where it joins the upper body and twist off the large claws. Split the body of the lobster in half lengthwise, then remove and discard the gelatinous sac (stomach) in the head and the long intestinal vein attached to it. Scoop out and set aside the greenish brown tomalley (or liver) and the black roe (or coral) if any. Cut the tail crosswise into 2-inch-thick slices. Cut the body shells in half crosswise. Separate the claws at the joint and crack each large claw with a blow of a heavy knife.

In a heavy, deep 12-inch skillet, preferably a 12-inch sauté pan, melt 3 tablespoons of the butter over moderate heat. Add the celery, carrots, onions, thyme, bay leaf, cayenne, white pepper and salt. Stirring frequently, cook for 5 minutes, or until the vegetables are soft but not brown. Add the lobsters to the skillet. Turning them frequently, cook over high heat for 2 or 3 minutes, or until the shells are red. Warm ½ cup of the cognac in a small saucepan over low heat, ignite it with a match and slowly pour it flaming over the lobster, meanwhile sliding the pan gently back and forth until the flames die. Pour in the wine and bring to a boil over high heat. Baste the lobster with the pan juices, reduce the heat to low, and simmer tightly covered for about 10 minutes.

Lift out the pieces of lobster and place them on a plate; set the skillet aside. Remove the shell from the tail pieces, cut the meat into ½-inch dice and reserve it in a bowl. With a pick or small knife, remove all the meat from the claws and joints. Cut the meat into ¼-inch dice and add them to the skillet. Stir in 1 cup of the chicken stock, and then purée the mixture in an electric blender. Pour the purée into a heavy 4-quart enameled-iron casserole and set aside.

Chop the lobster shells into small pieces with a cleaver and place them in a 3- to 4-quart saucepan. Pour in the remaining 6 cups of chicken stock and bring to a boil over high heat. Reduce the heat to low and simmer uncovered for 15 minutes. Strain the stock through a fine sieve directly into the purée and discard the shells. Bring to a boil over high heat. Add the rice, tomatoes and tomato paste. Reduce the heat to moderate and cook partially covered for 20 minutes, or until the rice is soft. Purée the soup in a food mill with a fine disc or, with a spoon, rub the contents of the pan through a fine sieve set over a bowl and return it to the pan.

Combine the reserved tomalley and coral (if any) with the softened butter and rub them through a small sieve into a bowl. In a 6- to 8-inch skillet, melt the remaining tablespoon of butter over high heat. Drop in the reserved diced lobster and toss it about in the butter for a minute or so. Then remove the pan from the heat. Warm the remaining 3 tablespoons of cognac in a small pan, ignite it with a match, and pour it over the lobster. Slide the pan back and forth until the flames die.

Just before serving the bisque, bring it to a simmer over moderate heat. Stirring constantly with a whisk, add the tomalley-and-butter mixture a tablespoon at a time, and pour in the cream in a thin stream. Add the flamed lobster meat and all its juices, then taste for seasoning. Serve at once, from a heated tureen or in individual soup plates.

Potage crème de petits pois
CREAM OF FRESH PEA SOUP

To serve 4 to 6

4 cups fresh shelled green peas (about 4 pounds unshelled), or substitute 4 cups defrosted frozen peas (about three 10-ounce packages)
2 cups sauce béchamel (page 9)

2 cups fond blanc de volaille (page 6) or 2 cups canned chicken stock, chilled, then degreased
½ cup heavy cream
2 sprigs fresh chervil or ½ teaspoon crumbled dried chervil leaves
2 tablespoons unsweetened butter, chilled and broken into ½-inch bits

Drop the fresh peas into enough lightly salted boiling water to cover them. When the water returns to a boil, reduce the heat to moderate and cook uncovered for 5 to 10 minutes, or until the peas are almost tender but still slightly resistant to the bite. Drain the peas in a sieve or colander and plunge them into a pot of cold water to set their color. Drain and set aside. (Frozen peas need only to be thoroughly defrosted and drained.)

Combine the béchamel and chicken stock in a heavy 2- to 3-quart saucepan and, stirring constantly, bring to a simmer over moderate heat. Add the peas and cook for 5 to 10 minutes longer, stirring from time to time. When the peas are soft enough to be easily mashed with a spoon, purée the contents of the saucepan 2 or 3 cups at a time in the jar of an electric blender or through the finest blade of a food mill set over a bowl.

Return the purée to the saucepan and, over low heat, pour in the cream in a slow stream, whisking constantly. Simmer only long enough to heat the soup through, but don't let it boil. Add the chervil and taste for seasoning. Remove the pan from the heat, swirl in the butter bits and serve at once from a heated tureen or individual soup plates.

Consommé; consommé double; et gelée
CONSOMMÉ; DOUBLE CONSOMMÉ; AND ASPIC

To make about 7 cups

CONSOMMÉ
½ cup coarsely chopped fresh
   celery leaves
½ cup coarsely chopped green leek
   tops
½ cup coarsely chopped scraped
   carrots

¼ cup coarsely chopped fresh
   parsley leaves and stems
2 medium-sized firm ripe tomatoes,
   coarsely chopped
½ cup egg whites
3 or 4 egg shells, finely crushed
2 quarts of any of the stocks
   described, cold or cooled to room
   temperature

CONSOMMÉ: Drop the celery leaves, leek tops, carrots, parsley, tomatoes, egg whites and egg shells in a heavy 4- to 5-quart copper or enameled-iron saucepan, mix well and pour in the stock. Set the pan over high heat and, stirring constantly, bring to a boil.

Reduce the heat to low and simmer the stock undisturbed and uncovered for about 20 minutes. Then pour the contents of the pan slowly into a large sieve lined with a double thickness of dampened cheesecloth and set over a deep bowl. Allow the liquid to drain through without disturbing it. The consommé may be used at once as it is, or garnished *(Recipe Index),* or cooled to room temperature, covered tightly and stored in the refrigerator for 3 or 4 days or in the freezer for several months.

CONSOMMÉ DOUBLE
1 pound lean ground beef or 1 pound cut-up chicken wings and backs

CONSOMMÉ DOUBLE (DOUBLE CONSOMMÉ): To make a richer "double" consommé, mix 1 pound of raw meat with the basic vegetable ingredients. Use lean ground beef with beef stock; and chicken wings and backs with chicken stock. Pour in the stock and bring the mixture to a boil over high heat, stirring constantly. Cook undisturbed and uncovered for 45 minutes, then strain it following the directions above.

GELÉE
6 envelopes unflavored gelatin

GELÉE (ASPIC): Pour 2 cups of the cool stock into a heavy 4- to 5-quart copper or enameled-iron saucepan and sprinkle the gelatin evenly over it. When the gelatin has softened for several minutes, add the vegetables, egg whites and egg shells and mix well. Pour in the remaining 6 cups of stock, set the pan over high heat and, stirring constantly, bring to a boil. Then proceed as described in the basic consommé recipe.

Fish

Écrevisses à la nage
CRAYFISH WITH WHITE WINE AND VEGETABLES

To serve 6

COURT-BOUILLON

3 medium-sized carrots, scraped, cut along the entire length with four or five ¼-inch-deep V-shaped grooves or notches, and sliced into ⅛-inch-thick rounds

2 small onions, peeled and thinly sliced

2 medium-sized leeks, white part only, cut into strips about 1½ inches long and ⅛ inch wide and thoroughly washed to remove sand

2 unpeeled garlic cloves, crushed with the side of a cleaver or heavy knife

10 fresh parsley sprigs

3 medium-sized bay leaves

2 fresh thyme sprigs, or substitute ½ teaspoon crumbled dried thyme

2 tablespoons salt

1½ tablespoons freshly ground black pepper

2 cups dry white wine

7 cups water

5 pounds live fresh water crayfish (15 to 25 to the pound)

First prepare the court bouillon in the following fashion: Combine the carrots, onions, leeks, garlic, parsley, bay leaves, thyme, salt and pepper in a 12-inch enameled cast-iron skillet or sauté pan. Pour in the wine and water, and bring to a boil over high heat. Reduce the heat to low and let the court bouillon simmer for 15 minutes.

Meanwhile, wash the crayfish briefly under cold running water. To remove the intestines, grasp the body of each crayfish in one hand and with the other twist the middle section of the fanlike tail from side to side. When the tail section snaps at the base of the body, pull it straight out; it is attached to the intestines and will draw them out in one piece.

Return the court bouillon to a boil and drop in the crayfish. Stirring occasionally, cook briskly, uncovered, for 5 to 6 minutes. Let the crayfish cool to room temperature in the court bouillon. Remove and discard the garlic, and refrigerate until chilled. Then ladle the crayfish, liquid and vegetables into a tureen or deep platter. Arrange the crayfish on the top attractively and serve.

Alose à l'oseille

SHAD AND ROE WITH SOLE MOUSSE AND SORREL SAUCE

To serve 6

MOUSSE DE SOLE

2 slices stale homemade-type white
    bread, with crusts removed, torn
    into small pieces
½ pound skinned sole fillets, cut
    into 1-inch chunks
⅓ cup heavy cream

2 hard-cooked eggs, coarsely chopped
1 medium-sized fresh mushroom,
    cut into small pieces
2 tablespoons coarsely chopped
    shallots
½ cup finely chopped fresh parsley
½ teaspoon salt
⅛ teaspoon freshly ground white
    pepper

MOUSSE DE SOLE (SOLE MOUSSE): Preheat the oven to 400°. Prepare the sole mousse in the following fashion. Pulverize the bread in the jar of an electric blender. Then add the sole, ⅓ cup cream, the hard-cooked eggs, mushroom pieces and coarsely chopped shallots, and blend at medium speed for about 30 seconds. Turn off the machine and scrape down the sides of the jar with a rubber spatula. Blend again until the mixture is a smooth purée. Then scrape it into a bowl and stir in the ½ cup parsley, ½ teaspoon salt and ⅛ teaspoon white pepper.

ALOSE

4 tablespoons unsalted butter, softened
2 tablespoons finely chopped shallots
1 teaspoon finely cut fresh thyme,
    or substitute ½ teaspoon
    crumbled, dried thyme
1 medium-sized bay leaf, crumbled
2 shad fillets, each about 1½ pounds
½ teaspoon salt

⅛ teaspoon freshly ground white
    pepper
1 pair shad roe
3 large fresh mushrooms wiped
    with a dampened cloth, trimmed
    and cut lengthwise through caps
    and stems into ⅛-inch-thick slices
1½ cups dry white wine

ALOSE (SHAD): With a pastry brush, spread 2 tablespoons of the softened butter over the bottom and sides of an 8-by-12-inch shallow baking dish. Scatter the finely chopped shallots, thyme and bay leaf evenly over the bottom of the dish.

On a flat surface arrange five 15-inch-long pieces of white kitchen string parallel to each other and about 1½ inches apart. Pat the shad fillets completely dry with paper towels and place them skin down and side by side lengthwise across the row of strings so that the ends of string extend beyond the fish. Sprinkle the fillets with ½ teaspoon salt and ⅛ teaspoon white pepper, then spread the puréed sole mixture over the center of the fillets with a metal spatula.

Slit the membranes connecting the pair of shad roe with scissors or a small, sharp knife and place one half of the roe lengthwise along the center of each shad fillet. Gently lift up one fillet and invert it on top of the other, roe side down. Then tie the strings around the shad to make as neat and secure a package as possible. Butter the surface of the fish with 2 tablespoons of softened butter.

Place the shad in the buttered baking dish and scatter the sliced mushrooms over it. Pour in the wine and cover the dish with aluminum foil. Braise in the middle of the oven for 45 minutes, or until the fish feels firm when pressed lightly with your finger. Transfer the shad to a heated platter and drape it loosely with foil to keep it warm while you prepare the sorrel sauce.

SAUCE

2 cups heavy cream
2 tablespoons unsalted butter, softened
½ pound fresh sorrel, washed, trimmed and shredded (see potage Germiny, page 18)

½ cup *sauce velouté (page 8)* made with *fumet de poisson,* or substitute *beurre manié* made with 1½ tablespoons butter, softened and rubbed to a paste with 1½ tablespoons flour

SAUCE: Strain the braising liquid through a fine sieve into a 1- to 1½-quart enameled saucepan, pressing down hard on the mushrooms and shallots with the back of a spoon to extract all their juice before discarding them. Bring to a boil over high heat and cook briskly until the liquid is reduced to about ½ cup. Reduce the heat to moderate and pour in the 2 cups of heavy cream. Stirring from time to time with a wire whisk, simmer for 8 to 10 minutes until the sauce is reduced to about 1½ cups.

Meanwhile, in a heavy 6- to 8-inch skillet, melt 2 tablespoons of butter over moderate heat. Add the sorrel and, stirring frequently, cook for 3 or 4 minutes. Then set the skillet aside off the heat.

Whisk the *velouté* or *beurre manié* into the 1½ cups of reduced sauce and continue to simmer, still whisking, for 2 or 3 minutes until the sauce thickens and is smooth. Then stir in the sorrel. Taste for seasoning.

Carefully cut and discard the strings from the shad. Mask the fish with a few tablespoonfuls of the sauce and pour the rest of the sauce into a small bowl or sauceboat. Serve the shad and sauce at once.

Mousse de sole
BAKED SOLE MOUSSE

To serve 6 to 8

2½ pounds skinned Dover sole, or substitute other sole fillets, cut into 1-inch pieces
3 egg whites
2 tablespoons butter, softened
2 cups heavy cream, chilled
⅛ teaspoon ground hot red pepper (cayenne)

1½ teaspoons salt
⅛ teaspoon freshly ground white pepper
1 black truffle (see Glossary), thinly peeled, sliced ⅛ inch thick and cut into strips about 1 inch long and ⅛ inch wide
Sauce vin blanc (page 14) or sauce Nantua (page 12)

Place about one third of the sole and 1 egg white at a time in the jar of an

Continued on next page

electric blender and blend at high speed for 30 seconds. Turn off the machine, scrape down the sides of the jar with a rubber spatula and blend again until the sole is a smooth purée. As you proceed, with the remaining sole and egg whites, transfer the puréed sole to a deep bowl. Cover and refrigerate until the fish is thoroughly chilled.

Preheat the oven to 350°. With a pastry brush, spread the softened butter over the bottom and sides of a 6-cup charlotte mold.

Place the bowl of puréed fish in a large pot half filled with crushed ice or ice cubes and water. A tablespoon at a time, beat the cream into the purée, making sure each addition is thoroughly absorbed before adding the successive tablespoons of cream. Beat in the red pepper, salt and white pepper. To check the seasoning, drop a teaspoonful of the purée into a pan of boiling water and poach for 2 or 3 minutes. Taste, and season the mousse more definitely if desired.

Spoon the mousse into the buttered mold, spreading it evenly and smoothing the top with a spatula. Cover tightly with a piece of buttered wax paper. (At this point the mousse may be refrigerated for several hours or overnight.) To bake, place the mold in a deep roasting pan set in the middle of the oven. Pour enough boiling water into the roasting pan to come about halfway up the sides of the mold. Bake for 30 minutes, or until the mousse is firm when pressed gently with a finger.

To unmold and serve the mousse, remove the wax paper and run a knife around the edge of the mold. Place a heated platter upside down over the mold. Grasping the platter and mold firmly together, invert them. The mousse should slide out easily. Stir the truffle strips into the *sauce vin blanc* or *sauce Nantua* and then spoon some of the sauce over the mousse. Serve the remaining sauce separately in a sauceboat.

Filets de sole à la florentine
FILLET OF SOLE WITH SPINACH AND MORNAY SAUCE

To serve 6

Salt

2 pounds fresh spinach, trimmed and thoroughly washed

8 tablespoons butter, softened

A pinch of nutmeg, preferably freshly grated

2 tablespoons finely chopped shallots

Six 6-ounce sole fillets, lightly pounded with the side of a cleaver to a uniform thickness of about ¼ inch

Freshly ground white pepper

¼ cup *fumet de poisson (page 5)*

¼ cup dry white wine

In an enameled or stainless-steel 5- to 6-quart pot, bring 3 quarts of water and 1 teaspoon of salt to a boil over high heat. Drop in the spinach, return the water to a boil and cook briskly, uncovered, for 4 to 5 minutes. Drain the spinach in a large sieve or colander and run cold water over it to set the color. A handful at a time, squeeze the spinach vigorously to remove all the excess liquid. Chop the leaves and set aside.

Preheat the oven to 325°. With a pastry brush, spread 2 tablespoons of the softened butter evenly over the bottom and sides of an 8-by-12-inch baking dish. Scatter the shallots in the bottom of the dish. Season the fillets lightly with salt and pepper, and fold them crosswise in half, white side out. Lay the fillets side by side in the baking dish. Pour the *fumet de poisson* and wine down the sides of the pan. Cover the fish with a sheet of buttered wax paper cut to fit flush against the sides of the baking dish. Bring to a simmer over moderate heat, then place the dish in the middle of the oven. Poach the fillets for 10 to 12 minutes, or until they are tender enough to flake easily when prodded gently with a fork. Do not overcook.

Meanwhile, in a heavy 10- to 12-inch skillet, heat the remaining 6 tablespoons of softened butter over moderate heat until it browns lightly. Add the spinach and nutmeg and, stirring constantly, sauté for 1 or 2 minutes until almost all of the liquid in the pan has evaporated. With a fork, transfer the spinach to an ovenproof serving platter or large *gratin* dish and spread it out evenly. Carefully lift the poached fillets out of the baking dish and arrange them attractively in one layer on top of the spinach. Drape loosely with foil to keep the fish and spinach warm while you make the sauce.

SAUCE MORNAY
1 cup *sauce béchamel (page 9)* ¼ cup grated imported Parmesan
½ cup heavy cream   combined with ¼ cup freshly
1 egg yolk   grated imported Gruyère cheese

SAUCE MORNAY (MORNAY SAUCE) : Heat the broiler to its highest setting. Working quickly, strain the liquid remaining in the baking dish through a fine sieve into a heavy 1- to 2-quart saucepan, pressing down hard on the shallots with the back of a spoon to extract all the juices before discarding. Boil the liquid briskly until it is reduced to about ½ cup. Reduce the heat to moderate and, with a wire whisk, stir in the béchamel and cream. Simmer for 5 minutes, or until the sauce is smooth, whisking all the while. Remove the pan from the heat. Whisk in the egg yolk. Then stir in 6 tablespoons of the grated cheese. Taste for seasoning.

Spoon the sauce evenly over the fillets, masking them completely, and sprinkle the top with the remaining 2 tablespoons of cheese. Slide the dish under the broiler for 30 seconds or so, until the topping is lightly browned. Serve at once.

Paupiettes de sole Dugléré

ROLLED FILLETS OF SOLE IN CREAMY VELOUTÉ SAUCE WITH TOMATO

To serve 6

4 large firm ripe tomatoes
4 tablespoons cold butter, plus 4
    tablespoons softened butter
¼ cup finely chopped shallots
¼ cup finely chopped onions
Salt
Freshly ground white pepper
Six 6-ounce sole fillets, cut
    lengthwise into halves and lightly
    pounded with the side of a
    cleaver to a uniform thickness of
    about ¼ inch
3 tablespoons finely chopped fresh

parsley
½ cup dry white wine
½ cup *fumet de poisson (page 5)*
⅔ cup *sauce velouté (page 8)*
    made with *fumet de poisson*
¼ cup heavy cream

OPTIONAL GARNISH
tomato balls made from six small
    ripe tomatoes *(see selle d'agneau
    Armenonville, page 94)*
1 teaspoon finely chopped fresh
    parsley
12 *fleurons (page 144)*

Drop the tomatoes into a pan of boiling water and remove them after about 10 seconds. Run them under cold water, and peel the tomatoes with a small, sharp knife. Cut out the stems and slice the tomatoes in half crosswise. Squeeze the halves gently to remove the seeds and juice and chop the tomatoes coarsely. In a small enameled or stainless-steel saucepan, melt 2 tablespoons of the cold butter over moderate heat. When the foam begins to subside, drop in the tomatoes. Stirring frequently, cook briskly until most of the liquid in the pan evaporates and the tomatoes are reduced to a thick purée. Set aside off the heat.

Preheat the oven to 350°. With a pastry brush, spread the 4 tablespoons of softened butter evenly over the bottom and sides of a 12-by-7-inch enameled or glass baking dish. Scatter the shallots and onions over the bottom of the dish and sprinkle them with a little salt and white pepper. Spoon about half the tomato purée into the dish, smoothing it to the edges with the back of the spoon.

To make each *paupiette,* roll a strip of sole lengthwise into a tight cylinder and fasten the ends securely with a plain wooden toothpick. Stand the *paupiettes* upright side by side in the dish, then spread the remaining tomato purée on top and sprinkle with the parsley. Pour the white wine and *fumet de poisson* down the sides of the dish. Cover the fish with a sheet of buttered wax paper cut to fit snugly inside the dish. Bring to a simmer over moderate heat, then place the dish in the middle of the oven. Poach the *paupiettes* for 10 to 12 minutes, or until they are tender enough to flake easily when prodded gently with a fork.

With a slotted spoon or spatula, carefully lift the *paupiettes* from the dish and arrange them attractively on a heated platter. Remove and discard the toothpicks, then drape foil loosely over the fish to keep it warm while you prepare the sauce.

Transfer the entire contents of the dish to a small, heavy saucepan. Bring to a boil over high heat and, stirring occasionally with a wire whisk, cook briskly until the liquid is reduced to about 1 cup. Whisk in the velouté and ¼ cup of heavy cream and simmer slowly, stirring for about 5 minutes, until the sauce is smooth and heated through. Taste for seasoning. Remove the pan from the heat and swirl in the remaining 2 tablespoons of cold butter.

With a bulb baster, remove any trace of liquid that has accumulated around the *paupiettes* and stir it into the sauce. Pour the sauce evenly over them and serve at once. If you like, you may garnish the top of each *paupiette* with a tomato ball and sprinkle parsley over it. Arrange the *fleurons,* if you wish to serve them, in a ring around the edge of the platter.

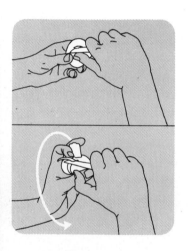

To flute a mushroom, hold it in your left hand with your thumb on the edge of the cap and the stem pointing away from your palm *(left)*. Using a small knife with a rounded blade, cut from the center to the edge of the cap, rotating your left hand toward you *(left, below)*. By repeating this process, you can flute a mushroom as shown at right.

Turban de sole Nantua

POACHED SOLE RING FILLED WITH PIKE MOUSSE SERVED WITH NANTUA SAUCE

To serve 8

2 tablespoons butter, softened, plus 2 tablespoons unsalted butter, cut into bits
¼ cup finely chopped shallots
7 eight-ounce sole fillets, preferably Dover sole, skinned
Salt
Freshly ground white pepper
Uncooked *quenelles de brochet* mixture *(page 49)*
8 fresh-water crayfish, or substitute 8 large shrimp (15 to 20 to the pound)
1 cup water

1 tablespoon strained fresh lemon juice
Eight 1½-inch mushroom caps, wiped with a dampened towel and fluted *(see diagram above)*, plus 4 two-inch mushroom caps, cut into julienne strips about ⅛ inch wide
Sauce Nantua (page 12), freshly made
1 large black truffle, thinly peeled and cut into ⅛-inch-thick slices *(see Glossary)*
1 small black truffle, thinly peeled and cut into julienne strips about ⅛ inch thick *(see Glossary)*

Continued on next page

Preheat the oven to 350°. With a pastry brush, spread the 2 tablespoons of softened butter over the bottom and sides of a 7- to 8-cup ring mold. Sprinkle the shallots evenly all over the mold.

Cut each of the sole fillets in half lengthwise. One at a time, place a fillet half between 2 sheets of wax paper and gently pound it with the smooth side of a kitchen mallet or the flat of a cleaver until it is flattened to a uniform thickness of about ¼ inch.

Season the fillets on both sides with a little salt and a few grindings of white pepper. Holding a fillet at both ends, place it in the mold with the whiter side down, letting one end drape over the outside and the other end over the center ring of the mold. Repeat with the remaining fillets, laying them side by side and overlapping them somewhat to completely cover the inside surfaces of the mold. Fill the fish-lined mold with the *quenelles de brochet* mixture, spreading it and smoothing the top with a spatula. Then bring the ends of the fillets up and over the *quenelle* mixture. Cover the top of the mold with a sheet of buttered wax paper.

Place the mold in a large, shallow roasting pan set in the middle of the oven and pour in enough boiling water to come halfway up the sides of the mold. Bake for 30 minutes, or until the *turban de sole* feels firm when prodded gently with a finger. Remove from the oven and set the *turban* aside for 5 to 10 minutes before unmolding. Drop the crayfish or shrimp into enough lightly salted boiling water to cover them completely and cook briskly, uncovered, for 3 or 4 minutes. Drain the crayfish or shrimp well, shell them and set aside on a plate, draped with foil to keep them warm. Keep the heads on several of the crayfish to make a more impressive garnish.

Meanwhile, combine the cup of water, the lemon juice and ⅛ teaspoon of salt, and the 2 tablespoons of butter bits in a small enameled saucepan. Bring to a boil over high heat, add the fluted mushroom caps, and turn them about with a spoon until they are evenly moistened. Reduce the heat to moderate, cover the pan tightly, and cook for about 3 minutes. Do not overcook.

With a slotted spoon, transfer the fluted mushroom caps to a plate. Add the strips of mushrooms to the cooking liquid remaining in the pan, stir them about, cover and cook for about 2 minutes. Drain them in a sieve and set them aside in a bowl.

To unmold and serve the *turban de sole,* run a thin-bladed knife around the edges of the mold. Place an inverted serving plate on top of the mold and, grasping plate and mold together firmly, turn them over. The *turban* should slide out easily. Drain off and discard any liquid that accumulates around the *turban* on the platter.

Arrange the crayfish or shrimp at evenly spaced intervals around the top of the ring. Place the fluted mushroom caps between them. Gently but firmly press the truffle rounds against the sides of the *turban* ring. Stir the mushroom and truffle strips into the previously prepared *sauce Nantua* and pour it over and around the *turban*. Serve at once.

Bar braisé aux aromates

BASS BRAISED WITH HERBS

To serve 6

5 tablespoons butter, softened, plus
    8 tablespoons (1 quarter-pound
    stick) unsalted butter, chilled and
    cut into ¼-inch bits
½ pound fresh mushrooms,
    trimmed and cut lengthwise
    through the stems into ⅛-inch-
    thick slices
½ cup finely chopped shallots
¼ cup finely chopped onions
½ teaspoon finely chopped garlic
1 tablespoon finely chopped fresh
    parsley plus 3 sprigs fresh parsley
A 3- to 3½-pound striped bass,

cleaned but with head and tail intact
1 teaspoon finely cut fresh rosemary,
    or substitute ¼ teaspoon
    crumbled dried rosemary
½ teaspoon finely cut fresh thyme,
    or substitute ¼ teaspoon
    crumbled dried thyme
1 medium-sized bay leaf
½ teaspoon salt
¼ teaspoon freshly ground black
    pepper
1 cup dry white wine
1½ tablespoons strained fresh
    lemon juice

Preheat the oven to 450°. With a pastry brush, spread 1 tablespoon of the softened butter over the bottom and sides of a shallow glass or enameled baking dish large enough to hold the bass comfortably. Scatter the mushrooms, shallots, onions, garlic and 1 tablespoon chopped parsley evenly in the bottom of the dish.

Wash the bass quickly under cold running water and pat it dry, inside and out, with paper towels. Place the 3 parsley sprigs, the rosemary, thyme and bay leaf in the cavity of the fish. Then sprinkle the skin with the salt and pepper and brush it with the remaining 4 tablespoons of softened butter. Place the bass on top of the mushroom mixture and pour the wine down the sides of the dish. Cover tightly with foil and braise in the middle of the oven for 15 minutes. Remove the foil and, basting the fish 2 or 3 times with the braising liquid, bake for 15 minutes longer, or until the fish feels firm when prodded gently with a finger. With a spatula, carefully transfer the fish to a heated platter and drape it loosely with foil while you prepare the sauce.

Strain the entire contents of the baking dish through a fine sieve into an enameled or stainless-steel saucepan, pressing down hard on the vegetables with the back of a spoon to extract all their juices before discarding them. Bring the liquid to a boil over high heat and cook briskly until it is reduced to about 1 cup. Remove the pan from the heat, stir in the lemon juice, and briskly whisk in the chilled butter bits, a few tablespoonfuls at a time. Taste for seasoning.

With a small, sharp knife, remove the top layer of skin from the fish. Pour the sauce over the bass and serve at once.

Homard à la parisienne

COLD LOBSTER STUFFED WITH MIXED VEGETABLE SALAD

To serve 6

COURT-BOUILLON

1 cup coarsely chopped onions
1 cup coarsely chopped leeks,
   including 2 inches of the green
   tops, thoroughly washed to
   remove any sand
½ cup coarsely chopped celery,
   including the leaves
¼ cup coarsely chopped, scraped carrots
¼ cup coarsely chopped fresh parsley
2 sprigs fresh thyme, or substitute
   ½ teaspoon crumbled dried thyme
1 medium-sized bay leaf
1 tablespoon whole black peppercorns
3 tablespoons salt
2 cups dry white wine
8 quarts water
Two 3- to 3½-pound live lobsters

NOTE: As an aid to preparing, decorating and presenting the lobsters, see the photograph on pages 12 and 13 of the main volume.

COURT-BOUILLON (POACHING LIQUID): In a 12-quart fish poacher or deep roasting pan large enough to hold one of the lobsters and the court bouillon, combine the coarsely chopped onions, leeks, celery, carrots, parsley, thyme, bay leaf, peppercorns and 3 tablespoons of salt. Pour in the wine and water and bring to a boil over high heat. Reduce the heat to low and simmer, partially covered, for 30 minutes.

Meanwhile, to keep the tails of the lobsters flat when they are poached, tie them one by one to a board the length and width of the body—about 14 inches by 3 inches. Tie string around the board and lobster in 3 or 4 places to hold them securely together.

Return the court bouillon to a boil and lower the lobster on the board into it. The court bouillon should cover the lobster completely. Add up to 2 quarts of boiling water if necessary. If some shell still protrudes above the water, drape a dampened kitchen towel over the lobster. Reduce the heat to low and poach for 20 to 25 minutes. Transfer the cooked lobster to a cutting board, untie it and discard the string. Tie the second lobster to the board and poach it in identical fashion.

As soon as each lobster is poached, place it on its stomach. With kitchen scissors remove the top of the tail shell and a strip of the upper body shell. Start cutting just above the fanning end-section of the tail and follow the ridges along the sides where the tail shell joins the feelers. Continue cutting in straight lines through the upper body shell toward the head and to the natural depressed line which encircles the back of the head. Cut along this line to neatly remove the strip of upper body shell.

Carefully lift out the tail meat in one piece, then slice it crosswise into ¼-inch-thick medallions. Trim off any ragged edges from the medallions. Keep the medallions in the order in which they were cut. Cover them with foil or plastic wrap and chill. Coarsely chop any uneven pieces and scraps, cover them with plastic wrap and refrigerate. With a fine butcher's saw, remove the top of the main joint of each claw, following the outline of the claw. Draw out the claw meat in one piece. Slice the wider part of the claw meat crosswise into 2 or 3 medallions but leave the slender tip whole. Wrap the meat of each claw separately in plastic wrap and chill. Wrap the lobster carcasses and refrigerate until you are ready to assemble the dish.

GELÉE 2 quarts of the *court-bouillon (opposite)*

GELÉE (ASPIC) : Measure off and strain 2 quarts of the remaining court bouillon. Discard the rest of it or refrigerate or freeze it for another use. Prepare aspic with the court bouillon following the directions and using the additional ingredients specified for *gelée* on page 24. Set aside at room temperature to keep the aspic fluid.

LÉGUMES	
1 cup fresh green peas (about ½ pound unshelled), or substitute 1 ten-ounce package frozen peas	trimmed
	½ pound medium-sized carrots, scraped
½ pound fresh green string beans,	½ pound medium-sized white turnips, peeled

LÉGUMES (VEGETABLES) : Cook the vegetables one at a time in the same pan, using the following cooking times and techniques. Bring 2 quarts of lightly salted water to a boil over high heat. (Replenish the water with more boiling water when necessary.) Drop in the peas and boil briskly for 8 to 10 minutes, or until they are tender to the bite. Scoop them out of the pan with a slotted spoon and drop them into a bowl of cold water to set their color. When cool, transfer them to another bowl and set aside. (Frozen peas need only be defrosted and drained.) Add the green beans to the same water, a handful at a time so the water does not stop boiling, and cook for 8 to 10 minutes until they are tender. Scoop the beans into a sieve, run cold water over them for a minute, drain and set them aside in a separate bowl. Add the carrots to the boiling water and cook for 30 minutes, or until they are tender when pierced with the tip of a small, sharp knife. Remove them from the pan with a slotted spoon, drop them into a bowl of cold water for a few minutes, then drain and set them aside separately. Finally, drop the turnips into the boiling water and cook for 30 minutes, or until they are tender when pierced with the tip of a small, sharp knife. Immediately drop them into cold water for a few minutes, drain and set aside. Cut the beans into ½-inch lengths, and cut the carrots and turnips into neat ¼-inch dice. Combine all the vegetables in a large bowl, cover with foil or plastic wrap and refrigerate. (You may cook the vegetables at the same time in different pans.)

SAUCE MAYONNAISE	
2 egg yolks at room temperature	teaspoons wine vinegar
1 teaspoon Dijon-style prepared mustard	1 teaspoon salt
	⅛ teaspoon freshly ground white pepper
1½ teaspoons strained fresh lemon juice, or substitute 1½	1 cup vegetable oil

Continued on next page

SAUCE MAYONNAISE (MAYONNAISE): With a wire whisk or a rotary or electric beater, beat the egg yolks together with the mustard, lemon juice or vinegar, salt and pepper until the mixture thickens and clings to the beater. Then beat in ½ cup of the oil, ½ teaspoon at a time; make sure each addition is absorbed before adding more. By the time ½ cup of the oil has been beaten in, the sauce should be the consistency of very thick cream. Pour in the remaining oil in a thin stream, beating constantly. Taste for seasoning.

GARNITURE

2 tablespoons finely chopped onions
2 or 3 large green leaves from the top of a leek or scallion, blanched and cut into fine strips *(see oeufs en gelée, page 84)*
Five ⅛-inch-thick slices of thinly peeled black truffle *(see Glossary)*
2 loaves stale unsliced white bread
3 hard-cooked eggs
1½ tablespoons unsalted butter, softened
Salt
Pepper
Six 2½-inch firm ripe tomatoes, dropped into boiling water for 10 seconds, cooled in a pot of cold water, then peeled
6 *fonds d'artichaut* cooked *à blanc,* then chilled *(see selle d'agneau Armenonville, page 94)*
6 capers

GARNITURE: Set the pan of aspic in a large pot half-filled with crushed ice or ice cubes and water, and stir the aspic with a large metal spoon until it thickens enough to flow sluggishly off the spoon. Beat 2 table-spoons of the aspic into the mayonnaise. Set 1 tablespoon of the mayonnaise aside to use for filling the eggs. Then add the remaining mayonnaise and 2 tablespoons finely chopped onions to the carrots, turnips, peas and beans and toss gently but thoroughly together. Stir in any reserved chopped pieces of lobster meat.

Remove the medallions of lobster meat and the thin claw tips from the refrigerator and in the order in which you cut them, place them on a rack over a jelly-roll pan. Coat them evenly with aspic and return them to the refrigerator until the aspic has set. Dip the blanched leek or scallion strips in aspic and wrap them, one at a time, around the upper edge of each medallion. Reserve the leftover strips. Cut tiny dots with a round truffle cutter from the truffle slices, then dip the dots in aspic and set one on each medallion just above the center. Return the medallions to the refrigerator until the decorations have set.

(Keep the remaining aspic at room temperature so that it remains liquid and ready to use; if it begins to set, warm briefly over low heat to soften it, then stir it over ice again until it reaches the same thick but still fluid consistency as before.)

Meanwhile, cut 2 loaves of stale unsliced white bread into 2 loaf-length wedges for stands on which to display the lobsters. See pages 12 and 13, main volume. Set them end to end and wrap them with a white linen towel so they form a single solid base. Set the base in the center of the tray on which you wish to serve the lobsters.

Remove the lobster shells from the refrigerator. Arrange them on the base and anchor them to it with toothpicks. Once the lobsters are in place, carefully spoon the vegetable mixture into the open tails and claws, dividing the vegetables evenly among them.

Take the medallions of lobster meat from the refrigerator and return them and the slender tips of the claws to the lobsters in the order in which they were removed, overlapping the medallions slightly. Spoon a layer of aspic about ⅛ inch thick around the lobsters on the tray, first making sure the tray is perfectly clean and dry. With a brush, coat the lobster shells evenly with liquid aspic and refrigerate the tray until the aspic has set firmly. Brush the shell with a second coat of aspic and refrigerate once more. (Melt the aspic and rechill it over ice as necessary.) With a spatula return any aspic that was under the medallions in the jelly-roll pan to the aspic in the saucepan.

Cut the hard-cooked eggs in half lengthwise and carefully remove the yolks. Force the yolks through a fine sieve with the back of the spoon, then beat in the reserved tablespoon of mayonnaise and 1½ tablespoons of softened butter. Taste for salt and pepper. Spoon the egg-yolk mixture into a pastry bag fitted with a decorative tube and pipe the egg yolks into the egg-white halves. Set the eggs on a rack over a jelly-roll pan.

Wash off the artichoke bottoms and pat them dry with paper towels. Place a tomato on each of the artichoke bottoms and set them on the rack as well. Lightly brush the eggs and the tomatoes with a coating of aspic and refrigerate them until the aspic is firm. Then dot the top of each egg half with a caper. Dip the remaining strips of leek or scallion into aspic and wrap a strip in a long spiral coil around each peeled tomato. Refrigerate again until the aspic has set.

Pour the remaining aspic into a small loaf pan and refrigerate for at least an hour, or until firmly set. Dip the bottom of the pan in hot water. Place an inverted plate over the top of the mold and, holding the pan and the plate together firmly, turn them over. The aspic should slide out easily. Cut the aspic into ¼-inch slices and then into ¼-inch dice.

Set the egg halves and the artichoke bottoms with tomatoes in a pattern around the lobsters. Scatter the aspic dice around the lobsters and garniture and return the tray to the refrigerator for at least 2 hours, or until ready to serve.

Just before serving you may want to decorate the tray with lettuce leaves and with a whole head of lettuce, fancifully cut tomato and lemon baskets, and a whole black truffle on a decorative skewer (attelet) as shown in the photograph. Lobster elaborately presented in this fashion is often called homard en bellevue parisienne.

Soufflé de homard à l'américaine

LOBSTER SOUFFLÉ WITH LOBSTER SAUCE

To serve 4 to 6

6 black truffle rounds from a thinly
    peeled truffle, sliced ⅛ inch thick
6 tablespoons cognac
Two 1½- to 2-pound live lobsters
1¾ cups dry white wine
6 tablespoons flour
½ cup clarified butter *(page 13)*,
    plus 5 tablespoons unsalted butter,
    cut into ¼-inch bits and chilled
1 cup *fumet de poisson (page 5)*
⅔ cup finely chopped onions
⅓ cup finely chopped scraped carrots
1 large firm ripe tomato, washed,

stemmed and coarsely chopped
3 tablespoons canned tomato paste
2 tablespoons finely chopped celery
1 teaspoon coarsely chopped garlic
½ cup fresh parsley leaves
1 medium-sized bay leaf
1 teaspoon finely cut fresh tarragon,
    or substitute ½ teaspoon
    crumbled dried tarragon
¼ teaspoon finely cut fresh thyme,
    or substitute ⅛ teaspoon
    crumbled dried thyme
1 tablespoon salt
Freshly ground black pepper
1¼ cups heavy cream

Place the truffle rounds in a small, shallow bowl and pour 3 tablespoons of the cognac over them. Set aside at room temperature.

With a cleaver or large, heavy knife, chop off the tail section of each lobster at the point where it joins the body and twist off the large claws. Slice each tail crosswise into 4 or 5 pieces, and make a gash on the flat side of each of the large claws.

Split the body shells in half lengthwise and remove and discard the gelatinous sac (stomach) in the head and the long intestinal vein attached to it. Scoop out the greenish-brown tomalley (or liver) and the black caviarlike coral (or eggs) if any. Place the tomalley and coral in a small bowl, add ¼ cup of the wine, any juice left from cutting up the lobster and 6 tablespoons of flour and mix well. Set aside.

In a heavy 12-inch sauté pan, heat the ½ cup of clarified butter over high heat for 10 seconds. Add the pieces of lobster and turn them about with a slotted spoon until they are evenly coated on all sides and the shells have begun to turn red. Add the remaining 1½ cups of wine, 2 tablespoons of cognac, the *fumet de poisson,* onions, carrots, tomato, tomato paste, celery, garlic, parsley, bay leaf, tarragon, thyme, salt and a liberal grinding of pepper. Stirring constantly, bring to a boil. Reduce the heat to low, cover the pan tightly and simmer for 15 minutes. With tongs or a slotted spoon, transfer the pieces of lobster to a large platter to cool.

Stirring constantly with a whisk, add the reserved tomalley-and-flour mixture to the mixture remaining in the pan. Still whisking, bring to a boil over high heat, then set the pan aside off the heat.

Shell the tail pieces and the lobster claws with a pick or small knife, and cut all the meat into small pieces. Set the meat aside. Remove the small lobster legs and chop them and the body shells coarsely.

Add all the chopped shells to the sauté pan and, stirring constantly, bring to a boil over high heat. Reduce the heat to low and, stirring occasionally, simmer uncovered for about 10 minutes, or until the sauce thickens. Strain the entire contents of the pan through a fine sieve lined with a double thickness of dampened cheesecloth and set over a deep bowl. Press down hard on all the vegetables and lobster shells with the back of a spoon to extract their juices before discarding them. There should be about 1¾ to 2 cups of *américaine* sauce.

Ladle ¾ cup of the sauce into a heavy 1- to 1½-quart enameled-iron or tin-lined copper saucepan and stir in ¾ cup of the heavy cream with a wire whisk. Whisking constantly, pour in the remaining tablespoon of cognac and cook over moderate heat for 2 or 3 minutes. Remove the pan from the heat, dot the surface of the sauce with about 1 tablespoon of butter bits and set aside.

Ladle the remaining *américaine* sauce into a 3- to 4-quart enameled or stainless-steel saucepan and stir in ½ cup of heavy cream. Taste for seasoning. Then add the reserved lobster meat and turn the pieces about with a spoon until they are evenly coated. Set aside.

SOUFFLÉ

1 tablespoon butter, softened	5 egg whites
1 cup *sauce béchamel (page 9)*	¼ cup freshly grated imported
3 egg yolks	Gruyère cheese

SOUFFLÉ: Preheat the oven to 400°. With a pastry brush, spread the tablespoon of softened butter evenly over the bottom and sides of a 2-quart *gratin* or baking dish about 2½ inches deep.

In a heavy 2- to 3-quart saucepan, warm the *sauce béchamel* over low heat for a minute or so. Whisk in the egg yolks, one at a time. Remove the pan from the heat and set aside.

With a large balloon whisk, beat the egg whites in an unlined copper bowl (glass or ceramic will do) until they are stiff enough to form unwavering peaks on the beater when it is lifted from the bowl. Stir 2 heaping tablespoons of the whites into the waiting sauce, then stir in the grated cheese. Scoop the remaining egg whites over the sauce and, using an over-under cutting motion rather than a stirring one, fold them together gently but thoroughly.

Pour the lobster and its sauce into the buttered dish, spreading the lobster meat out evenly. Spoon the soufflé mixture over the top and gently spread and smooth it to the edges of the dish with a spatula. With the dull side of a large knife, quickly and carefully make crisscrossing diagonal lines about 2 inches apart and ¼ inch deep over the surface of the soufflé. Bake in the middle of the oven for about 25 minutes, or until the soufflé has risen an inch or more above the edge of the dish and the top of the soufflé is golden brown.

Meanwhile, warm the reserved lobster sauce over low heat and swirl in the remaining 4 tablespoons of butter bits. Taste for seasoning.

Just before serving, pat the truffle rounds dry with paper towels and gently place them in a ring around the center of the soufflé. Serve at once, accompanied by the sauce presented separately in a sauceboat.

Coulibiac

BRIOCHE LOAF FILLED WITH SALMON, MUSHROOMS, VELOUTÉ AND CRÊPES

The "coulibiac" is easier to prepare if you allow two days. Make the salmon, crêpes, eggs and rice and the brioche dough a day ahead. The next day combine the eggs and rice with the tapioca, then assemble the loaf.

To serve 8

SAUMON
2 tablespoons unsalted butter, softened
3 tablespoons finely chopped shallots
2 teaspoons salt
¼ teaspoon plus ½ teaspoon
    freshly ground black pepper
2 pounds center-cut salmon fillets,
    boned carefully with tweezers,
    then skinned and cut diagonally
into ¼-inch-thick slices
½ pound fresh mushrooms, wiped
    clean, trimmed and cut into ⅛-inch
    thick slices (about 2 cups)
¼ cup finely cut fresh dill leaves
1 cup dry white wine
1 cup *sauce veloutée (page 8)* made
    with *fumet de poisson*
5 egg yolks
2 tablespoons strained fresh lemon juice
⅛ teaspoon ground hot red pepper

SAUMON (SALMON): Preheat the oven to 350°. Spread 2 tablespoons of softened butter on the bottom and sides of a 7½-by-12-by-2-inch glass baking dish. Scatter the shallots over the bottom of the dish and season them with ½ teaspoon of the salt and ¼ teaspoon of the black pepper. Arrange the salmon in two parallel rows the length of the dish, overlapping the slices at the middle of the dish. Spread the mushroom slices over the salmon, and sprinkle them with ¼ cup of dill, 1 teaspoon of salt and ½ teaspoon of black pepper. Pour the wine over the fish. Cover tightly with foil and bake in the middle of the oven for 20 minutes, or until the salmon flakes easily when prodded with a fork.

With a bulb baster or spoon, transfer as much of the cooking liquid as possible to a heavy 10- to 12-inch skillet. Let the salmon rest for about 15 minutes, then draw up any additional liquid that accumulates around it and add it to the skillet. Bring the liquid to a boil over high heat and cook briskly until it is reduced to about ½ cup. Reduce the heat to moderate and, stirring constantly with a wire whisk, slowly pour in the *sauce veloutée* and continue to cook for 4 to 5 minutes. Beat the 5 egg yolks lightly with a fork and whisk them into the sauce. Bring to a simmer, stirring all the while with the whisk and remove the skillet from the heat. Stir in the lemon juice, ½ teaspoon of salt and the red pepper. Taste for seasoning and pour the sauce over the salmon, spreading it (smoothly) with a spatula. As the sauce runs into the dish, spoon it back over the salmon until it is collected on the fish. Cool to room temperature, then cover and refrigerate until the fish is firm to the touch; preferably, overnight.

CRÊPES (to yield 20)
1¼ cups all-purpose flour
4 eggs
1 cup milk
1¼ cups cold water
3 tablespoons unsalted butter,
melted and cooled, plus 6
    tablespoons melted clarified
    butter *(page 13)*
½ teaspoon salt
3 tablespoons finely chopped parsley
3 tablespoons finely cut fresh dill leaves

CRÊPES: To make the batter with a blender, combine 1¼ cups of flour, 4 eggs, 1 cup of milk, 1¼ cups of cold water, 3 tablespoons of melted butter and ½ teaspoon of salt in the blender jar. Blend at high speed for a few seconds. Turn off the machine, scrape down the sides of the jar with a rubber spatula and blend again for 40 seconds. Pour the batter into a bowl and stir in 3 tablespoons of parsley and 3 of dill.

To make crêpe batter by hand, stir the flour and eggs together in a mixing bowl and gradually stir in the milk, water and salt. Beat with a whisk or a rotary or electric beater until smooth, then rub through a fine sieve into another bowl and stir in the melted butter, parsley and dill. Cover and refrigerate the batter for at least two hours before using it.

Heat a 6-inch crêpe pan over high heat until a drop of water flicked into it splutters and evaporates instantly. With a hair-bristled (not nylon) pastry brush, grease the bottom and sides of the pan with a little of the clarified butter. Stir the batter lightly. Using a small ladle, pour about 2 tablespoons of the batter into the pan and tip the pan so that the batter quickly covers the bottom; the batter will cling to the pan and begin to firm up almost immediately. At once tilt the pan over the bowl and pour off any excess batter; the finished crêpe should be paper-thin.

Cook the crêpe for a minute or so until the underside turns golden. Turn it over with a spatula and cook the other side for a minute. Slide the crêpe onto a plate. Brush clarified butter on the pan again and make the remaining crêpes similarly, stacking them on the plate. The crêpes may be made a day ahead of time, cooled to room temperature, covered with plastic wrap and refrigerated. (In this case, they should be brought back to room temperature before they are separated and used.) Or they may be made several hours ahead and kept at room temperature.

MÉLANGE D'OEUFS DURS ET DE RIZ
1 tablespoon minute tapioca
½ cup cold water
1 tablespoon unsalted butter
1 teaspoon finely chopped onions
½ cup uncooked long-grain white
    rice (not the converted variety)
1½ cups *fond blanc de volaille*

(page 6), or substitute 1½
    cups canned chicken stock,
    chilled, then degreased
3 hard-cooked eggs, rubbed through
    a fine sieve with the back of a spoon
3 tablespoons finely chopped parsley
1 teaspoon salt
¼ teaspoon freshly ground black pepper

MÉLANGE D'OEUFS DURS ET DE RIZ (EGG-AND-RICE MIXTURE): In a small saucepan or skillet, sprinkle the tapioca over ½ cup of cold water and set aside to soften for 5 minutes. Then, stirring frequently, bring to a boil over high heat. Reduce the heat to low and simmer uncovered for 6 to 8 minutes, until the mixture is very thick. Pour the tapioca into a fine sieve and let it drain for at least 10 minutes.

Meanwhile, in a heavy 1- to 1½-quart saucepan, melt 1 tablespoon of butter over moderate heat. When the foam begins to subside, add the

Continued on next page

onions and stir for about 2 minutes until they are soft but not brown. Stirring constantly, add the rice in a slow stream and continue to cook until the grains glisten. Do not let the rice brown. Pour in the chicken stock and, still stirring, bring to a boil. Reduce the heat to low, cover tightly, and simmer for 20 minutes, or until the grains are soft and have absorbed all the liquid. Remove the pan from the heat.

In a mixing bowl, combine the sieved hard-cooked eggs, 3 tablespoons of parsley, 1 teaspoon of salt and ¼ teaspoon of black pepper. Add the tapioca and rice and toss gently but thoroughly together.

BRIOCHE

¾ cup lukewarm milk (110° to 115°)
3 packages active dry yeast
½ teaspoon sugar
3½ to 4½ cups all-purpose flour
2 teaspoons salt
12 egg yolks plus 2 lightly beaten
   egg yolks

½ cup unsalted butter, softened
   and cut into ¼-inch bits
2 tablespoons soft fresh crumbs
   made from homemade-type white
   bread, trimmed of crusts and
   pulverized in a blender or finely
   shredded with a fork

BRIOCHE: Pour the lukewarm milk into a small, shallow bowl and sprinkle it with the yeast and sugar. Let the mixture stand for 2 or 3 minutes, then stir well. Set in a warm, draft-free place (such as a turned-off oven) for about 5 minutes, or until the mixture almost doubles in volume.

Place 3½ cups of the flour and the 2 teaspoons of salt in a large deep mixing bowl, and make a well in the center. Add the yeast mixture, 12 egg yolks and ½ cup of softened butter to the well and, with a wooden spoon, gradually incorporate the flour into the center ingredients. Stir vigorously until the dough is smooth and can be gathered into a ball.

Place the dough on a lightly floured surface, and knead by pushing it down with the heels of your hands, pressing it forward and folding it back on itself. Repeat for 10 to 15 minutes. A little at a time incorporate only enough flour to keep the dough from becoming shiny on the surface. It should be smooth and elastic. (You may need as much as 1 cup, depending on the brand of flour you use.)

When blisters form on the surface of the dough, shape it into a ball and place it in a buttered bowl. Drape with a kitchen towel and set in the warm place for about 1 hour, or until the dough doubles in bulk.

Punch the dough down with a blow of your fist. Then knead it for a minute, shape it into a ball and return it to the bowl to rise and to double its bulk once more. Use at once or cover and refrigerate overnight.

6 tablespoons softened butter plus 1½ cups warm melted butter

FINAL ASSEMBLY: Preheat the oven to 400°. With a pastry brush spread 1 tablespoon of the softened butter evenly over a large baking sheet.

Punch the dough down and, on a lightly floured surface, roll it out into a rectangle 19 inches long, 15 inches wide and ¼ inch thick.

Lay 6 of the crêpes in two parallel rows the length of the rectangle, overlapping the crêpes slightly in the center to leave a 2-inch-wide band of uncovered dough all around the rectangle. Sprinkle the crêpes evenly with about ⅓ of the egg-and-rice mixture.

Cut the salmon in half lengthwise and, with the aid of a large wide metal spatula, gently lift one half from the baking dish and turn it mushroom-coated side down over the center of the crêpes. Arrange 6 more crêpes on top as before, sprinkle them with half of the remaining egg-and-rice mixture, and place the remaining half of the salmon on top with the mushroom-coated side up. Scatter the remaining egg-and-rice mixture over the salmon and cover it with 6 more crêpes.

Lightly brush the edge of one of the exposed long sides of the brioche rectangle with the beaten egg yolk. Lift the opposite side over the filling, then fold the egg-coated side on top of it and press gently to seal the sides together along the top. Trim both ends of the *coulibiac* to extend no more than 3 inches beyond the filling. Brush the tops of the ends with beaten egg yolk and tuck the ends snugly over the top of the filled cylinder.

Carefully turn the loaf upside down on its seam and place it on the buttered baking sheet. With a small, round cookie cutter or sharp knife, make two holes 1 inch in diameter, centered about 3 inches from each end of the loaf. Gather the scraps of brioche dough into a ball and roll it out ¼ inch thick. Cut two ½-inch-wide and 4-inch-long strips out of the dough, moisten the bottom of each with egg yolk and fit the strips like collars around the openings, pressing gently to secure them. Score the loaf lightly with a knife in an attractive pattern or, if you prefer, with cookie cutters or a small knife cut the remaining dough into decorative leaf and flower shapes. Moistening the bottom of each decorative piece with egg yolk, arrange them attractively on top of the loaf. Brush the surface with the remaining egg yolk and sprinkle with the bread crumbs.

Cut a strip of aluminum foil about 5 feet long, fold it lengthwise in half and grease one side lightly with 5 tablespoons of softened butter. Wrap the foil around the loaf like a collar and tie it in place with 2 or 3 turns of kitchen string. Place small cylindrical funnels made from a double thickness of heavy foil into each pastry opening. Set the loaf aside in a warm, draft-free place for 30 minutes. Preheat the oven to 400°.

Bake the *coulibiac* in the middle of the oven for 15 minutes. Lower the heat to 375° and continue baking for 30 minutes. Cut off the string and remove the collar of foil and bake for 15 minutes longer, or until the loaf is a rich golden brown. Slide it onto a heated platter and let it rest at room temperature for 15 to 20 minutes before serving. Just before slicing the *coulibiac* pour ¼ cup melted butter into each of the openings in the top of the loaf, and remove the foil funnels. Serve the remaining cup of melted butter separately as a sauce.

NOTE: The tapioca used to thicken the egg-and-rice mixture above is a substitute for the traditional fresh *vesiga,* or sturgeon marrow. If *vesiga* is available, replace the tapioca with 3 ounces of it. Wash the *vesiga* in cold water, then simmer it for 1½ hours in enough lightly salted water to cover it completely. Chop the *vesiga* fine.

43

Saumon à la norvégienne flaunts a shrimp "fin" and a bouquet of butter daisies.

Saumon à la norvégienne

COLD POACHED SALMON WITH STUFFED BEETS, CUCUMBERS, EGGS AND
TOMATO BALLS

To serve 8

COURT-BOUILLON
4 quarts water
2 cups dry white wine
1½ cups coarsely chopped onions
1 cup coarsely chopped leeks,
   including the green tops,
   thoroughly washed to remove any
   sand
½ cup coarsely chopped celery,
   including the leaves

¼ cup coarsely chopped scraped
   carrots
¼ cup coarsely chopped parsley,
   including the stems
1 large bay leaf
1 teaspoon finely cut fresh thyme,
   or substitute ½ teaspoon
   crumbled dried thyme
3 tablespoons salt
1 tablespoon whole black
   peppercorns

COURT-BOUILLON (POACHING LIQUID): Combine 4 quarts of water,
the wine, onions, chopped leeks, celery, carrots, parsley, bay leaf, thyme,
3 tablespoons salt and peppercorns in an 8-quart enameled pot or casserole and bring to a boil over high heat. Reduce the heat to low, cover
partially and simmer for 30 minutes. Turn off the heat and let the court
bouillon cool to room temperature.

SAUMON
A 5- to 6-pound salmon, cleaned
   through the gills instead of

through the stomach and with
head and tail intact

SAUMON (SALMON): Wrap the fish in a long, doubled piece of dampened cheesecloth, leaving at least 6 inches of cloth at each end to serve as
handles for lifting the fish in and out of a fish poacher. Twist the ends of
the cloth and tie them with string, then tie the fish to the rack of the
poacher and place the rack in the pan.
   Pour in the court bouillon and add enough cold water to cover the fish
by at least 2 inches. Place the lid on the poacher and bring to a simmer

over moderate heat; immediately reduce the heat to the lowest possible point and simmer gently for 45 minutes, or until the fish feels firm when prodded gently with a finger. Let the fish cool to room temperature, then refrigerate it—still in the court bouillon—until it is thoroughly chilled.

When the fish is cold, remove the cheesecloth and carefully set the salmon on its stomach in its "swimming" position on a platter large enough for you to work on. If necessary, prop it up on one side with tightly rolled kitchen towels. Strain the court bouillon through a fine sieve lined with a double thickness of dampened cheesecloth. Reserve 2 quarts for making the *gelée;* chill or freeze the rest for another use.

With a small knife, skin the fish from the tail to the gills and across the back, leaving a notched border of skin in front of the tail and around the neck. Gently peel off the skin in strips. Then carefully scrape off the gray-ish fat underneath the skin with a spoon until the pink meat is evenly exposed. Refrigerate the salmon while making the *gelée.*

GELÉE 2 quarts of the *court-bouillon*

GELÉE (ASPIC): Prepare the *gelée,* using the reserved 2 quarts of strained court bouillon with the ingredients and method described on page 24. Set the pan of *gelée* in a large bowl or pot half filled with crushed ice or ice cubes and water. Stir with a large metal spoon until it thickens enough to flow sluggishly off the spoon. Pour a film of *gelée* about ⅛ inch thick over the bottom of a large serving platter or tray and refrigerate until firm. Then slowly spoon *gelée* over the salmon on its platter; the gelée should cling to the salmon and cover it with a thin translucent glaze. Return the fish to the refrigerator.

(Keep the remaining *gelée* at room temperature so that it remains liquid and ready to use; if it begins to set, warm briefly over low heat to soften it, then stir it over ice again until it reaches the same thick but still fluid consistency as before.)

GARNITURE
5 large green leek leaves
2 hard-cooked egg yolks
1 tablespoon unsalted butter,
softened
1 small black truffle *(see Glossary),*
 thinly peeled and cut into ⅛-
 inch-thick slices

GARNITURE: To prepare the decorations for the fish, drop the leek leaves into a pot of boiling water and boil for 2 or 3 minutes. Drain the leaves in a sieve, run cold water over them to set their color, then spread them on paper towels and pat dry. With a small, sharp knife, cut the leaves into 8 leaf blades, two 6- to 8-inch-long strips about ½ inch wide, and 20 to 25 long thin strips to use as thin stems for daisies, to outline the border of skin remaining on the salmon and to decorate the tomatoes. Reserve one large piece of leaf to cover the hole at the gill where the fish was cleaned. (The ingredients for decoration are given for one side of the

Continued on next page

fish, presuming it will be seen from only one side. If you prefer to decorate both sides, increase the leek tops, yolk mixture for the daisies and
the truffle accordingly.)

When the aspic on the salmon is firm, dip the thin green strips of leek
one by one into the liquid aspic and outline the head and tail notches,
trimming the strips neatly as you proceed. Then dip some of the remaining thin strips one by one into the aspic and set them as daisy stems on one
side of the fish. Next, dip the petal blades into the aspic and set them in
place one at a time. Then dip the long ½-inch strips and place them
along the bottom of the fish so it looks as if the other stems branch from
there. Dip the large piece of leek into the aspic to cover the gill and set it
in place. Refrigerate the fish while you prepare the egg mixture.

Force the 2 hard-cooked egg yolks through a fine sieve with the back
of a spoon. Beat in 1 tablespoon of softened butter, cover tightly and
chill until the aspic on the fish has set. Then spoon the egg-yolk-and-but-
ter paste into a pastry bag fitted with a small tube and pipe daisies in the
spots you have designed for them on the side of the fish. Cut out truffle
rounds ½ inch in diameter from the truffle slices and gently press one in
the center of each flower. Reserve the remaining truffle pieces.

Spoon another coating of aspic over the salmon and refrigerate it while
you prepare the other garniture.

BETTERAVES ROUGES FARCIES AU
    SAUMON FUMÉ

8 small fresh firm beets	small pieces
¼ pound smoked salmon, cut into	¼ cup heavy cream, chilled
	2 tablespoons of the *gelée*

BETTERAVES ROUGES FARCIES AU SAUMON FUMÉ (BEETS STUFFED
WITH SMOKED SALMON): With a small, sharp knife cut the tops from the
beets, leaving about 1 inch of stem on each. Scrub the beets under cold
running water, then drop them into a pot of boiling water. The water
should cover them by at least 2 inches. Return to a boil, reduce the heat to
low, cover the pan and simmer until the beets show no resistance when
pierced deeply with the point of a small skewer. (This may take anywhere from 30 minutes for young beets to as long as 2 hours if you have
to use older ones. The beets should be kept constantly covered with water;
add boiling water if necessary.)

Drain the beets in a colander and, when they are cool enough to handle, slip off the skins. Cut off the stems and bottoms of the beets so they
will stand straight, then with a small, sharp spoon hollow out the top of
each beet to make a bowllike shell about ¼ inch thick. Purée the smoked
salmon in an electric blender, then scrape it into a mixing bowl. Beating
constantly with a spoon, add the heavy cream to the salmon a tablespoon
at a time. Beat in the 2 tablespoons of *gelée* and taste for seasoning. Then
fill the beets with the smoked salmon mixture, dividing it evenly among
them. Cut 8 small truffle circles ¼ inch in diameter from the reserved

truffle pieces, and place one on top of each beet. Refrigerate the beets on a large rack set over a jelly-roll pan.

CONCOMBRES FARCIS AUX
    CREVETTES
2 large cucumbers
¼ cup finely chopped plus 32
    whole shelled, cooked tiny fresh
    crevettes (see Glossary) or
    shrimp (60 or more to the

pound), or substitute ¼ cup
finely chopped, plus 32 whole
drained, canned tiny shrimp
2 tablespoons *sauce mayonnaise*
    (page 13)
1 tablespoon of the *gelée*

CONCOMBRES FARCIS AUX CREVETTES (CUCUMBERS STUFFED WITH SHRIMP): Scrub the unpeeled cucumbers under cold water and pat them completely dry with paper towels. Cut off the ends and slice each cucumber crosswise into 4 cylinders. With a small, sharp knife, score and decorate the green peel of each cylinder as fancifully as you like. Hollow out the cylinders with a spoon to make round tubes about ¼ inch thick. Combine the chopped shrimp, 2 tablespoons of mayonnaise and 1 tablespoon of *gelée* in a bowl and mix well. Fill the cucumbers with the shrimp mixture, dividing it evenly among them and garnish the top of each one with 4 small shelled shrimp, equally spaced with tails to the center. Between each one place a small ¼-inch-wide truffle circle cut from the remaining truffle slices. Place the cucumbers on the rack next to the beets in the refrigerator.

TOMATES 4 large firm ripe tomatoes

TOMATES (TOMATOES): Drop the tomatoes into a pan of boiling water and boil briskly for about 10 seconds. Run cold water over them and peel them with a small, sharp knife. Cut out the stems, then slice the tomatoes in half lengthwise. Squeeze the halves gently to remove the seeds and juices. One at a time, place a tomato half on a kitchen towel cut side up. Pull the towel up tightly around the tomato, enclosing it completely; twist the ends of the towel together and squeeze gently to shape the tomato into a compact ball. Dip the reserved blanched leek strips into the *gelée* and arrange them attractively in rings or coils around the tomato balls. Chill the tomatoes on the rack with the beets and cucumbers.

OEUFS MIMOSA
4 hard-cooked eggs
4 tablespoons unsalted butter,
    softened
½ teaspoon salt
⅛ teaspoon freshly ground white
    pepper

8 capers
14 shelled, cooked medium-sized
    crevettes with the heads on *(see*
    Glossary), or substitute 14
    shelled medium-sized shrimp
    (about 21 to 25 to the pound)
    with or without the heads on

Continued on next page

OEUFS MIMOSA (STUFFED EGGS): With a small knife, cut each of the 4 hard-cooked eggs in half crosswise and carefully remove the yolks. Trim off a thin slice from the end of each egg-white half so it will stand on end. (Use these egg white pieces to make eyes for the fish.) Force the yolks through a fine sieve with the back of a spoon, then beat in the 4 tablespoons of softened butter a little at a time. Add the ½ teaspoon salt and ⅛ teaspoon white pepper; taste for seasoning. Spoon the egg-yolk mixture into a pastry bag fitted with a decorative tube and pipe it into the egg-white halves. Dot the top of each one with a caper. Remove the jelly-roll pan with the rack of beets, cucumbers and tomatoes from the refrigerator. Set the eggs on the rack, and then spoon a coating of aspic over the garnishes. Return them to the refrigerator until the aspic is firm.

FINAL ASSEMBLY: Very carefully transfer the salmon to the serving platter, again placing it in the "swimming" position, and neatly freeing it from any aspic that may have jelled around it before you set it on the platter. Arrange the stuffed beets and cucumbers, the tomato balls and the stuffed eggs attractively around the salmon. One by one set the whole *crevettes* or shrimp on their heads facing forward in a row down the back of the salmon to resemble a fin. Anchor them by pushing their pointed spiky heads gently into the flesh of the salmon. Brush them with aspic and refrigerate the salmon for at least two hours before serving. (If you are using shrimp without heads on anchor them on the head end in the salmon with a toothpick.)

Transfer any remaining aspic on the jelly-roll pan to the saucepan of aspic and warm it until it is fluid. Pour the aspic into a small loaf pan and chill until firm. Dip the pan briefly into hot water, place an inverted plate over it, and, grasping pan and plate firmly together, turn them over. The aspic should slide out easily. Cut it crosswise into ¼-inch-thick slices, and then into ¼-inch dice. Scatter the dice around the salmon and the garniture before serving.

SAUMON POCHÉ MOUSSELINE (POACHED SALMON WITH MOUSSELINE SAUCE): Prepare the court bouillon as described in this recipe and in it poach a 5- to 6-pound salmon. As soon as the fish is cooked, remove it from the pan and set it on its side. Open the cheesecloth and remove the skin and gray fat underneath it from the top side of the fish from tail to gill. Carefully transfer the salmon to a heated platter. Garnish the platter with peeled boiled potatoes and parsley sprigs. Present the *sauce mousseline* separately in a bowl or sauceboat and serve immediately.

Quenelles de brochet mousselines

POACHED PIKE MOUSSE DUMPLINGS

To serve 8 to 10

9 tablespoons unsalted butter,
    softened, plus 2 tablespoons
    unsalted butter, cut into ½-inch
    bits
½ cup cold water
Salt
½ cup all-purpose flour
1 pound skinned pike fillets, cut

into 2-inch pieces
1 whole egg
2 egg whites
¾ cup heavy cream, chilled
¼ teaspoon ground nutmeg,
    preferably freshly grated
⅛ teaspoon freshly ground white
    pepper
Sauce Nantua (page 12) or *sauce*
    vin blanc (page 14), freshly made

With a pastry brush, spread 1 tablespoon of the softened butter over the bottom and sides of a flat-bottomed dish about 4 inches in diameter.

In a heavy 1-quart saucepan, bring the water, 2 tablespoons of butter bits and a pinch of salt to a boil over high heat, stirring occasionally. As soon as the butter has melted, remove the pan from the heat and pour in the flour. Beat vigorously with a wooden spoon for a few seconds until the mixture (known as a *panade*) is smooth. Then return to moderate heat, and still beating vigorously, cook until the *panade* is thick enough to pull away from the bottom and sides of the pan into a solid mass. Spoon the *panade* into the buttered dish, spreading it evenly. Cover with a piece of buttered wax paper and refrigerate until thoroughly chilled.

Meanwhile, purée the fish in the jar of an electric blender, 5 or 6 pieces at a time, or put it through the finest blade of a food grinder. As it is puréed, transfer the fish to a bowl. When all the fillets have been blended or ground, add 6 tablespoons of softened butter, a few tablespoonfuls at a time, beating vigorously with a wooden spoon. Refrigerate for at least 30 minutes.

Then transfer the *panade* to a deep chilled bowl and, one at a time, beat in the whole egg and the egg whites. When all of the eggs have been absorbed, beat in the puréed fish a little at a time. Then force the mixture through the finest disc of a food mill into a clean bowl set in a pot of crushed ice or ice and water. Beating constantly, add the cream a tablespoon at a time. Beat in the nutmeg, pepper and 1½ teaspoons salt. Cover with foil or plastic wrap and chill for at least 30 minutes.

Spread the remaining 2 tablespoons of butter evenly over the bottom and sides of a heavy 12-inch sauté pan. Bring two 1½- to 2-quart saucepans half filled with water to a boil over high heat.

To shape each *quenelle,* fill a soupspoon generously with the fish mixture. Dip another soupspoon into one pan of boiling water and invert it

Continued on next page

over the first spoon to mold the fish mixture into an oval shape. Then use the second spoon to push the *quenelle* gently into the buttered skillet.

When all the *quenelles* have been shaped, pour the second pan of boiling water down the sides of the skillet and add 1 teaspoon of salt. Cover the pan at once and poach over low heat for 10 minutes, or until the *quenelles* feel firm when pressed lightly with a finger. With a slotted spoon, carefully transfer the *quenelles* to a heated platter. Pour the *sauce vin blanc* or *sauce Nantua* over them and serve.

NOTE: If you wish to prepare the *quenelles* in advance, you may transfer them to ice water as soon as they are poached. Let them cool completely and then transfer them to a dampened towel spread out on a jelly-roll pan. Cover with plastic wrap or foil and refrigerate until ready to serve. To reheat them, bring 1 quart of water to a simmer in a 2-quart saucepan, drop in the *quenelles* and simmer for 3 or 4 minutes.

Filets de sole Marguery

FILLET OF SOLE WITH MUSSELS, SHRIMP AND WHITE WINE SAUCE

To serve 6

1 tablespoon butter, softened, plus
  2 tablespoons unsalted butter
6 eight-ounce sole fillets (preferably
  Dover sole), skinned
24 mussels in their shells
½ cup *fumet de poisson (page 5)*

½ cup dry white wine
1 pound imported *crevettes (see
  Glossary),* or substitute 1 pound
  small shrimp (about 60 or more
  to the pound), shelled and
  deveined

Preheat the oven to 350°. Spread the tablespoon of softened butter over the bottom and sides of a *gratin* dish large enough to hold the sole in one layer. Fold the fillets lengthwise in half, white side out, arrange them side by side in the buttered dish, and set aside.

Scrub the mussels thoroughly under cold running water with a stiff brush or scouring pad. With a small, sharp knife scrape or pull off the black ropelike tufts from the shells. Combine the mussels, *fumet de poisson* and wine in a 3- to 4-quart enameled or stainless-steel saucepan, cover tightly and bring to a boil over high heat. Reduce the heat to low and simmer for about 2 minutes, shaking the pan from time to time until the mussels open. Discard those that remain closed.

With a slotted spoon, transfer the mussels to a plate; remove and discard their shells and pull off and discard the dark filament that surrounds them. Place the mussels in a bowl and cover with foil to keep them warm. Strain the broth through a fine sieve lined with a double thickness of dampened cheesecloth and pour it evenly over the sole. Cover with buttered wax paper, cut to fit snugly inside the dish. Bring to a simmer on top of the stove, then poach the sole in the middle of the oven for about 10 minutes, or until the fish flakes easily when prodded with a fork.

Wash the *crevettes* or shrimp under cold water and pat them completely dry with paper towels. In a heavy 8- to 10-inch skillet, melt the 2 tablespoons of unsalted butter over moderate heat. When the foam begins to subside, drop in the *crevettes* or shrimp and, turning them frequently with a slotted spoon, sauté for 3 to 4 minutes, or until they turn pink and feel firm to the touch. Transfer the *crevettes* or shrimp to the plate with the mussels.

Carefully pour the poaching liquid from the sole through a fine sieve set over a heavy tin-lined copper or enameled-iron saucepan. Ring the sole in the serving dish with a circle of the *crevettes* or shrimp and a circle of mussels. Drape with foil to keep them warm while you prepare the sauce. Preheat the broiler to its highest setting.

SAUCE VIN BLANC

4 large egg yolks	juice
1¼ cups warm clarified butter	¼ teaspoon salt
(page 13)	⅛ teaspoon freshly ground white
2 teaspoons strained fresh lemon	pepper

SAUCE VIN BLANC (WHITE WINE SAUCE) : Bring the poaching liquid to a boil over high heat. Cook briskly until the liquid is reduced to 4 tablespoons. Remove the pan from the heat. With a wire whisk, beat the egg yolks into the pan and continue to beat briskly for 2 or 3 minutes until the yolks begin to thicken. Place the pan over low heat and cook until the yolks almost double in volume. Lift the pan from the heat from time to time, still whisking, to prevent the egg yolks from curdling.

Off the heat, whisking, pour in the 1¼ cups of clarified butter in a slow, thin stream. After about ¼ cup of the butter has been absorbed the sauce will begin to thicken again and you may whisk in the remaining butter more rapidly. Stir in the lemon juice, salt and pepper.

Taste for seasoning. Then pour the sauce evenly over the sole, shrimp and mussels. Slide the baking dish under the broiler for about 30 seconds, or until the top is lightly browned. Serve at once.

Fowl & Eggs

Poulet sauté Boivin

SAUTÉED CHICKEN WITH ARTICHOKE HEARTS, ONIONS AND POTATOES

To serve 4

3 young artichokes, each about
   2 inches in diameter
1 lemon, cut in half
2 tablespoons plus 1 teaspoon
   strained fresh lemon juice
8 to 10 tablespoons clarified butter
   (page 13)
12 peeled white onions, about 1½
   inches in diameter

A 3- to 3½-pound chicken, cut
   into 8 serving pieces (see diagrams
   opposite)
16 small new potatoes, peeled and
   shaped into balls about 1½
   inches in diameter
Salt
Freshly ground black pepper
1 cup fond brun de veau (page 4)
2 tablespoons glace de viande (page 7)

Cut off the stems of the artichokes and snap off the small bottom leaves and any bruised outer leaves. Lay each artichoke on its side, grip it firmly, and slice about 1 inch off the top. With scissors, trim ¼ inch off the points of the remaining leaves. (Rub all the cut edges with the cut lemon as you proceed to prevent discoloring.) Slice each artichoke lengthwise into quarters and, with a small knife or the tip of a small spoon, scrape out the hairy chokes and the small white and pale purple leaves.

Drop the artichokes into a 12-inch sauté pan or skillet filled with enough boiling water to cover them completely. Add 2 tablespoons of lemon juice, reduce the heat to moderate and cook uncovered for 10 minutes. Drain the artichoke quarters in a sieve or colander and run cold water over them to stop their cooking. Set them aside on paper towels to drain completely.

With paper towels wipe the pan and in it warm 4 tablespoons of the clarified butter over moderate heat. Add the onions and, sliding the pan back and forth frequently to roll the onions about, brown them lightly on all sides. As they brown, transfer them to a plate with a slotted spoon.

Preheat the oven to its lowest setting. Place the chicken, skin side down, in the butter remaining in the pan and brown it over high heat, turning the pieces with tongs or a slotted spoon and regulating the heat so that they color richly and evenly without burning. Add up to 2 more tablespoons of clarified butter, if necessary. When the chicken is browned, return the onions to the pan. Cover tightly and sauté over low heat for 20 to 25 minutes, or until the chicken is tender.

Meanwhile, in another heavy 10- to 12-inch skillet, warm the remaining 4 tablespoons of clarified butter for about 10 seconds. Drop in the potatoes and, sliding the pan back and forth over the burner constantly, brown them lightly but richly and evenly on all sides. Add the artichokes, season with salt and pepper, cover tightly and cook over the lowest possible heat for about 15 minutes, shaking the pan from time to time. The potatoes and artichokes are done if they show no resistance to the point of a skewer or the tip of a small, sharp knife. Remove the pan from the heat and set aside.

When the chicken is cooked remove the bones from the breast pieces, and arrange all the pieces attractively on a heated ovenproof platter. Cover loosely with foil, and keep the chicken warm in the oven while you prepare the sauce. With a slotted spoon transfer the onions to the pan of potatoes and artichokes.

With a large spoon, skim as much fat as possible from the liquid remaining in the pan in which the chicken was sautéed. Pour in the *fond brun de veau* and bring to a boil over high heat, stirring constantly and scraping in the browned particles that cling to the bottom and sides of the pan. Reduce the heat to low and stir in the *glace de viande* and 1 teaspoon of lemon juice. Taste for seasoning. Strain the sauce over the onions, potatoes and artichokes and turn them about gently with a slotted spoon until they are evenly glazed with the sauce. Arrange the vegetables as formally as you like around the chicken, pour the sauce over the entire contents of the platter and serve at once.

How to Cut an Uncooked Bird into Eight Serving Pieces

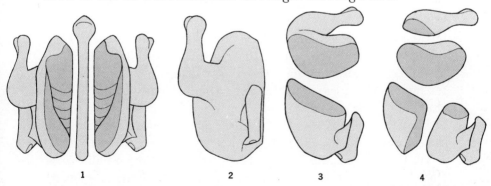

1   **2**   **3**   **4**

Before a bird is sautéed, poached or braised, you may cut it into serving pieces as shown above. (1) Place the bird breast side up and, with a sharp carving knife or chef's knife, cut along the length of the breast bone and along each side of the back bone. Remove the back bone in one piece. (2) One at a time, lay each half of the bird flat, flesh side up. (3) Gently pull the leg away from the breast and, following the outline of the leg, cut the half of the bird in two. (4) Cut the leg into two pieces at the joint between the drumstick and thigh. Separate the wing and the top part of the breast from the main breast section. Repeat the procedure with the other half of the bird to produce eight serving pieces in all. After the bird is cooked, remove the breast and rib bones.

Canard à l'orange

ROAST DUCK WITH ORANGE SAUCE

To serve 8

2 medium-sized oranges
Two 5- to 6-pound ducks
Salt
Freshly ground black pepper
4 cups *fond lié (page 10)*

⅓ cup sugar
⅓ cup white wine vinegar
⅓ cup fresh lemon juice
2 teaspoons red currant jelly
  (optional)
3 tablespoons unsalted butter,
  chilled and cut into ½-inch bits
1 tablespoon Grand Marnier or
  other orange-flavored liqueur

With a small, sharp knife, remove the peel from one of the oranges in long strips as wide as possible, without cutting into the bitter white pith. Cut the peel into julienne strips 1½ to 2 inches long and no more than ¹⁄₁₆ inch wide. You should have ¼ cup. If less, use part of the peel of the second orange. Drop the peel into boiling water and boil for 1 or 2 minutes, then drain the julienne in a sieve and run cold water over the strips to set their color. Spread the strips on paper towels to dry. Squeeze enough juice from the oranges to make ⅓ cup and set aside.

Preheat the oven to 450°. Pat the ducks completely dry inside and out with paper towels. With a sharp knife, cut off each wing tip at the joint. Rub the cavities of both ducks with salt and pepper and sprinkle the skin of the ducks lightly with salt. Truss the ducks following the diagrams on page 58, and prick the skin around the thighs, the backs and the lower part of the breasts with the point of a skewer or sharp knife.

Place the ducks breast side up, as far apart as possible, on a rack set in a large, shallow roasting pan. Roast in the middle of the oven for 20 minutes until the skin browns lightly. Draw off the fat from the pan with a bulb baster, and turn the ducks on one side.

Reduce the heat to 350° and roast for about 30 minutes; turn the birds on the other side and continue roasting for about 30 minutes more. Place the ducks breast side up again and continue roasting for about 30 minutes longer, occasionally removing the fat as it accumulates in the pan. To test for doneness, pierce the thigh of each bird with the point of a small, sharp knife. The juice that trickles out should be a clear yellow; if it is pink, roast the ducks for another 5 to 10 minutes. Transfer the ducks to a heated platter and drape them with foil while you make the sauce.

Tilt the pan and, with a large spoon, remove and discard all the fat from the juices that remain. Pour in the *fond lié* and bring to a simmer over moderate heat, meanwhile scraping in the browned particles clinging to the bottom and sides of the pan. Set aside off the heat.

In a 2- to 3-quart enameled-iron or copper saucepan, stir the sugar and vinegar together and bring to a boil over high heat. Cook briskly until the mixture thickens to a tealike gold syrup. Be careful not to let the sugar burn; it will color very quickly. Pour in the warm *fond lié,* reduce the heat to low and, stirring all the while, simmer 3 or 4 minutes. Stir in the reserved orange juice, the lemon juice and the currant jelly, if you are using it. Continue to simmer for 3 to 4 minutes longer.

Strain the sauce through a fine sieve into another saucepan. Swirl in the 3 tablespoons of butter bits and when they are completely absorbed, add the Grand Marnier. Season to taste with salt and pepper. If you wish, pour some of the sauce around the birds and serve the remainder in a sauceboat. Scatter the orange peel attractively over the ducks and serve.

Or, garnish the ducks with peeled orange segments and orange baskets cut as fancifully as you like. You may also insert into the ends of the birds decorative silver skewers *(attelets)* garnished with artfully cut oranges, lemons and miniature oranges.

Poulet reine sauté à l'archiduc
SAUTÉED CHICKEN WITH MADEIRA-FLAVORED CREAM SAUCE

To serve 4

A 3- to 3½-pound chicken, cut into 8 serving pieces *(see diagrams page 53)* with neck and backbone reserved
8 tablespoons clarified butter *(page 13)*
½ cup finely chopped onions
2 tablespoons cognac
½ cup *sauce velouté (page 8)*

½ cup heavy cream
¼ teaspoon salt
⅛ teaspoon ground white pepper
1 tablespoon dry Madeira
2 tablespoons strained fresh lemon juice
2 tablespoons unsalted butter, chilled and cut into ½-inch bits
1 black truffle, thinly peeled and sliced into ⅛-inch-thick rounds

Pat the chicken completely dry with paper towels. Then, in a 12-inch sauté pan or heavy skillet, warm the clarified butter over moderate heat. Add the chicken pieces skin side down and sauté for 3 or 4 minutes on each side, or until they are firm and white. Do not let them brown. Transfer the chicken to a plate and set aside.

Add the onions to the butter remaining in the skillet and, stirring frequently, cook for about 5 minutes, or until they are soft and transparent but not brown. Return the chicken and the liquid that has accumulated around it to the pan, add the uncooked neck and backbone, and cover tightly. Simmer over low heat for about 25 minutes, basting occasionally with the juices that will soon accumulate in the pan. When the chicken is tender, discard the neck and backbone and transfer the chicken pieces to a plate. With a small knife, remove and discard the skin and the rib bones. Arrange the chicken attractively on a heated platter and drape loosely with foil to keep it warm while you prepare the sauce.

Skim as much fat as possible from the liquid remaining in the pan and pour in the cognac. Bring to a boil over moderate heat and cook until the liquid is reduced to about ¼ cup. Whisk in the velouté, cream, salt and white pepper, and continue to stir until the sauce is smooth and hot. Strain the sauce through a fine sieve into a small saucepan and warm it briefly over low heat. Stir in the Madeira and lemon juice, and taste for seasoning. Remove the pan from the heat and swirl in the butter bits.

To serve, pour the sauce over the chicken and arrange the truffle slices decoratively around it.

Poularde Derby
ROAST CHICKEN WITH RICE, FOIE GRAS AND TRUFFLE STUFFING

To serve 6

FARCE
4 tablespoons unsalted butter
2 teaspoons finely chopped onions
1 cup uncooked converted long-
  grain white rice
1½ cups *fond blanc de volaille (page*
6), or substitute 1½ cups canned
  chicken stock, chilled, then degreased
½ teaspoon salt
¼ teaspoon freshly ground white pepper
5 tablespoons finely chopped black
  truffles *(see Glossary)*
5 tablespoons finely chopped foie
  gras *en bloc (see Glossary)*

FARCE (STUFFING): First prepare the *farce* in the following fashion: Preheat the oven to 375°. Melt 4 tablespoons of butter in a heavy 2- to 3-quart casserole over moderate heat. Add the 2 teaspoons of chopped onion and, stirring frequently, cook for 1 or 2 minutes. When the onion is soft, add the rice and stir for a few minutes until the grains glisten with butter, but do not let the rice brown. Then pour in the stock, add the ½ teaspoon of salt and ¼ teaspoon of white pepper and bring to a boil.

Cover the casserole tightly and bake in the middle of the oven for about 20 minutes, or until the grains are softened but still somewhat resistant to the bite. Drain the rice in a sieve, fluffing the grains with a fork to remove excess moisture, then place it in a bowl and stir in the chopped truffles and chopped foie gras. Taste for seasoning.

MIREPOIX
3 tablespoons unsalted butter
1¼ cups finely chopped onions
½ cup finely chopped carrots
⅓ cup finely chopped celery
2 tablespoons finely chopped lean
  cooked ham
1 tablespoon finely chopped fresh parsley
½ large bay leaf
1 sprig fresh thyme, finely cut, or
  ¼ teaspoon crumbled dried thyme
½ teaspoon salt
⅛ teaspoon freshly ground white
  pepper

MIREPOIX: Meanwhile, in a heavy copper or enameled cast-iron casserole large enough to hold the two birds comfortably, melt 3 tablespoons of butter over moderate heat. When the foam begins to subside, add the 1¼ cups of chopped onions, the carrots, celery, ham, parsley, bay leaf, thyme, ½ teaspoon of salt and ⅛ teaspoon of white pepper. Stirring frequently, cook the mirepoix mixture for about 5 minutes, or until the vegetables are soft but not brown. Set the casserole aside off the heat.

POULARDE
Two 3½-pound roasting chickens
2 tablespoons softened butter
Salt
3 cups *fond brun de veau (page 4)*
1 tablespoon arrowroot dissolved in
  ¼ cup dry Madeira
2 tablespoons chilled unsalted
  butter cut in ½-inch bits

POULARDE (CHICKEN): Reduce the oven heat to 350°. Pat the chickens completely dry inside and out with paper towels. Spoon the *farce* loosely into the chickens. Close the openings by lacing them with skewers or by sewing them with heavy white thread. Fasten the neck skin to the back of each chicken with a skewer and truss the birds securely *(see page 58)*. Rub each bird with 1 tablespoon of softened butter and lightly salt it.

Place the chickens on their backs side by side on top of the mirepoix and pour ½ cup of the *fond brun de veau* into the casserole. Bring to a simmer on top of the stove, then cover the casserole tightly and braise the chickens in the middle of the oven for about 45 minutes, basting them every 15 minutes with the cooking liquid.

Increase the oven temperature to 500°. Carefully transfer the chickens from the casserole to a rack set in a large, shallow roasting pan and roast in the middle of the oven for 10 to 15 minutes, or until richly browned.

Meanwhile, strain the liquid remaining in the casserole through a fine sieve set over a heavy 1- to 2-quart saucepan, pressing down hard on the vegetables with the back of a spoon to extract all their juices before discarding them. Let the liquid rest for a minute or so, then skim as much fat as possible from the surface. Add 2½ cups of *fond brun de veau* to the roasting liquid and boil briskly until reduced to 2 cups. Lower the heat. Stirring constantly, pour in the arrowroot-and-Madeira mixture in a thin stream and simmer for several minutes until the sauce thickens lightly. Swirl in the 2 tablespoons of butter bits. Taste for seasoning. Add the slices of foie gras and both the sliced and whole truffles for the garniture and simmer for a few minutes, basting them constantly with the sauce.

GARNITURE
Six ½-inch-thick slices foie gras *en bloc (see Glossary)*
Six ⅛-inch-thick slices of black truffle, thinly peeled *(see Glossary)*
6 large whole black truffles
6 cylinders cut out of a loaf of stale

homemade-type white bread, each about 1½ inches in diameter and 3 inches long
6 two-inch *pâte brisée* tartlet shells *(page 140)*
6 tablespoons melted butter
3 large green leek leaves

GARNITURE: To garnish and serve, arrange the previously prepared *socles (below)* and the tartlet shells around the birds. Top each *socle* with a slice of foie gras and a slice of truffle and moisten them with a little of the sauce. Place a whole truffle in each tartlet shell. Pour the remaining sauce into a bowl and serve at once.

SOCLES (PEDESTALS): Cut diagonal grooves about ¼ inch deep and ¼ inch wide around the long sides of each bread cylinder. Stand the cylinders on a baking sheet and brush them evenly with 6 tablespoons of melted butter. Toast in a preheated 375° oven until golden.

Blanch the leek leaves by dropping them into boiling water and letting them boil for 1 or 2 minutes. Drain in a sieve or colander under cold water to set their color, then pat them dry with paper towels and cut them into fine strips about 4 inches long and ⅛ inch wide. Slide a strip of the blanched leek into each groove of the *socles* and trim off any excess top and bottom. These "pediments" of toasted bread may be served at room temperature and can be made hours in advance if necessary.

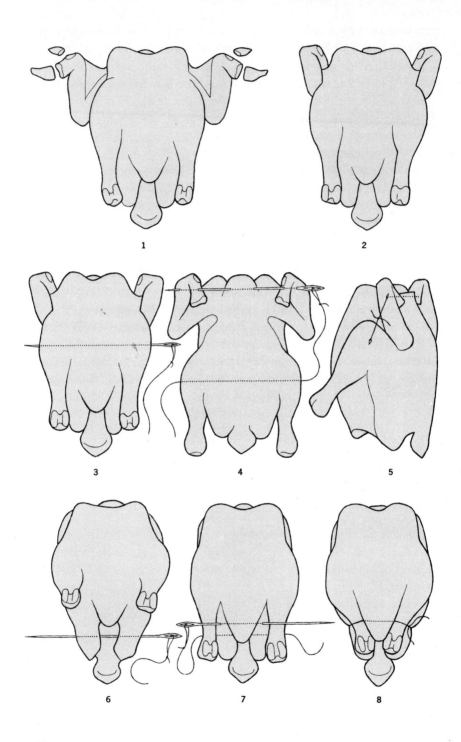

How to Truss a Large Bird

In trussing a bird that weighs more than three pounds, start by turning it breast side up. Then (1) with a sharp knife, cut off the ends of the wing tips and the small bony pieces at the joint of the first and second sections of each wing. (2) Bend the first section of each wing backward and tuck it behind the flap of skin holding the wing to the body. (3) Thread a trussing needle with kitchen string and insert the tip of the needle into the joint between the thigh and drumstick at one side of the bird. Push the needle through the bird and out the drumstick joint on the opposite side. (4) Draw all but 4 inches of string through the bird and turn the bird breast side down. Now push the needle into the nearer wing through its first and second sections, through the skin over the back of the neck, and then through the same two sections of the opposite wing. (5) Turn the bird on its side, draw the string taut, knot it tightly and clip off the ends. (6) Turn the bird breast side up and lift the legs up toward the wings. Thread the needle with another string and insert the needle into the soft spot below the bone in the lower part of the back near the tail. Push the needle through the same spot on the opposite side of the back and draw all but 4 inches of string through the bird. (7) Return the legs to their natural position and loop the string over the nearer drumstick. Lift the tip of the breastbone and put the needle through both sides of the skin joining the bone to the carcass. Loop the string over the second drumstick. (8) Push the legs of the bird forward, tightly against the breast, and pull the string taut. Knot the string tightly, and clip off the ends.

Poularde à la Néva
COLD CHICKEN WITH CHICKEN MOUSSE IN JELLIED VELOUTÉ SAUCE AND ASPIC

To serve 10 to 12

COURT-BOUILLON
5 quarts water
1 medium-sized onion, peeled and pierced with 4 whole cloves
2 medium-sized carrots, scraped and cut into 3-inch lengths
1 medium-sized celery stalk, including the leaves, trimmed and coarsely chopped
½ cup coarsely chopped fresh parsley, including the stems
2 medium-sized bay leaves
2 sprigs fresh thyme, or substitute 1 teaspoon crumbled dried thyme
2 teaspoons whole black peppercorns
2 tablespoons salt

Two 4- to 4½-pound chickens, cleaned and dressed with the smallest possible opening, preferably chickens with the heads removed but the feet intact

The preparation of this elaborate dish should be scheduled over a two-day period. On the first day, prepare the court bouillon, truss the chickens, poach them in the court bouillon, skin and refrigerate them. Then make the "gelée" and "chaud-froid" sauce. On the second day, carve the birds and make the mousse. Then coat the birds with the "chaud-froid" sauce, reassemble them and coat them with the "gelée." Once finished, "poularde à la Néva" may safely be kept in the refrigerator for a day or so before it is served.

At least one chicken with its feet intact is essential to a classic "poularde à la Néva." The feet of one bird are trimmed and tied to simulate the head—as seen in the cover photograph. If you cannot buy such chickens, the finished "poularde" will still be impressive though not as classic.

Continued on next page

COURT-BOUILLON (POACHING LIQUID): Combine the water, onion, 2 carrots, celery stalk, ½ cup parsley, bay leaves, thyme, peppercorns and 2 tablespoons of salt in a heavy 8- to 10-quart stock pot or casserole. Bring to a boil over high heat, reduce the heat to moderate and cook gently for 30 minutes. Turn off the heat and let the liquid cool to room temperature.

Meanwhile, prepare the chickens for poaching. One bird at a time, singe the legs of both birds over a gas or alcohol burner. Grasp the bird firmly in one hand and turn the legs constantly above the flame to char the foot and leg up to the first joint. As soon as the skin is evenly blackened, rub it off with a dampened kitchen towel.

Grasp the bird with the more perfect shape firmly and with scissors or a small, sharp knife cut off all but the longest center toe of each foot. (Be sure to remove the small vestigial toe above and behind the middle of each foot.) Following the diagrams on page 58, truss the chicken with a trussing needle and white string. Then make an incision across the back of each leg at the main joint, bend the legs straight up at right angles to the bird and tie the legs together at that joint. Tie the feet together at the ankles (just above the toes) and then cross the toes and tie them tightly in place. At this stage, the legs should extend in a perpendicular line straight up from the body of the bird. Wrap the legs in a double sheet of foil to hold them firmly in place and then make a final tie of the string once around the length of the body, to ensure that the bird holds its shape when it is poached. Refrigerate the chicken until ready to poach it.

Truss the second bird as shown in the diagrams, but do not bother to cut off its toes or tie its legs. Place it in the cooled court bouillon. The liquid should cover the breast of the bird by at least 1 inch; if necessary add cold water. Bring to a simmer over moderate heat, reduce the heat to low and poach the chicken partially covered for 1 hour. Turn off the heat and let the chicken cool to room temperature in the court bouillon, then transfer the bird to a platter. With a small, sharp knife, remove the trussing strings and cut away and discard all the skin. Cover the bird tightly with plastic wrap and refrigerate.

Place the chicken with the tied feet on its back in the liquid left in the casserole. The court bouillon should cover the breast by at least 1 inch; if necessary, add cold water. The ends of the legs, however, may stick up out of the liquid and should be basted every 10 minutes during the entire poaching time; the legs will not be served but need to be cooked enough to make them firm.

Bring to a simmer over moderate heat, reduce the heat to low and poach the chicken for 1 hour. Turn off the heat and let the bird cool to room temperature in the court bouillon. Then carefully transfer the chicken to a platter. Remove and discard the trussing strings and the skin. Cover the bird tightly with plastic wrap and refrigerate. Then skim as much fat as possible from the court bouillon. Measure the court bouillon, add enough cold water to make 5 quarts, and set aside in a large bowl.

GELÉE

20 envelopes unflavored gelatin	leek tops, thoroughly washed to
10 egg whites	remove any sand
10 egg shells, finely crushed	1 cup coarsely chopped fresh
3 medium-sized firm ripe tomatoes,	parsley, including the stems
coarsely chopped	1 cup coarsely chopped celery leaves
1½ cups coarsely chopped green	¾ cup coarsely chopped carrots

GELÉE (ASPIC): Pour 1 quart of the court bouillon back into the casserole. Sprinkle the gelatin over the court bouillon and let it soften for 2 or 3 minutes. Then stir in the egg whites, egg shells, tomatoes, leek tops, 1 cup parsley, celery leaves and chopped carrots. Mix well and then pour in the remaining 4 quarts of court bouillon. Stirring constantly, bring to a boil over high heat.

Reduce the heat to low and simmer undisturbed and uncovered for about 20 minutes. Then pour the entire contents of the casserole into a large sieve lined with a double thickness of dampened cheesecloth and set over a deep pan. Allow the clear liquid to drain through without stirring it at any point. Cool to room temperature, then use at once or cover tightly and refrigerate overnight. (If the aspic is refrigerated, melt it over low heat before using it.)

SAUCE CHAUD-FROID

8 tablespoons butter (1 quarter-	2 cups heavy cream
pound stick), cut into ½-inch bits	Salt
10 tablespoons flour	Freshly ground white pepper

SAUCE CHAUD-FROID (JELLIED VELOUTÉ SAUCE): In a heavy 3- to 4-quart saucepan, melt the butter bits over low heat. When the foam begins to subside, remove the pan from the heat and stir in the flour with a wire whisk to make a smooth roux. Then return to low heat and, stirring constantly, cook for about 2 minutes, or until the roux foams.

Pour in 6 cups of the aspic and beat vigorously with a whisk until the roux has dissolved. Increase the heat to moderate and, still stirring, cook until the sauce comes to a boil.

Reduce the heat to the lowest possible point and simmer the sauce for about 10 minutes, whisking it every few minutes. Pour in 2 cups of heavy cream and bring to a boil again over moderate heat, whisking frequently. Cook for 2 or 3 minutes, stirring constantly, then strain the *chaud-froid* through a fine sieve into another saucepan. Taste and season with as much salt and white pepper as you think it needs. The *chaud-froid* may be used immediately or refrigerated. If chilled, warm it again in a sauce pan, stirring constantly until it is fluid and smooth.

CARVING THE CHICKENS: Place the chicken with the tied feet on a cutting board. With a long, sharp knife, carefully remove each side of the breast in one piece. Holding the knife blade at a diagonal, cut each breast lengthwise and horizontally into 5 thin slices as equal as possible. Trim

Continued on next page

any rough edges from the slices and gently press each one flat with your hand. Set the slices aside separately in the order in which they were cut. Wrap the slices and the carcass of the bird and refrigerate them.

Then place the chicken with the untied feet on the board. Carve off both sides of the breast, each in one piece, and cut each piece, holding the knife at a diagonal, lengthwise and horizontally into 3 slices. Trim any rough edges from the slices and set them aside separately in the order in which they were cut. Carve both legs from the bird and separate the thighs from the drumsticks. Remove the thigh bones and press each piece of meat flat with your hand. Holding the meat flat, cut two ¼-inch-thick slices off the top of each thigh. Again, trim any rough edges from the slices. Wrap the breast and thigh slices separately and return them to the refrigerator.

Gather up the scraps of breast and thigh meat remaining on the board. Then, with a small knife or your fingers, remove all the remaining meat from the second bird. Discard the carcass. Chop the meat coarsely.

MOUSSE DE VOLAILLE AU FOIE GRAS

5 ounces foie gras *en bloc (see Glossary)*

1 black truffle *(see Glossary)*, thinly peeled and finely diced

1 tablespoon cognac

Salt

Freshly ground black pepper

¾ cup heavy cream, chilled

MOUSSE DE VOLAILLE (CHICKEN MOUSSE): Melt the aspic over low heat if it has been refrigerated and pour ¾ cup of it into the jar of an electric blender. Add a handful of the chopped chicken meat to the aspic and purée it. Gradually add the remaining meat. From time to time turn off the machine and scrape down the sides of the jar.

When the purée is smooth rub it, together with the foie gras, through a fine sieve with the back of a spoon into a deep bowl. Stir in the diced truffle and cognac, then taste and season with salt and pepper. In a chilled bowl, beat ¾ cup of heavy cream with a wire whisk or a rotary or electric beater until stiff enough to form soft peaks on the beater when it is lifted from the bowl. Fold the whipped cream gently but thoroughly into the chicken mousse.

With a spatula dipped in cold water from time to time, smoothly spread each slice of chicken breast and thigh with 2 tablespoons of the mousse, mounding it slightly in the center. As you coat the slices, arrange them mousse side up in order on wire racks, carefully keeping the 10 slices from the first bird in their original order. Spread the entire breast area of the reserved chicken carcass with the remaining mousse to re-create the original shape of the bird, again dipping the spatula in cold water occasionally to make the surface smooth. Chill the slices and carcass for at least 30 minutes until the mousse is firm.

FINAL ASSEMBLY: Place the racks of chicken slices over a jelly-roll pan, and turn the slices mousse side down; put the whole chicken carcass on a rack over another jelly-roll pan.

Set the pan of *chaud-froid* in a large bowl or pot half-filled with crushed ice or ice cubes and water, and stir the sauce with a large metal spoon until it thickens enough to flow sluggishly off the spoon. Spoon a coating of *chaud-froid* evenly over each chicken slice. It should cling and cover the surface with an opaque white glaze. Then coat the entire chicken including the tied feet liberally with *chaud-froid,* using a bulb baster to glaze the parts of the bird that are difficult to reach with a spoon. With a spatula scrape the excess *chaud-froid* that falls into the jelly-roll pans back into the bowl. Return the slices and carcass to the refrigerator until the *chaud-froid* is set, then coat them again and chill. The slices should only need two coats of *chaud-froid* to cover them well, but the carcass will probably need three coats.

(Keep the *chaud-froid* at room temperature throughout the glazing process so that it remains liquid and ready to use. If it begins to set, warm briefly over low heat to soften it, then stir the *chaud-froid* over ice again until it reaches the same thick but still fluid consistency as before.)

Using toothpicks to hold them in place, arrange the 10 thin slices of breast meat back on the bird as shown in the cover photograph; start at the breast end and place the slices on the glazed carcass in the same order they were carved, laying them mousse side down and overlapping them slightly as you proceed.

GARNITURE

2 large black truffles *(see Glossary),* thinly peeled, cut into ⅛-inch-thick slices, and cut into flower petals with truffle cutters or a small, sharp knife

4 or 5 large green leaves from the top of a leek or scallion, washed to remove the sand, then blanched and cut into ⅛-inch-wide strips *(see oeufs en gelée, page 84)*

Warm the remaining aspic in a saucepan over low heat, set it in a pot of crushed ice or ice and water, and stir until it is thick and syrupy. Dip truffle petals and blanched green leaf strips one at a time into the aspic and arrange them as fancifully as you like on the reassembled bird and on the remaining slices of chicken. Use the tip of a small, sharp knife to set them in place. Refrigerate again until the decorations are anchored firmly. Carefully and evenly pour spoonfuls of aspic over the bird and the slices, then chill them well to set the aspic.

With a rubber spatula, scrape up the aspic from the jelly-roll pans under the bird and sliced meat and add it to the aspic remaining in the saucepan. Warm briefly over low heat to melt it, then pour a "mirror" glaze to a depth of ⅛ inch into a large serving tray about 18 by 22 inches. Refrigerate until set. Pour the rest of the aspic into a loaf pan and chill until the aspic is firm.

Arrange the *poularde à la Néva* on the serving tray with the 10 slices of breast and thigh meat from the other chicken around it. Unmold the aspic from the loaf pan by dipping the bottom in hot water, then inverting the pan. Cut the block of aspic into ¼-inch slices and then into ¼-inch dice. Spoon the dice around the bird and refrigerate the *poularde à la Néva* until 30 minutes before serving.

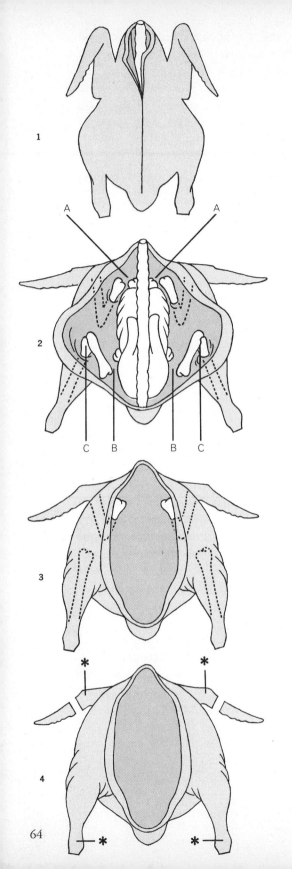

How to Bone a Chicken or Duck in the French Manner

The first step in boning a duck or chicken is to place the bird on its breast and slit the skin along the backbone from neck to tail (1). With tiny cuts of a sharp, thin boning knife, free the meat around the neck cavity from the backbone. Then, folding the skin and flesh back as you proceed, continue to cut and scrape the meat away from the carcass. Work from the neck toward the tail, turning and lifting the carcass when necessary.

Always cut as close to the bones as you can and try not to pierce the bird's skin. Wiggle each wing to find where the joint meets the carcass, then with knife or scissors cut through the joint to detach the wingbone (2A). Free the meat around each thighbone and cut the joints attaching the thighbones to the carcass (2B). With the knife separate the thighbones from the drumsticks (2C). Then lift out the carcass (3). Working from the cavity, free the meat from the two large bones of each wing and the drumsticks without piercing the skin (4). With a kitchen mallet or the side of a heavy cleaver, strike the wing tips and drumstick joints on the outside (at the points starred in number 4). Remove the bones. Next carefully remove all the meat from the bird, without piercing the skin. Finally, spread the skin out, breast side down. It is now ready to be filled. (If you are making a galantine, the wing tips are cut off after the galantine is cooked.)

Galantine de canard

DUCK SKIN STUFFED WITH DUCK, PORK, VEAL, TRUFFLES AND PISTACHIOS

To serve 15 to 20

2 five-pound ducks

MARINADE

A 7-ounce can black truffles *(see Glossary)*, thinly peeled and cut into neatly squared-off strips about ¼ inch wide and ½ inch thick

The liquid from the truffles *(see Glossary)*

¼ teaspoon Spice Parisienne *(see Glossary)*

The breast meat of the 2 ducks

¼ pound lean cooked ham, cut into neatly squared-off strips about 4 inches long, ½ inch wide and ¼ inch thick

5 ounces fresh pork fatback, cut into neatly squared-off strips the size of the ham strips

The livers of the 2 ducks, each cut into halves

4 strips fresh pork fatback (or side pork) sliced parallel to the rind, each about 8 inches long, 2½ to 3 inches wide, and ⅛ inch thick, then pounded as thin as possible between 2 sheets of wax paper

Following the diagrams at left, bone and skin both ducks. Try not to pierce the skins of the birds while you remove the meat and bones; wrap both skins in a damp kitchen towel and refrigerate until ready to use. Set the duck bones and the carcasses aside. Save the livers, gizzards and hearts, but discard any large globules of fat. Cut the breast meat of the ducks lengthwise into neat strips about ½ inch wide. Then coarsely chop any scraps of breast and all the rest of the duck meat and reserve.

MARINADE: In a glass loaf dish or deep bowl, combine the truffles, truffle liquid and ¼ teaspoon Spice Parisienne, and stir together gently. Add the duck breast, ham, 4-inch-long fatback strips and the duck livers, and turn them carefully about with a spoon until they are evenly moistened. Cover with the 8-inch slices of fatback and then with plastic wrap or foil and marinate in the refrigerator for 2 or 3 days.

FOND

The carcasses, gizzards and hearts of the two ducks

4 to 5 quarts cold water

1 large onion, peeled and pierced with 2 whole cloves

1 large carrot, scraped

1 large leek, including 2 inches of the green top, trimmed, slit lengthwise in half and thoroughly washed to remove any sand

1 large bay leaf

4 fresh parsley sprigs

2 fresh thyme sprigs or ½ teaspoon crumbled dried thyme

8 whole black peppercorns

1 tablespoon salt

FOND (STOCK): Place the duck bones, carcasses, gizzards and hearts in

Continued on next page

a heavy 6- to 8-quart casserole. Pour in 4 quarts of water; add more if necessary to cover the bones by at least 2 inches. Bring to a simmer over moderate heat, skimming off the foam and scum as they rise to the surface.

Add the onion, carrot, leek, bay leaf, parsley, thyme, peppercorns and 1 tablespoon salt, and reduce the heat to low. Simmer partially covered for 3 hours, or until the stock has developed an intense and definite flavor. With a slotted spoon, pick out and discard the duck pieces and vegetables. Then strain the stock through a fine sieve lined with a double thickness of dampened cheesecloth and set over a deep bowl.

When the stock has cooled to room temperature, refrigerate uncovered until the surface is coated with a layer of solidified fat. Sealed with the fat, the stock may safely be kept in the refrigerator for 3 or 4 days. Before using it, carefully lift off and discard all the fat.

FARCE

The coarsely chopped meat of the 2 ducks

5 ounces lean cooked ham, coarsely chopped

¾ pound fresh pork fat, coarsely chopped

¾ pound lean pork, cut into 1-inch pieces

½ pound lean veal, cut into 1-inch pieces

½ cup finely chopped shallots

1 cup dry white wine

¼ cup dry Madeira

3 egg yolks

1 teaspoon Spice Parisienne *(see Glossary)*

¼ teaspoon saltpeter *(see Glossary)*

5 teaspoons salt

½ teaspoon freshly ground black pepper

5 to 6 tablespoons butter, softened

½ cup shelled blanched unsalted pistachios

3 cups dry white wine

FARCE (STUFFING): Put the chopped duck meat, chopped ham, pork fat, lean pork, veal and shallots through the finest blade of a meat grinder 3 or 4 times and then beat in the white wine. Or grind the meat and shallots once, then purée them in an electric blender, about 1 cup at a time, using ¼ cup of the wine with each cup of meat. Transfer the purée to a deep bowl and mix thoroughly.

Add the Madeira, egg yolks, 1 teaspoon of Spice Parisienne, ¼ teaspoon saltpeter, 5 teaspoons salt and ½ teaspoon freshly ground black pepper to the purée. Knead vigorously with both hands, then beat with a wooden spoon until the *farce* is light and fluffy. To check the seasoning, drop a spoonful of the *farce* into a small pan of simmering water. Poach it for 3 to 4 minutes, taste, and add more salt and pepper to the raw *farce* if necessary. Cover the bowl tightly with foil or plastic wrap and marinate in the refrigerator for 2 or 3 days.

ASSEMBLY: Coat a double thickness of dampened cheesecloth about 36 inches long and 22 inches wide with the softened butter. Spread out the more perfect of the two duck skins with the outside surface down on the cheesecloth. If there are any punctures in the surface of the duck skin, cut oversized square patches out of the second skin and set them outside surface down over the holes to conceal them. Discard the remainder.

With a spatula, spread a layer of *farce* about ¼ inch thick on the duck skin and stuff the wing and leg cavities. Place alternating rows of pistachios, marinated duck, ham, truffle and 4-inch-long fatback strips end to end lengthwise on top of the *farce,* spacing the rows about 1 inch apart. Cover the strips with a layer of *farce* about ½ inch thick. Then place one 8-inch slice of fatback lengthwise down the center and form a groove in it with the side of your hand. Lay the pieces of duck liver down the length of the groove and cover them with another 8-inch slice of fatback. Make sure the livers are completely and smoothly surrounded by the fatback. If you need more of these fatback slices to cover the livers, use the two remaining 8-inch slices or save them for another use.

Arrange alternate rows of meat strips and pistachios along both sides of the fat-wrapped livers, add another ½-inch layer of *farce* and place the remaining pistachios, marinated strips of truffles, meat and 4-inch-long fatback in lengthwise rows on top. Cover with the rest of the *farce.*

Carefully lift up the side edges of the duck skin and pull them together tightly over the filling, thus forming a thick compact roll, or galantine. Sew the seams together with a needle and heavy thread; turn the neck skin back over the seam and stitch it to the roll. (If you have used a bird with the legs left on, bend them forward, press them close against the body and tie them in place.)

Wrap the cheesecloth around the roll, twist the ends of the cheesecloth together and tie each one securely with kitchen cord close to the galantine. Then tie the cord loosely around the bird in 3 or 4 places to keep the galantine in shape.

Place the galantine in a 15-quart fish poacher or a casserole just large enough to hold it comfortably. Pour in the degreased stock and the 3 cups of white wine. The liquid should cover the galantine; if necessary, add *fond blanc de volaille (page 6),* canned chicken stock, or even water. If the galantine rises above the surface of the water, set a heatproof platter over it to submerge it.

Bring to a simmer over moderate heat, cover partially and reduce the heat to low. Poach the galantine for 1½ hours, then turn off the heat and let it cool to room temperature in the poaching liquid. Transfer the galantine to a large platter and, while it is still warm, remove the cheesecloth. Cover the galantine with foil or plastic wrap and refrigerate for 2 or 3 days before serving. Strain the poaching liquid into a deep bowl through a fine sieve lined with dampened cheesecloth. Let it cool to room temperature and refrigerate.

NOTE: As an aid to decorating and presenting the galantine, refer to the photograph on page 44 of the main volume.

Remove and discard all the fat from the chilled poaching stock and make aspic, following the directions on page 24. Save the remaining stock for another use.

Continued on next page

Set a saucepan containing the aspic in a large bowl or pot half-filled with crushed ice or ice cubes and water, and stir the aspic with a large metal spoon until it thickens enough to flow sluggishly off the spoon. Pour aspic to a depth of about ¼ inch into the large platter on which the galantine is to be served, and refrigerate. Set the galantine on a wire rack over a jelly-roll pan. Spoon more aspic from the saucepan over the galantine to cover the surface with a thin translucent glaze. Then refrigerate the galantine, still on the jelly-roll pan, until the glaze is firm. (Keep the remaining aspic in the saucepan at room temperature so that it stays liquid and ready to use; if it begins to set, warm briefly over low heat to soften it, then stir it over ice again until it reaches the same thick but still fluid consistency as before.)

2 or 3 large green leaves from the top of a leek or scallion	1 black truffle thinly peeled 2 small firm ripe tomatoes

Meanwhile, following the directions for the garniture for *oeufs en gelée (page 84),* blanch the leek or scallion tops and cut them into leaf or blade shapes as desired. Slice the truffle thin and cut it into triangles and diamonds with truffle cutters or a small, sharp knife. Peel the tomatoes in a spiral fashion to make long continuous strips about ¾ inch wide. Shape one of the tomato strips into a roselike coil; cut the other into triangles, diamonds or other decorative shapes.

Carve a dozen slices, each about ¼ inch thick, off one end of the galantine, set them on a rack placed in a second jelly-roll pan and spoon a layer of aspic over them. Refrigerate until the aspic is firm and then coat and chill them once more. Arrange the slices in an overlapping circle at one end of the aspic-coated platter. Coat the tomato rose lightly with liquid aspic and chill until firm, then place it in the center of the circle of galantine slices. Return the platter to the refrigerator.

Dip the decorative pieces of leek or scallion top, truffle and tomato skin into the aspic remaining in the saucepan and arrange them attractively on the unsliced section of the galantine. Refrigerate until the garniture is anchored firmly, then carefully pour spoonfuls of aspic over the uncut galantine once or twice more, chilling it each time. When the galantine is well glazed transfer it to the serving platter.

Meanwhile, with a rubber spatula, scrape up the aspic from both jelly-roll pans and return it to the aspic remaining in the saucepan. Warm briefly over low heat to melt it, then pour the aspic into a small loaf pan. Refrigerate for at least 1 hour, or until firmly set. Remove the loaf pan from the refrigerator, dip the bottom in hot water, cover the top with an inverted plate. Grasping the loaf pan and plate firmly together, turn them over. The aspic should slide out easily. Cut the aspic into ¼-inch slices and then into ¼-inch dice. Scatter the dice around the galantine on the platter and refrigerate again until ready to serve.

Suprêmes de volaille Polignac
CHICKEN BREASTS, MUSHROOMS AND TRUFFLES WITH CREAM SAUCE

To serve 6

3 one-pound chicken breasts, skinned and halved
1 teaspoon plus 2 tablespoons strained fresh lemon juice
Salt
Freshly ground white pepper
4 tablespoons clarified butter *(page 13)* plus 1 tablespoon unsalted butter, plus 2 tablespoons unsalted butter, chilled and cut into ½-inch bits
¼ pound fresh mushrooms, trimmed, wiped with a dampened towel, stems removed and both caps and stems cut into ⅛-inch-wide julienne strips
1 large black truffle, thinly peeled, sliced ⅛-inch thick, and cut into ⅛-inch-wide strips *(see Glossary)*
1½ tablespoons flour
1 cup *fond blanc de volaille (page 6),* or substitute 1 cup canned chicken stock, chilled, then degreased
1 cup heavy cream

Preheat the oven to 450°. Remove the breastbones from the chicken pieces. With paper towels pat the chicken breasts completely dry and rub them on both sides with ½ teaspoon of the lemon juice, a little salt and a few grindings of white pepper.

In a 12-inch sauté pan or heavy skillet with an ovenproof handle, warm the clarified butter over moderate heat for about 10 seconds. Add the chicken and, turning it frequently with tongs or a slotted spatula, sauté until the pieces are firm and white, but do not allow them to brown. Remove the pan from the heat and cover it with a lid or foil. Then cook the chicken breasts in the middle of the oven for 7 to 8 minutes, or until they are tender and show no resistance when pierced deeply with the point of a small skewer. Arrange the chicken on an ovenproof platter. Reduce the oven heat to the lowest point. Place the pan over moderate heat on top of the stove and add the mushroom and truffle strips and 2 tablespoons of lemon juice. Stirring constantly, cook for 3 minutes. With a slotted spoon, remove the mushroom and truffle strips from the pan and scatter them over the chicken breasts. Cover the platter with foil and keep the chicken warm in the oven, while you prepare the sauce.

With a wire whisk, stir the tablespoon of butter into the liquid remaining in the pan. When the butter melts, add the flour and continue to whisk over moderate heat until it is completely absorbed. Pour in the chicken stock and, still whisking constantly, cook over high heat until the sauce comes to a boil and thickens lightly. Reduce the heat to the lowest possible point and simmer for 8 to 10 minutes. Then pour in the cream in a slow, thin stream and, stirring frequently, continue to simmer until the sauce is reduced to about 1 cup. Remove the pan from the heat and swirl in the 2 tablespoons of chilled butter bits and the remaining ½ teaspoon of lemon juice. Taste for seasoning. Strain the sauce through a fine sieve directly over the chicken to mask it completely and serve at once.

How to Carve a Cooked Bird into Four Serving Pieces

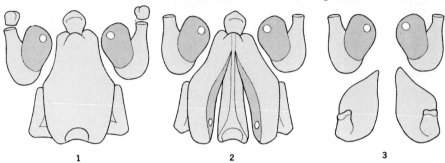

After the whole bird has been cooked, place it breast side up on a cutting board. (1) With a cleaver or heavy knife, chop off and discard the tips of both drumsticks. Pull each leg gently out from the body and, with a large, sharp knife, carve off the entire leg at the joint where the thigh meets the carcass. (2) Following the contours of the wishbone, cut through the joints where the wings meet the body. Continue to cut along the length of the breast bone and cut down each side of the back bone to free the back bone completely from the rest of the bird. (3) Remove all but the meatiest parts of the wing sections that are nearest the breast and trim the ragged flaps of skin from the lower part of each breast piece. Remove the breast and rib bones. You should now have four neatly shaped servings. If the bird was unusually large, you can carve the drumsticks from the thighs and cut the breast pieces in half to make eight serving pieces.

Faisan Souvaroff
ROAST PHEASANT BAKED WITH TRUFFLES AND FOIE GRAS IN MADEIRA SAUCE

To serve 4

A 3- to 3½-pound oven-ready
   young pheasant
1 teaspoon salt
½ teaspoon ground black pepper
6 tablespoons melted clarified butter
   (page 13) plus 2 tablespoons
   butter, softened

¾ cup foie gras *en bloc* (see
   Glossary), cut into ½-inch dice
⅓ cup coarsely chopped black truffles
The pheasant neck and gizzard
¼ cup dry Madeira
1½ cups *fond lié* (page 10)
4 cups all-purpose flour
1 cup cold water
1 egg yolk, lightly beaten

Preheat the oven to 400°. Pat the pheasant dry inside and out with paper towels. Sprinkle the cavity and skin with the salt and pepper, and truss the bird neatly with white kitchen string (*see page 58*). Brush the surface of the pheasant with 2 tablespoons of the clarified butter. Lay the bird on its side on a rack set in a shallow roasting pan.

Roast the pheasant in the middle of the oven for 10 minutes. Turn it over, brush it with 2 more tablespoons of the clarified butter and roast for 10 minutes longer. Then turn the bird breast side up, brush it with the remaining clarified butter and continue roasting for 15 to 20 minutes longer, or until it is golden brown on all sides but still somewhat undercooked. To test for doneness, pierce a thigh with the point of a skewer or small, sharp knife; the juices that trickle out should be pale pink. If they are still red, roast the bird for 5 minutes longer.

Transfer the pheasant to a platter. Discard the trussing string and, with

How to Carve a Cooked Bird into Five Serving Pieces

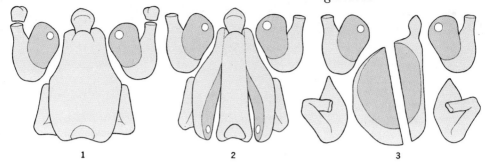

1   2   3

After the whole bird has been cooked, place it breast side up on a cutting board. (1) With a cleaver or heavy knife, chop off and discard the tips of both drumsticks. Pull each leg gently out from the body and, with a large, sharp knife, carve off the entire leg at the joint where the thigh meets the carcass. (2) Following the contours of the wishbone, cut through the joints where the wings meet the body. Then, leaving about 1 inch of meat on either side of the breast bone, cut along its length and through the back (dotted lines). Carefully lift each side piece from the center piece. (3) Chop off the wing tips and trim the ragged flaps of skin from the lower part of each flat breast piece. Turn the carcass on its side and cut the back bone away from the long top length of breast meat. Discard the backbone, ribs and breast bones. You should now have five neatly shaped servings. If the bird was unusually large, you can carve the drumsticks from the thighs and cut the remaining pieces in half to make ten serving pieces.

a sharp knife, carve the bird into 5 pieces, as shown above. Chop the backbone into small pieces and set aside.

Brush the softened butter over the bottom and sides of a 2-quart cocotte equipped with a tight-fitting cover. Arrange the pieces of pheasant in the cocotte and scatter the foie gras and truffles on top. Set aside.

Pour into the roasting pan any juices that have accumulated on the platter around the pheasant. Add the chopped backbone and the uncooked neck and gizzard. Stirring constantly and scraping in the brown particles that cling to the bottom and sides of the pan, cook over moderate heat for 4 or 5 minutes. Then add the Madeira and stir for a minute or so longer. Pour in the *fond lié* and stir until the sauce is smooth and heated through. Skim as much fat as possible from the surface. Strain the sauce through a fine sieve into the cocotte, pressing down hard on the bones to extract all their juices before discarding them. Cover and set aside.

Combine the flour and water in a bowl and beat to a smooth paste with a whisk or spoon. Cover with plastic wrap and let the dough rest in the refrigerator for 30 minutes, or until it is firm but malleable.

Preheat the oven to 400°. On a lightly floured surface, roll the dough out ¼ inch thick. With a 1½-inch round cookie cutter—preferably a fluted one—cut the dough into circles. Overlapping them by about ½ inch, arrange the circles of dough in a ring around the lid so they completely seal the cocotte. Lightly moisten the bottom of each circle with water as you proceed. Brush them with egg yolk and bake the *faisan Souvaroff* in the middle of the oven for 15 minutes. Serve at once, directly from the cocotte. Cut through the pastry seal at the table.

Salmis de faisan

PHEASANT WITH MUSHROOMS AND TRUFFLES IN RED WINE SAUCE

To serve 4 to 5

A 3- to 3½-pound oven-ready
   young pheasant
1 teaspoon salt
Freshly ground black pepper
6 tablespoons clarified butter (page
   13), plus 2 tablespoons softened
   butter
1 black truffle, thinly peeled and cut

into ⅛-inch-thick rounds (see
   Glossary)
3 tablespoons cognac
¼ pound fresh mushrooms,
   trimmed, wiped with a damp
   cloth, and cut lengthwise through
   caps and stems into ⅛-inch-thick
   slices

Preheat the oven to 400°. Pat the pheasant completely dry inside and out with paper towels. Sprinkle the cavity and skin evenly with 1 teaspoon salt and a few grindings of pepper, and truss the bird, following the directions on page 58.

In a heavy 10-inch skillet with an ovenproof handle heat 4 tablespoons of clarified butter over high heat for 10 seconds. Add the pheasant to the pan and brown it evenly and lightly, turning it first on one side and then the other. When the pheasant is browned place the skillet in the oven and roast the bird for 40 minutes, turning it in the pan and basting it about every 10 minutes. To test for doneness, pierce the thigh with the point of a skewer or small, sharp knife. The juices that trickle out should be pale pink. If they are still red, roast the bird for 5 more minutes.

Meanwhile place the truffle rounds in a deep saucer and sprinkle them with 1 tablespoon of the cognac.

Warm another 2 tablespoons of clarified butter in a small skillet and drop in the mushrooms. Stirring constantly, sauté for 4 or 5 minutes until the mushrooms are soft. Do not let the mushrooms brown. Then set them aside off the heat.

When the pheasant is roasted, remove the pan from the oven and set aside, but leave the oven heat on. Transfer the bird to a cutting board and, with a sharp knife, carve it into 5 pieces, as shown in the diagram on page 71. Remove the skin and chop the skin and backbone into small pieces and reserve. Set the skillet aside.

Brush a large ovenproof platter with the softened butter. Arrange the pieces of pheasant meat on the platter and scatter the mushrooms over them. Sprinkle with another tablespoon of cognac and arrange the truffle rounds attractively on top.

FARCE

The pheasant liver, finely chopped, and the fat trimmed from the gizzard

⅛ teaspoon finely chopped shallots

½ medium-sized bay leaf broken into 3 or 4 small pieces

⅛ teaspoon finely cut fresh thyme, or substitute a pinch of crumbled, dried thyme

¼ teaspoon salt

⅛ teaspoon freshly ground black pepper

FARCE (STUFFING): In a small, heavy skillet or saucepan, combine the pheasant liver, fat and 2 tablespoons of the pheasant cooking liquid from the skillet. Stirring constantly, cook over moderate heat for 2 or 3 minutes until the liver is firm. Add the shallots, bay leaf, thyme, ¼ teaspoon salt and ⅛ teaspoon pepper and stir over low heat for 3 or 4 minutes longer. Add the remaining tablespoon of cognac, then rub as much of the mixture as possible through a fine sieve into a bowl with the back of a spoon. Cover the *farce* with foil or plastic wrap and refrigerate.

SAUCE

The pheasant skin and backbone

The pheasant neck, heart and gizzard, coarsely chopped

3 tablespoons finely chopped onions

2 tablespoons finely chopped scraped carrots

1 medium-sized garlic clove, peeled

and crushed with the side of a cleaver or heavy knife

3 sprigs fresh parsley

1½ cups dry red wine

1 cup *fond lié (page 10)*

1 tablespoon chilled unsalted butter

2 slices homemade-type white bread, trimmed of crusts

SAUCE: Add the pheasant skin and chopped backbone, and the uncooked neck, heart and gizzard to the skillet in which the bird was roasted. Stirring constantly, and scraping in the brown particles that cling to the bottom and sides of the pan, cook the pieces of pheasant over moderate heat until they are evenly browned on all sides. Pour off the excess fat, leaving about 3 tablespoons of liquid in the pan. Add the onions, carrots, garlic and parsley sprigs to the pan and cook, stirring occasionally, until the vegetables are lightly browned. Pour in the wine and, stirring constantly, cook briskly for about 5 minutes. Stir in the *fond lié* and bring the sauce to a boil. Reduce the heat to low and simmer for 5 or 6 minutes.

Strain the entire contents of the skillet through a fine sieve into another saucepan, pressing down hard on the bits of pheasant and vegetables to extract all their juices before discarding them. Reheat the sauce briefly. Taste for seasoning, then swirl in 1 tablespoon of chilled butter. Pour the sauce over the pheasant.

Cover the *salmi de faisan* with foil and warm it in the middle of the oven for about 5 minutes. To serve, toast the trimmed bread slices, then spread with the *farce,* cut them diagonally into 4 triangles and arrange them in a ring around the pheasant.

Pâté de faisan en croûte

PHEASANT PÂTÉ BAKED IN A PASTRY CRUST

To serve 10 to 12

A 2-pound oven-ready pheasant

MARINADE
⅓ cup truffle juice *(see Glossary)*
3 tablespoons cognac
½ teaspoon Spice Parisienne *(see Glossary)*
The strips of pheasant breast

The pheasant liver, trimmed of any fat or bits of green, and cut in half
2 fresh chicken livers, trimmed of any fat or bits of green, and cut in half
4 large black truffles, thinly peeled and cut in half *(see Glossary)*
6 strips fresh pork fatback (or side pork) each about 6 inches long, ½ inch wide and ¼ inch thick

Start the pâté at least six or seven days in advance to allow the ingredients to marinate and develop flavor.

Ask your butcher to remove each side of the pheasant breast as neatly as possible in one piece. Strip off the skin and cut the breast meat into 6 or 8 long strips of equal width. Set aside.

Cut the thighs, drumsticks and wings from the bird; skin them and remove all the meat from the bones. Then peel the skin from the pheasant carcass and remove any clinging bits of meat. Chop all the meat coarsely and reserve. (There should be about ½ cup.) With a cleaver, chop up all the bones and set them aside with the skin.

MARINADE: In a glass loaf dish or deep bowl, combine the truffle juice, 3 tablespoons of cognac and ½ teaspoon Spice Parisienne. Add the strips of pheasant breast, the pheasant and chicken livers, the truffle halves and the 6-inch strips of pork fat, turning them about gently in the marinade until they are evenly moistened. Cover tightly with foil or plastic wrap and marinate in the refrigerator for 3 days.

GLACE DE FAISAN
The skin and bones of the pheasant
The pheasant heart
1 medium-sized leek, including 3 inches of the green top, trimmed, coarsely chopped and washed thoroughly in a sieve set under running water
1 medium-sized onion, peeled and coarsely chopped
1 medium-sized carrot, scraped and coarsely chopped
2 medium-sized unpeeled garlic cloves, crushed with the side of a cleaver or large knife
1 medium-sized bay leaf
1 fresh thyme sprig or ⅛ teaspoon crumbled dried thyme

GLACE DE FAISAN (PHEASANT GLAZE): In a heavy 6- to 8-quart enameled cast-iron casserole, sauté the pheasant skin and bones, the pheasant heart, the leek, onion and carrot over moderate heat, stirring constantly until they are all lightly colored. Pour in enough cold water to cover the contents by 2 inches, and add the 2 crushed garlic cloves and the bay leaf.

Bring to a boil over moderate heat, skimming off and discarding the foam and scum as they rise to the surface. Add the sprig of fresh thyme or ⅛ teaspoon crumbled dried thyme. Then boil undisturbed and uncovered for about 1 hour. Strain the entire contents of the casserole through a fine sieve into a deep bowl, pressing down hard on the skin, bones and vegetables with the back of a large spoon to extract all their juice before discarding them.

Skim all fat from the surface of the stock. Pour the stock into a small, heavy saucepan and boil briskly, uncovered, until it is reduced to about 1 cup. Turn the heat to low and, stirring occasionally, reduce the stock to ½ cup of thick syrupy glaze, or *glace de faisan*.

FARCE
The chopped pheasant meat
½ cup shallots, peeled and thinly sliced
1 large garlic clove, peeled and crushed with the side of a cleaver or large knife
1 teaspoon Spice Parisienne *(see Glossary)*
1 fresh thyme sprig or ⅛ teaspoon crumbled dried thyme
½ teaspoon freshly ground white
pepper
1 tablespoon salt
⅓ cup cognac
½ cup dry white wine
1 pound lean boneless pork, trimmed of all fat and cut into small chunks
½ pound fresh pork fatback, cut into small chunks
2 ounces foie gras, preferably *en bloc (see Glossary)*, optional
⅛ teaspoon saltpeter

FARCE (STUFFING) : To prepare the *farce,* or ground-meat stuffing mixture, drop the reserved chopped pheasant meat, shallots and crushed garlic clove into a heavy 12-inch skillet.

Stirring constantly, cook for about 5 minutes over moderate heat until the meat is lightly browned. Then stir in the 1 teaspoon Spice Parisienne, the sprig of fresh thyme or ⅛ teaspoon crumbled dried thyme, white pepper and salt, and add the cognac and the white wine. Stirring all the while and scraping in the brown particles that cling to the bottom of the pan, bring to a boil over high heat.

Strain the entire contents of the skillet through a fine sieve and set the liquid aside. Put the strained meats and seasonings, the boneless pork, the fatback chunks, and the foie gras (if you are using it) through the finest blade of a food grinder.

Add the reserved liquid, the *glace de faisan* and the saltpeter. Knead vigorously with both hands, then beat with a wooden spoon until the *farce* is smooth and fluffy. (There should be about 4 cups.) Cover tightly and refrigerate for 3 days.

PÂTE FINE
4 cups all-purpose flour
8 tablespoons unsalted butter (1 quarter-pound stick), chilled and cut into ¼-inch bits
8 tablespoons lard, chilled and cut
into ¼-inch bits
4 egg yolks
4 to 8 tablespoons ice water
1 egg yolk combined with 1 tablespoon water

PÂTE FINE (FINE PASTRY) : In a large chilled mixing bowl, combine the flour, butter and lard. With your fingertips rub the flour and fat to-

Continued on next page

gether until they look like flakes of coarse meal. Add the egg yolks and mix them thoroughly into the dough.

Pour 4 tablespoons of the ice water over the mixture all at once, knead vigorously, and gather the dough into a ball. If the dough crumbles, add up to 4 more tablespoons of ice water, a spoonful at a time, until the particles adhere. Dust the dough with a little flour and wrap it in wax paper. Refrigerate for at least 1 hour before using. (The dough may be made 1 or 2 days in advance, if you prefer. In that event, let it soften at room temperature just long enough to become malleable.)

1½ pounds fresh pork fatback, cut horizontally with the rind into thin, wide slices about ⅛ inch	thick, 9 inches long and 3 inches wide, then pounded between 2 sheets of wax paper until paper-thin

FINAL ASSEMBLY: Separate the sides and bottom of a fluted oval *pâté en croûte* mold 9¼ inches long and 4 inches deep. On a lightly floured surface, roll the dough out into a rough rectangle about ⅛ inch thick.

With a ruler and pastry wheel or sharp knife, cut two rectangles each 11 inches long and 5 inches wide. Place the sides of the mold next to one another, concave surfaces up. Then press the dough rectangles into the concave sides of the mold, leaving a ½-inch overhang on the top long edges but trimming off the rest of the excess dough.

Place the bottom of the mold on the remaining rolled dough and use it as a guide to cut out two ovals, one exactly the size of the mold and the other about ½ inch wider all around. Cover the larger oval with wax paper and set aside; gather the scraps of dough into a ball and refrigerate.

Hinge the two sides of the lined mold and press the ends of the dough together where they meet to join them securely. Lift the sides of the mold and carefully snap them into the base. Set the smaller oval of dough into the bottom of the mold. Join it to the sides by pressing the pieces of dough firmly together and smoothing the seam with a moistened finger.

Line the bottom and sides of the mold with paper-thin slices of fatback, overlapping the slices slightly where they meet and arranging them so that no dough shows through in any area.

Pour the marinade from the meat and truffles into the *farce* and beat it. Set the meats and truffles aside on a plate. To test the *farce* for seasoning, fry 1 teaspoon of it over moderate heat for 2 or 3 minutes, taste, then add salt or pepper to the raw *farce* if necessary.

Spoon 1 cup of the *farce* into the mold and smooth the top with your hands. Place 2 strips of the marinated fatback lengthwise over the *farce* and lay 3 or 4 strips of pheasant meat end to end in rows between them.

Spoon in another cup of *farce,* smooth it to the edges of the mold, then place a thin, wide slice of fatback lengthwise down the center. Press a groove down the length of the slice with the side of your hand and set the truffle halves into it end to end. Cover the truffles with the pheasant and chicken livers. Set another thin, wide slice of fatback over the livers and place a strip of the marinated fatback along each side of them.

Add a cup of the *farce* and smooth it to the sides of the mold. Place the remaining 2 strips of fatback along the sides and arrange the rest of the pheasant strips between them. Now spoon in all the remaining *farce,* spreading it evenly over the entire surface and mounding it in the center. Cover the *farce* with a layer of the thin, wide slices of fatback. Trim off any excess. (Discard any leftover fat slices or save them for another use.)

Place the reserved, larger oval of dough gently on top of the filled mold, pressing it gently but snugly toward the rim. Fold the overhanging dough to meet the top evenly and trim off the excess. Then moisten the seam with water and smooth it with a knife or your fingers.

On a lightly floured surface, roll out the reserved dough to a thickness of ⅛ inch and cut off 2 strips about ½ inch wide and 12 inches long. Moisten the edges of the pastry-covered mold with water and carefully lay the strips around the edge of the oval, rounding the edges of the strips with your fingers as you proceed and pressing them gently to secure them. Cut off the excess where the strips overlap and crimp the dough attractively.

With the base of a pastry tube or a sharp knife cut a hole about 1 inch in diameter in the middle of the top. If you like you may form a little ring of pastry and anchor it around this opening, moistening the dough before setting it in place.

Using small pastry or cookie cutters, or cutting out designs with a small, sharp knife, decorate the top as fancifully as you like with flower and leaf shapes. Moisten the bottom of each decoration lightly with water before setting it in place. Then brush the entire top surface of the pastry with the egg-yolk-and-water mixture. Insert a 1-inch cylinder, made from a double thickness of heavy duty foil, into the hole in the crust.

Preheat the oven to 375°. Insert the tip of a meat thermometer at least 2 inches into the pâté through the hole in the top and set the mold on a jelly-roll pan to collect the fat that will bubble out when the pâté bakes. Bake in the middle of the oven for 10 minutes, then reduce the heat to 350° and continue baking for 2 hours longer, or until the thermometer registers 160° to 165°.

Remove the pâté from the oven and set it aside at room temperature for 15 to 20 minutes.

gelée de fond blanc de volaille (page 24)

GELÉE (ASPIC): Meanwhile, set the pan or bowl of *gelée de fond blanc de volaille* into a pot half filled with crushed ice or ice cubes and water and stir the aspic with a large metal spoon until it thickens enough to flow sluggishly off the spoon. With a funnel, pour about 2 cups of the aspic very slowly into the hole in the pâté until the liquid reaches the top. If any aspic runs out of the bottom of the mold, seal the leaks with cold butter and then set the molded pâté on a tray or plate in the refrigerator.

(Keep the remaining aspic at room temperature so that it remains liquid and ready to use; if it begins to set, warm briefly over low heat to

Continued on next page

soften it, then stir it over ice again until it reaches the same thick but still fluid consistency as before.)

After an hour or so, add another 1 to 2 cups of aspic to the pâté to fill the pastry shell as completely as possible, pouring it slowly into the foil cylinder. Cover the pâté tightly with plastic wrap and refrigerate it in the mold for about 24 hours. Cover and chill the remaining aspic.

The next day, check the level of the aspic in the chilled pâté; it probably will have settled somewhat. If so, melt the reserved pan of aspic over low heat and cool it in a pot of ice as described above. When the aspic is syrupy, pour it slowly through the hole in the pâté to again fill the shell completely. Tightly cover and return to the refrigerator for another day or two to allow the flavors to develop further. Pour the leftover aspic into a small loaf pan, cover, and chill.

To serve, carefully lift the sides of the mold from the base and set the *pâté en croûte* on a chilled platter. Unhinge and remove the sides of the mold. Dip the loaf pan of aspic briefly into hot water, then place an inverted plate over the top. Grasping dish and plate together firmly, turn them over and the aspic should slide out easily.

Slice the aspic ¼ inch thick and cut some of the slices into triangles or other decorative shapes to ring the edge of the platter. Cut the remaining slices of aspic into strips and then into cubes. Scatter the cubes around the *pâté en croûte.*

TERRINE DE FAISAN (TERRINE OF PHEASANT): Lacking the *pâté en croûte* mold, or the time to prepare *pâté en croûte,* you may make a terrine of pheasant as described above, using the same ingredients except for the pastry and the aspic.

Line a 6-cup terrine with the thin slices of fatback and assemble the *farce* and marinated meats and truffles in the fashion outlined in the recipe. Top the final layer of fat with a large bay leaf, cover the terrine tightly with foil, and place it on a jelly-roll pan.

Insert a meat thermometer into the center of the terrine and bake on the middle shelf of a preheated 350° oven for about 2 hours, or until the thermometer reaches a temperature of 160-165°. Do not remove liquid fat from the terrine; it will solidify when chilled and seal the terrine. Cool to room temperature, then refrigerate the *terrine de faisan* for 2 to 3 days until the flavors have developed. Serve directly from the terrine.

Chartreuse de perdreaux
PARTRIDGES MOLDED WITH CABBAGE AND DECORATED WITH VEGETABLES

The "Chartreuse de perdreaux" is named for La Grande Chartreuse Convent near Grenoble—where the entrée was invented many centuries ago by the vegetarian Carthusian monks. Originally a chartreuse was made solely of vegetables, cooked in a mold. Over the years, the term came to be applied to similarly molded compositions that included meat, game birds or poultry.

To serve 8

4 one-pound oven-ready young
   partridges
Salt
Freshly ground black pepper
4 to 5 tablespoons melted clarified
   butter *(page 13),* plus 6
   tablespoons unsalted butter,
   softened, plus 2 tablespoons
   unsalted butter, chilled and cut
   into ¼-inch bits
½ cup dry white wine
½ cup fresh green peas (about ½
   pound unshelled), or substitute
   ½ cup frozen peas
½ pound fresh green string beans,
   trimmed, washed and cut into
   1½-inch lengths
2 medium-sized white turnips, each
   about 2½ inches in diameter,
   peeled and cut into strips about
   1½ inches long, ½ inch wide
   and ¼ inch thick
3 large carrots, scraped and cut into
   strips about 1½ inches long, ½
inch wide and ¼ inch thick
4 medium-sized heads Savoy
   cabbage (about 2 pounds each)
1½ pounds lean mildly cured salt
   pork in one piece
The partridge necks, hearts,
   gizzards and livers
½ cup finely chopped onion
½ teaspoon finely chopped garlic
½ cup finely chopped carrots
½ cup finely chopped celery
2 sprigs fresh thyme or ½ teaspoon
   crumbled dry thyme
2 whole cloves
1 medium-sized bay leaf
6 whole black peppercorns
2 cups *fond blanc de volaille (page
   6),* or substitute 2 cups canned
   chicken stock, chilled then degreased
1½ pounds *saucisson à l'ail,* or
   substitute 1½ pounds *cotechino*
   or *kielbasa (see Glossary)*
16 medium-sized boiling potatoes,
   trimmed as in *filet de boeuf
   Richelieu, page 88*
2 teaspoons finely chopped parsley

Preheat the oven to 425°. Sprinkle the partridge cavities lightly with the salt and a few grindings of pepper, and truss the birds neatly with white kitchen string *(see page 81)*. With a pastry brush, coat the entire outside surface of each partridge evenly with 3 or 4 tablespoons of the clarified butter. Lay the birds on their backs side by side on a rack set in a shallow roasting pan. Then roast in the middle of the oven for about 15 to 20 minutes, or until they are golden brown, brushing them once or twice with the remaining clarified butter. Transfer them to a plate, cut off the trussing strings, and with a long, sharp knife slice each bird in half lengthwise. With scissors, remove the main carcass bones, leaving the legs and wings intact. Set the birds and bones aside.

Lower the oven heat to 350°. Pour off the fat remaining in the roasting pan and in its place add the white wine. Bring to a boil on the top of the stove over high heat, scraping in the brown bits clinging to the pan. Strain the sauce through a sieve into a bowl and set it aside.

Cook the fresh peas, green beans, turnip and carrot strips in the following fashion: Drop the fresh peas into 2 quarts of lightly salted boiling water, boil briskly for about 8 to 10 minutes, then scoop them out with a slotted spoon and drop them into a bowl of cold water to set their color. (Frozen peas need only be thoroughly defrosted and drained.) When cool, transfer the peas to another bowl and set aside. Add the green beans

Continued on next page

to the same saucepan of boiling water and cook for 8 to 10 minutes until they are slightly tender. Scoop the beans into a sieve, run cold water over them and set them aside in a separate bowl. Finally, drop the turnip and carrot strips into the boiling water and boil for 8 to 10 minutes, or until the vegetables are tender. Then scoop them into a bowl of cold water and reserve separately.

Remove the tough or bruised outer leaves of the cabbages, wash the heads under cold running water, and cut each head lengthwise into quarters. Blanch the quarters by dropping them into boiling water for 1 minute, then place them in a colander and run cold water over them.

Combine the salt pork and 1 quart of cold water in a 2- to 3-quart saucepan, bring to a boil over high heat, and boil for 3 minutes. Drain the pork and run cold water over it. Then pat it dry with paper towels.

In a heavy 10-quart enameled cast-iron casserole, cook the salt pork over moderate heat for 4 or 5 minutes until it is lightly browned on all sides. Stir in the reserved partridge bones, necks, hearts, gizzards and livers, the onion, garlic, chopped carrots, celery, thyme, cloves, bay leaf and peppercorns, and continue cooking until the partridge pieces are delicately colored and the vegetables soften slightly. Set the cabbage quarters side by side over the meat-and-vegetable mixture, pour in the chicken stock and bring to a boil over high heat. Cover tightly and braise in the middle of the oven for 1 hour and 45 minutes.

Prick the sausages in 5 or 6 places with the point of a small skewer or sharp knife and add them to the casserole. Braise tightly covered for 30 minutes longer.

Transfer the sausages and salt pork to a cutting board, and place the cabbage quarters on a large plate or platter. Strain the liquid remaining in the casserole through a fine sieve set over a saucepan, pressing down hard on the remaining vegetables and partridge pieces with the back of a spoon to extract all their juices before discarding them. Stir in the reserved sauce from the roasted partridges, then skim the fat from the surface of the liquid. Boil briskly until the sauce is reduced to about 1½ cups and then set it aside.

To assemble the *chartreuse de perdreaux,* raise the oven temperature to 450°. With your fingers, spread the remaining 6 tablespoons of softened butter generously and evenly over the bottom and sides of a 5-quart ovenproof bowl. If the butter is very soft, refrigerate the bowl for several minutes until the butter becomes firm.

With a sharp knife, skin the sausages and cut them diagonally into ovals slightly less than ¼ inch thick. Line the bottom of the buttered bowl with a slightly overlapping ring of sausage ovals, then cover the sides with alternating rows of beans, carrot strips, peas and turnip strips, pressing them gently into the butter to secure them. Spread half of the cabbage in a layer over the entire inside of the bowl, being careful not to disturb the arrangement you have just created. Press the leaves down gently. Prop the partridge halves on end around the sides of the bowl. Cut the salt pork into slices ¼ inch thick. Stand a slice against each half bird and set all but 12 of the remaining slices of the sausage at random around the inside of the bowl. Fill the bowl with the remaining cabbage, pressing it down gently over the birds. (Drape foil over the remaining sausage and salt pork slices to keep them warm.)

Cover the bowl tightly with foil and set it into a large, shallow pan. Place the pan in the middle of the oven and pour in enough boiling water to come 1½ inches up the sides of the bowl. Bake the *chartreuse* for 15 to 20 minutes. Meanwhile, drop the potatoes into enough lightly salted boiling water in a saucepan to cover them completely and boil briskly until they are tender. Drain the potatoes in a sieve or colander. Return them to the dry saucepan, cover and keep them warm off the heat.

To unmold and serve the *chartreuse de perdreaux,* remove the foil and place an inverted heated serving plate over the bowl. Grasping plate and bowl together firmly, carefully invert them. The mold should slide out easily. If any of the decorations stick to the sides of the bowl, pick them off and restore them to their original places on the mold. Arrange the remaining sausage and salt pork slices around the mold and place a potato on top of each sausage. Sprinkle the potatoes with the parsley. Reheat the reserved sauce briefly, stirring frequently. Taste for seasoning, and swirl in the 2 tablespoons of butter bits. Pour the sauce into a sauceboat and serve it at once with the *chartreuse.*

How to Truss a Small Bird

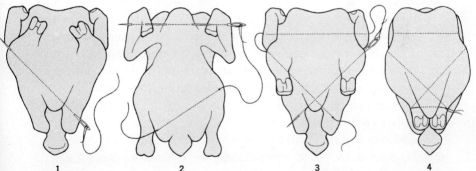

1   2   3   4

Small game birds or chickens that weigh 3 pounds or less may be trussed with a single length of kitchen string (about a yard) threaded into a large trussing needle. Place the bird on its back and trim the wing tips as shown in the diagram on page 58. Then turn the legs up toward the wings. (1) Insert the needle on one side into the soft spot below the bone in the lower part of the carcass near the tail and run the needle diagonally through the bird to the joint of the opposite drumstick and thigh. (2) Draw all but 4 inches of the string through and turn the bird over. Insert the needle into the nearer wing through the second and first sections, run it through the skin over the back of the neck, and then through the same two sections of the opposite wing. Draw the string tight and turn the bird on its back again. (3) Now reverse the process: insert the needle into the other drumstick joint, raise the legs and run the needle diagonally through the bird and out the soft spot on the opposite side of the lower back. (4) Return the legs to their natural position and loop the string over the nearer drumstick. Lift the tip of the breast bone and run the needle through both sides of the skin joining the bone to the carcass. Finally, loop the string over the second drumstick. Push the legs forward against the breast and pull the string taut. Knot the string and clip off the ends.

Cailles aux raisins en timbale
QUAIL WITH GRAPES IN A PASTRY SHELL

To serve 6

TIMBALE
3 cups all-purpose flour
A pinch of salt

12 tablespoons unsalted butter,
    chilled and cut into ¼-inch bits
    plus 1 tablespoon butter, softened
2 egg yolks
¼ to ½ cup ice water

TIMBALE (PASTRY SHELL): In a large chilled bowl, combine the flour, a pinch of salt and 12 tablespoons of butter bits. With your fingertips rub the flour and fat together until they look like flakes of coarse meal. Do not let the mixture become oily.

Add the egg yolks and ¼ cup of ice water, toss the mixture together lightly but thoroughly and gather the dough into a ball. If the dough crumbles, add up to ¼ cup more ice water, 1 tablespoon at a time, until all the particles adhere. Cover the bowl with wax paper and let the dough rest at room temperature for about 30 minutes.

Preheat the oven to 400°. With a pastry brush, spread the tablespoon of softened butter evenly over the bottom and sides of an 8- to 9-inch-square baking pan about 2 inches deep.

On a lightly floured surface, pat the dough into a rough square about 1 inch thick. Dust a little flour over and under it and roll it out into a large square, at least 15 to 16 inches, and ¼ inch thick. If the dough sticks to the board or table, lift it gently with a metal spatula and sprinkle a little flour under it.

Roll the dough gently around the rolling pin, lift it and unroll it slackly over the buttered pan. Press the dough against the bottom and sides and then into the corners of the pan, taking care not to tear it. With a pair of scissors cut off the excess dough from the edges, leaving a ¼-inch overhang all around the outside rim. Turn the overhang under the edge and crimp it attractively.

Spread two sheets of buttered heavy-duty aluminum foil across the pan at right angles to each other and press into the edges to support the sides of the pastry as it bakes.

Bake on the middle shelf of the oven for 20 minutes. Remove the foil, pick through any bubbles in the dough and continue baking for 20 minutes, or until the rim is golden brown. Let the pastry cool for 5 minutes to room temperature and then unmold it.

Run a thin knife around the sides to loosen them. Place an inverted wire cake rack over the pan and, grasping plate and rack together firmly, carefully turn them over. The pastry should slide out easily. Turn it over and set it aside on a serving platter.

1½ cups seedless or other green grapes, peeled and seeded	unsalted butter, chilled and cut into ½-inch bits
⅓ cup cognac	½ teaspoon salt
Six 6-ounce quail	¼ teaspoon freshly ground black pepper
4 tablespoons melted clarified butter (page 13), plus 2 tablespoons	1½ cups *fond lié (page 10)*

CAILLES (QUAIL): Combine the grapes and cognac in a small bowl and turn them about with a spoon until the grapes are well coated. Marinate at room temperature for at least 1 hour, stirring occasionally.

If you have freshly killed quail, remove the feathers and clip off the wing tips. Singe the feet over an open flame and rub off the skins. With a small, sharp knife, make an incision down the length of the back of the neck of each bird, cutting through to the neck bone. Free the bone from the surrounding skin with your fingers and then snip it out with scissors. Pull out the intestines through the same incision at the base of the neck. Discard the hearts, livers and gizzards. Truss the quail securely with kitchen string *(see page 81)*. Then push the head of each bird back against the body and anchor it deeply on both sides with wooden toothpicks. (If you buy quail from the butcher, they will already be eviscerated with the heads and feet removed. Pat the birds dry inside and out with paper towels and truss them securely.)

Preheat the oven to 500°. In a 12-inch skillet warm the clarified butter over high heat until a drop of water flicked into it splutters and evaporates instantly. Season the quail with the salt and pepper and place them in the skillet, turning them about with tongs or a spoon until they are evenly coated with butter.

Regulating the heat as necessary, continue to turn the birds until they color richly and evenly. As soon as the birds are brown, place the skillet on the middle shelf of the oven and roast the quail for 8 to 10 minutes. To test for doneness, pierce the thigh of a bird with the point of a small knife; the juices that trickle out should be pale pink. If they are still red, roast the birds for 2 or 3 minutes longer. Transfer the quail to a heated platter and quickly prepare the sauce.

Drain the grapes in a sieve over a bowl and put them aside. Pour off the fat from the skillet and in its place, add the liquid from the grapes. Bring to a boil over high heat, stirring constantly and scraping in the browned particles that cling to the bottom and sides of the pan.

Pour in the *fond lié* and, still stirring, continue to cook for 3 or 4 minutes until the sauce is smooth and thoroughly heated. Taste for seasoning and strain the sauce through a fine sieve into a small saucepan. Swirl in the 2 tablespoons of butter bits.

Arrange the quail attractively in the pastry shell and spoon the reserved grapes around them. Pour the sauce evenly over the birds and serve at once.

Oeufs en gelée
EGGS IN ASPIC

Only farm-fresh eggs will produce neat ovals when poached. If your eggs are more than a day or two old, make the "oeufs en gelée" in molds.

To serve 8 as a first course

OEUFS POCHÉS
¼ cup tarragon vinegar   8 fresh eggs

OEUFS EN GELÉE (EGGS IN ASPIC) : Pour cold water into a 12-inch sauté pan or skillet to a depth of about 2 inches, and add the vinegar. Bring to a simmer, then reduce the heat so that the surface of the liquid barely shimmers. Break 4 eggs into individual saucers. Gently slide one egg into the water, and with a large spoon, lift the white over the yolk. Repeat once or twice more to enclose the yolk in the white. One at a time, quickly slide the 3 other eggs from the saucers into the pan, enclosing them in their whites and spacing them at least 1 inch apart.

Poach the eggs for 3 or 4 minutes until the whites are set and the yolks still feel soft when prodded gently with the tip of your finger. With a slotted spoon, transfer the eggs to a bowl of cold water and let them cool completely. Repeating the procedure, poach the 4 remaining eggs. Then lift the eggs from the water and with scissors trim each egg into a smooth oval, being careful not to pierce the yolk. Place the eggs on a wire rack set in a jelly-roll pan and refrigerate for at least 2 hours.

GARNITURES POUR LES OEUFS EN
    GELÉE   1 black truffle *(see Glossary),*
2 or 3 large green leaves from the   thinly peeled
    top of a leek or scallion   1 small firm ripe tomato

Meanwhile prepare the decoration for the eggs. Drop the leek or scallion leaves into boiling water and boil for 1 or 2 minutes. Drain the greens in a sieve, run cold water over them, then spread them on paper towels and pat them dry. Cut the leek or scallion leaves into bladelike leaf shapes and a dozen or more thin strips to use as stems. Slice the truffle into rounds ⅛ inch thick. With a lily-of-the-valley truffle cutter, make truffle flowers and set them aside with the leaves and stems.

With a small, sharp knife, peel the skin of the tomato in spiral fashion to make a long continuous strip about ¾ inch wide. Shape the strip into a roselike coil and set aside. Coarsely chop the tomato and set aside.

GELÉE
1 small firm ripe tomato, coarsely
   chopped
¼ cup coarsely chopped leeks,
   including 2 inches of the green
   tops, thoroughly washed
3 envelopes unflavored gelatin
¼ cup egg whites

2 egg shells, finely crushed
2 tablespoons finely cut fresh
   tarragon leaves or 1 tablespoon
   crumbled, dried tarragon
1 quart cold *fond blanc de volaille*
   (page 6), or substitute 1 quart
   canned chicken stock, chilled,
   then degreased

GELÉE (ASPIC): Combine the chopped tomato, chopped leek, gelatin, egg whites, egg shells and tarragon in a heavy 2- to 3-quart enameled or stainless-steel saucepan and pour in the stock. Set the pan over moderate heat and, stirring constantly, bring the stock to a simmer.

When the mixture begins to froth and rise, remove the pan from the heat and let the stock rest for 10 minutes. Then pour the entire contents of the pan into a fine sieve lined with a double thickness of dampened cheesecloth and set over another enameled or stainless-steel pan. Allow the liquid to drain through undisturbed. Season with more salt if needed.

Set the pan in a large pot half-filled with crushed ice or ice cubes and water, and stir the aspic with a metal spoon until it thickens enough to flow sluggishly. Then spoon a little aspic over one of the eggs. It should cling and cover the surface with a thin translucent glaze. Coat the other eggs with aspic and return them to the refrigerator until the aspic is firm. (Keep the remaining aspic at room temperature so that it remains liquid and ready to use; if it begins to set, warm briefly over low heat to soften it, then stir it over ice again until it is thick but still fluid.)

Dip the truffle flowers and green leaf blades and stems one at a time into the aspic and arrange them fancifully on top of 7 of the eggs. Dip the tomato rose in aspic, place it in the center of the remaining egg and create a swirl of stems and leaves around it. Refrigerate again until the decorations are anchored firmly. Then carefully spoon aspic over the eggs two more times, chilling them to set the glaze after each coating.

With a rubber spatula, scrape up the aspic left in the jelly-roll pan and add it to the aspic remaining in the pan. Melt it over low heat, then pour a ⅛-inch layer of aspic over the bottom of a serving platter and pour the rest into a small loaf pan. Refrigerate the platter and pan until the aspic has firmly set. Remove the pan from the refrigerator, dip it in hot water, then place an inverted plate over it. Grasping pan and plate together firmly, turn them over. The aspic should slide out easily. Cut the aspic into ¼-inch slices, and then into diamonds or other shapes. Finely dice the scraps.

Arrange the eggs decoratively on the chilled platter with the tomato-topped egg in the center. Use the aspic diamonds to ring the platter and scatter the dice between the eggs. Refrigerate until ready to serve.

Continued on next page

GARNITURES POUR LES OEUFS EN
GELÉE EN MOULES
2 black truffles, thinly peeled (see

Glossary)
An 8-ounce chicken breast
¼ teaspoon salt

OEUFS EN GELÉE EN MOULES (EGGS MOLDED IN ASPIC): To prepare eggs in individual molds, select the smallest ones you can find. Pullet eggs are best if they are available. Poach and trim the eggs as described above.

Meanwhile, slice and cut the truffles in whatever shapes you wish, to decorate the top of the molded eggs, and chop the truffle scraps into ¼-inch dice and set aside. In a small heavy skillet, combine the chicken breast, ¼ teaspoon of salt and 2 cups of water. Bring to a simmer over moderate heat and poach partially covered for about 10 minutes, or until the chicken is tender. Remove the chicken from the pan and, with a small knife, pull off the skin and cut away the bones. Cut the meat into julienne strips about 1 inch long and ¼ inch wide and refrigerate covered with plastic wrap until ready to use.

Prepare the aspic as described above, cool it over ice and when it is a thick syrup, pour an ⅛-inch layer into each of 8 four-ounce egg molds. Chill until firm, then dip the truffle cutouts into the aspic and center one in each mold. Refrigerate again to anchor the truffle securely. Pour in another ⅛-inch layer of aspic and chill until it is firmly jelled.

Carefully set the eggs in the molds and pour enough aspic into each mold to reach about ¼ inch up the side of the egg. Chill, and when the jelly is firm, fill the molds with aspic to just cover the eggs. Refrigerate to set the jelly. Sprinkle the chopped truffle and the chicken into the molds, dividing the dice and julienne strips evenly among them. Now fill the molds with enough aspic to come to the rim. Refrigerate for at least 6 hours, or until very firm. (Any remaining aspic may be chilled in a loaf pan and used chopped or cut into decorative shapes to garnish the eggs.)

To unmold and serve, run a knife around the sides of each mold and dip the bottom in hot water for a few seconds. Wipe the mold dry, place an inverted plate over it and, grasping plate and mold together, turn them over. Rap the plate sharply on a table and the aspic should slide out. (If it does not, repeat the dipping and drying process once more.) Arrange the eggs on a chilled platter and refrigerate until ready to serve.

Meats

Steak au poivre
SAUTÉED PEPPER-COATED STEAK WITH COGNAC-FLAVORED BROWN SAUCE

To serve 4

4 six-ounce boneless shell steaks,
    each cut about 1 inch thick and
    trimmed of all excess fat
1 tablespoon salt
3 tablespoons whole black
    peppercorns, coarsely crushed
    with the side of a cleaver or heavy

knife or placed between sheets of
    wax paper and crushed with a
    rolling pin
3 tablespoons clarified butter *(page
    13)*
¼ cup cognac
1½ cups *fond lié (page 10)*
2 tablespoons unsalted butter,
    chilled and cut into ½-inch bits

Pat the steaks completely dry with paper towels. Rub the salt into both sides of each steak. One side at a time, sprinkle each steak with about 1 teaspoon of crushed peppercorns, pushing them firmly into the meat with your hands. In a 12-inch sauté pan or heavy skillet, warm the clarified butter over high heat for 10 seconds. Place the steaks in the pan and, turning them with a spatula, sauté them for 3 or 4 minutes on each side, or until they are done to your taste. Ideally they should be rare. Transfer the steaks to a heated platter and set them aside while you prepare the sauce.

    Pour the cognac into the fat remaining in the pan, let it warm for a few seconds and ignite it with a match. Slide the pan gently back and forth until the flames die. Pour in the *fond lié* and bring it to a boil over high heat, meanwhile scraping in the brown particles that cling to the bottom and sides of the pan. Taste for seasoning, strain the sauce into a small saucepan, and reheat. Remove the pan from the heat and swirl in the chilled butter bits.

    Pour the sauce over the steaks and serve at once.

Filet de boeuf Richelieu

ROAST FILLET OF BEEF WITH FILLED MUSHROOM CAPS, BRAISED LETTUCE,
CHÂTEAU POTATOES, AND TOMATOES

To serve 8

FILET

A 4-pound fillet of beef, center cut,
trimmed and tied at equal
intervals in 4 places around the meat
3½ teaspoons salt
½ teaspoon freshly ground black
pepper

2 tablespoons softened butter, and
4 tablespoons unsalted butter,
chilled and cut into ½-inch bits
¼ cup dry Madeira
⅓ cup thinly peeled and finely
chopped black truffles *(see Glossary)*
¼ cup truffle juice *(see Glossary)*
1 cup *fond lié (page 10)*
2 tablespoons cognac

FILET: Preheat the oven to 450°. Sprinkle the fillet evenly with 2 teaspoons of salt and ½ teaspoon of pepper and rub the 2 tablespoons of
softened butter into all sides of the meat. Insert a meat thermometer at
least 2 inches into one end of the beef. Place the fillet on a rack in a large,
shallow pan and roast in the middle of the oven for 30 minutes, or until
the thermometer reaches a temperature of 120° to 125°. (The fillet will
continue to cook internally after it is removed from the oven.) Transfer
the fillet to a heated platter, and let it rest at room temperature for 5 to
10 minutes before serving.

Prepare the sauce in the following fashion: Combine the Madeira, truffles, and truffle juice in a small, heavy skillet and bring to a boil over high
heat. Stirring occasionally, cook briskly for 2 or 3 minutes. Add the *fond
lié* and bring to a simmer, reduce the heat to low and cook for 8 to 10 minutes, stirring from time to time. When the sauce is as thick as heavy
cream, remove the skillet from the heat, add the remaining 1½ teaspoons salt and 3 or 4 grindings of fresh pepper and swirl in the 4 tablespoons of butter bits and the cognac.

To serve, arrange the previously prepared garniture *(below)* of filled
mushroom caps, braised lettuce, château potatoes and tomatoes in an attractive pattern around the beef. Moisten the fillet with a little sauce and
serve the rest separately in a sauceboat.

GARNITURE: The mushroom caps and *duxelles* filling may be prepared
3 or 4 hours ahead of time and then reheated. Braise the lettuce and par-
boil the potatoes at the same time. However, the final cooking of the potatoes and the tomatoes must be done while the fillet is roasting.

CHAMPIGNONS FARCIS
2 tablespoons clarified butter *(page 13)*
2 tablespoons finely chopped shallots
2 tablespoons finely chopped onions
1 cup finely chopped fresh
mushroom stems and caps (about
¼ pound)
2 teaspoons lemon juice
1 teaspoon freshly chopped parsley
8 fresh mushroom caps, each about

2 inches in diameter
5 tablespoons melted clarified butter
(page 13)
½ teaspoon salt
¼ teaspoon pepper
2 teaspoons soft fresh crumbs made
from homemade-type white
bread, trimmed of crusts and
pulverized in a blender or finely
shredded with a fork

CHAMPIGNONS FARCIS (MUSHROOM CAPS FILLED WITH DUXELLES):
To prepare ½ cup of *duxelles,* warm the 2 tablespoons of clarified butter over moderate heat for about 10 seconds. Add the shallots and onions and stir for 2 or 3 minutes until they are soft but not brown. Then drop in the chopped mushrooms, add the lemon juice and, stirring constantly, cook for about 3 to 4 minutes, or until they have released some of their liquid. Reduce the heat to low and, stirring from time to time, simmer for 10 to 15 minutes or even longer. The mushroom mixture is done when all its liquid has evaporated and the *duxelles* is fairly dry. Do not let the mushrooms brown. Stir in the teaspoon of parsley.

Wipe the mushroom caps clean with a damp cloth and brush them evenly with 3 tablespoons of the melted clarified butter. Arrange the caps stem side up in a lightly buttered baking dish just large enough to hold them comfortably, and then sprinkle them with ½ teaspoon salt and ¼ teaspoon of pepper. Bake in a preheated 450° oven for about 10 minutes, or until the mushrooms are tender but still firm. Remove them from the oven and fill each cap with about 1 tablespoon of the *duxelles,* mounding the top slightly. Sprinkle with bread crumbs and moisten with the remaining 2 tablespoons of melted clarified butter. Cover with foil and set aside. Just before serving reheat for 2 or 3 minutes in a 450° oven.

LAITUE BRAISÉE
5 firm 5- to 6-inch heads Boston lettuce
2 tablespoons butter
1 medium-sized carrot, scraped and finely chopped
1 medium-sized onion, peeled and finely chopped
1 medium-sized bay leaf
⅛ teaspoon finely chopped fresh or crumbled dried thyme
1 teaspoon salt
Freshly ground black pepper
¾ cup *fond lié (page 10)*

LAITUE BRAISÉE (BRAISED LETTUCE): Remove any wilted outer leaves from the lettuce and cut off the bottoms of the lettuce heads, but take care not to cut so deeply that the leaves separate. Rinse the heads in cold water, spreading the leaves apart gently to remove any traces of sand. Drop the lettuce in 3 or 4 quarts of boiling water and cook briskly for 2 or 3 minutes, or until the leaves are limp. Immediately remove the lettuce with tongs and plunge it into cold water for a few minutes to set its color. Gently squeeze each head, pat it dry with paper towels, and cut each head into quarters. (The inner leaves may have become somewhat brown after cooking.) Flatten each quarter by pressing it gently with the side of a cleaver or large knife blade. Trim the ragged side edges of the lettuce quarter with a knife to form a smooth-sided triangle, then cut off the heavy white stem at the core. Place the lettuce so the inside leaves are facing down, fold under the tops of the leaves and shape each triangle into an oblong packet. Set the lettuce aside on paper towels.

In a heavy 10- to 12-inch skillet, melt the 2 tablespoons of butter over moderate heat. Add the carrot, onion, bay leaf, thyme, salt and a liberal grinding of black pepper. Stirring frequently, cook for 3 or 4 minutes

89

Continued on next page

until the vegetables are slightly soft but not brown. Arrange the lettuce packets, inside leaves down, in one layer on top of the vegetables and pour the ¾ cup of *fond lié* over them. Cover with a circle of buttered wax paper or parchment paper cut to fit snugly into the skillet, reduce the heat to low and braise the lettuce for about 20 minutes until tender.

If you plan to use the lettuce at once, transfer it with a slotted spatula to a heated platter. Strain the sauce through a fine sieve set over a bowl and spoon it over the lettuce. If you make the lettuce earlier (it may safely be kept at room temperature for an hour or so), leave it undisturbed in the skillet. Just before serving, warm the lettuce over low heat for 3 to 4 minutes, basting it once or twice with its braising liquid.

POMMES CHÂTEAU
8 medium-sized boiling potatoes   ¼ cup clarified butter *(page 13)*

POMMES CHÂTEAU (CHÂTEAU POTATOES): With a small, sharp knife, peel the potatoes and cut them into egglike shapes about 2½ inches long and 1½ inches in diameter at the middle. Trim a ¼-inch slice off each end, then shape each potato into a faceted but slightly rounded oval by removing 7 thin lengthwise slices. Drop the potatoes into enough slightly salted water to cover them completely and boil briskly for 2 or 3 minutes. Drain the potatoes, then pat them completely dry with paper towels.

Just before serving, preheat the oven to 450°. In an 8-inch ovenproof skillet, heat the ¼ cup of clarified butter for about 10 seconds. Add the potatoes and, turning them frequently with a spatula, sauté over moderate heat for 4 or 5 minutes until they are lightly browned on all sides. Place the skillet in the oven and, turning the potatoes over occasionally, bake for 25 minutes, or until they are crisp and golden brown.

TOMATES ÉTUVÉES AU BEURRE   6 tablespoons clarified butter *(page 13)*
8 large firm ripe tomatoes, each   ½ teaspoon salt
    about 3 inches in diameter   Freshly ground white pepper

TOMATES ÉTUVÉES AU BEURRE (BAKED TOMATOES): Drop the tomatoes into a pan of boiling water and boil briskly for about 10 seconds. Run cold water over them and peel them with a small, sharp knife. Cut out the stems. Squeeze the tomatoes gently to remove the seeds and juice. One at a time, place a tomato on a kitchen towel. Pull the towel up tightly around the tomato, enclosing it completely. Twist the ends of the towel together close to the tomato and squeeze gently to shape the tomato into a compact ball. Brush the tomatoes with the clarified butter, set them in a baking dish and lightly salt and pepper them. Cover with foil and set aside for an hour or so before baking. Bake the tomatoes for 8 to 10 minutes in a 450° oven or until they are tender but still intact. Serve at once.

Tournedos Rossini
TOURNEDOS WITH FOIE GRAS, TRUFFLES AND MADEIRA SAUCE

To serve 4

½ cup plus ¼ cup dry Madeira
2 tablespoons truffle juice *(see Glossary)*
1 cup *fond lié (page 10)*
6 to 10 tablespoons clarified butter *(page 13)*
4 slices homemade-type white bread about ¼ inch thick, cut into rounds 2½ inches in diameter
4 six-ounce *tournedos,* each about 1½ inches thick

Salt
Freshly ground black pepper
4 round slices of foie gras *en bloc,* each about 2 inches in diameter and ¼ inch thick, at room temperature *(see Glossary)*
4 round slices of black truffle, each about 1 inch in diameter and ⅛ inch thick, thinly peeled *(see Glossary)*
2 tablespoons unsalted butter, chilled and cut into ½-inch bits

Combine ½ cup of the Madeira and the truffle juice in a small enameled saucepan and boil briskly until reduced to ¼ cup. Add the *fond lié* and stir over moderate heat for 2 or 3 minutes. Set aside off the heat and cover the pan to keep the sauce warm.

In a heavy 12-inch sauté pan or skillet, warm 3 tablespoons of the clarified butter over moderate heat for 10 seconds. Add the bread rounds and, turning them frequently with a slotted spoon, fry until they are crisp and golden brown on both sides, adding more butter to the pan if necessary. Arrange the croutons side by side on paper towels to drain, then transfer them to a large heated platter.

Add 3 more tablespoons of clarified butter to the skillet and raise the heat. Pat the *tournedos* completely dry with paper towels and season them with salt and pepper. Then sauté them in the hot butter for 3 to 4 minutes on each side, or until they are cooked to the state of doneness you prefer. Ideally they should be rare.

Place a *tournedos* on top of each crouton and set a round of foie gras and then a truffle slice on each one.

Working quickly, pour off the fat remaining in the skillet and in its place add the remaining ¼ cup of dry Madeira. Scrape in the browned particles clinging to the bottom and sides of the pan, stir in the reserved *fond lié* mixture, and cook over moderate heat for a minute or so to heat the sauce through.

Strain the sauce through a fine sieve into a small saucepan, swirl in the 2 tablespoons of butter bits and then taste for seasoning. Pour the sauce over the *tournedos* and serve at once.

Tournedos Henri IV

TOURNEDOS WITH BÉARNAISE SAUCE, ARTICHOKE BOTTOMS AND POTATOES

To serve 6

SAUCE BÉARNAISE
⅔ cup red wine vinegar
3 tablespoons finely chopped shallots
1 tablespoon finely cut fresh tarragon
  stems, or substitute 1½ teaspoons
  crumbled dried tarragon
12 white peppercorns, bruised with
  the side of a cleaver or heavy
  knife

8 fresh parsley sprigs
4 large egg yolks
1¼ cups warm clarified butter
  (page 13)
1 teaspoon salt
A pinch of ground hot red pepper
  (cayenne)
1 tablespoon finely cut fresh
  tarragon leaves
1 tablespoon finely chopped fresh
  parsley

SAUCE BÉARNAISE: Combine the vinegar, shallots, fresh tarragon stems or dried tarragon, peppercorns and parsley sprigs in a 1- to 1½-quart enameled cast-iron or copper saucepan and bring to a boil over high heat. Cook briskly until the liquid is reduced to about 2 tablespoons. Remove the pan from the heat, and let it cool for a minute or two.

With a wire whisk, quickly beat the egg yolks into the saucepan and continue to beat briskly for 2 or 3 minutes until the yolks thicken. Return the saucepan to low heat and, whisking constantly, cook long enough for the yolks to thicken further and double in volume. Lift the saucepan from the heat from time to time, still whisking, to prevent the egg yolks from becoming too hot and curdling.

Remove the pan from the heat again. Still whisking, immediately pour in the 1¼ cups of warm butter in a slow, thin stream. After about ¼ cup of the butter has been absorbed, the sauce will begin to thicken and you may whisk in the remaining butter more rapidly. The sauce should have the consistency of a light mayonnaise.

Strain the sauce through a fine sieve into a second pan, pressing down hard on the shallots and herbs with the back of a spoon to extract all their juices before discarding them. Taste the béarnaise and season it with salt and the cayenne. Add the tarragon leaves and chopped parsley and use at once or set aside in a warm place until ready to use. The sauce should not wait for more than an hour. Béarnaise is always served lukewarm so it should not be kept hot or reheated.

TOURNEDOS
6 six-ounce *tournedos,* each about
  1½ inches thick
Salt
Freshly ground black pepper
4 tablespoons melted clarified butter
  (page 13)
6 artichoke bottoms cooked *à blanc*
  (see selle d'agneau

Armenonville, page 94)
A bunch of fresh watercress,
  washed and trimmed
Pommes château (see *filet de boeuf*
  Richelieu, page 88),
  pommes pont neuf or *pommes
  Lorette (pages 114 or 111)*
4 tablespoons clarified butter *(page 13)*

TOURNEDOS: Light a layer of coals in a charcoal broiler and let them burn until a white ash appears on the surface.

Pat the *tournedos* completely dry with paper towels. Season them with salt and black pepper and brush them on both sides with 4 tablespoons of melted clarified butter. Grill the *tournedos* over charcoal for 2 or 3 minutes, then turn them at right angles so that the grill will form a criss-cross pattern on the surface of the meat. Turn the *tournedos* over and repeat this process on the other side, grilling them until the *tournedos* are cooked to the state of doneness you prefer. Ideally they should be rare.

Place the *tournedos* in a ring on a heated platter, and set an artichoke bottom on top of each one. Fill the artichoke bottoms with as much béarnaise sauce as they will hold. Set a bouquet of watercress in the center of the ring. Arrange the potatoes of your choice attractively on the platter and serve at once.

NOTE: In the event that you do not have a charcoal broiler, sauté the *tournedos* in a heavy skillet with 4 tablespoons of clarified butter, following the directions for *tournedos Rossini (page 91)*. It is not traditional in the French cuisine to use the broiler of a range as a substitute for a charcoal grill.

If the artichoke bottoms have been prepared hours ahead, warm them just before serving. Wash them off and pat them dry with paper towels. In a heavy 8- to 10-inch skillet, heat 4 tablespoons of clarified butter over moderate heat for 10 seconds. Reduce the heat to low and add the artichoke bottoms, concave side down. Then cover the skillet tightly and cook for about 5 minutes until the artichokes are heated through.

Côtes d'agneau sautées
SAUTÉED LAMB CHOPS

To serve 4

8 rib lamb chops, 4 to 5 ounces each, cut 1 inch thick and French style *(see page 130 main volume)*	Salt Freshly ground black pepper ¼ cup clarified butter *(page 13)*

Pat the lamb chops completely dry with paper towels and season them evenly on both sides with salt and a few grindings of pepper.

In a heavy 12-inch skillet, heat the clarified butter over high heat until a drop of water flicked into it splutters and evaporates instantly. Add the lamb chops and sauté them for 3 to 4 minutes on each side, or until they are cooked to the state of doneness you prefer. Ideally they should be medium rare. Arrange the chops attractively on a heated platter and serve at once accompanied, if you like, by any of the potato recipes.

Selle d'agneau Armenonville
ROAST SADDLE OF LAMB WITH GREEN BEANS, COCOTTE POTATOES AND
ARTICHOKE BOTTOMS FILLED WITH TOMATOES

To serve 6

SELLE D'AGNEAU

A 4- to 6-pound saddle of lamb (a
short double loin), with kidney
and inner fat removed and all
but ⅛ inch of fat removed from
the surface of the meat

1 teaspoon salt

¼ teaspoon freshly ground black
pepper

¼ cup soft fresh crumbs made
from homemade-type white
bread, trimmed of crusts and
pulverized in a blender or finely
shredded with a fork

2 tablespoons finely chopped fresh
parsley

1½ tablespoons finely chopped
shallots

½ teaspoon finely chopped garlic

¼ cup butter

1½ cups *fond brun de veau* or *fond
brun de boeuf (pages 4 and 2)*

1 tablespoon unsalted butter, cooked
over low heat until it is delicately
browned

SELLE D'AGNEAU (SADDLE OF LAMB): Ask the butcher to prepare the
lamb for roasting, or do it yourself in the following fashion: With a mallet or the flat of a cleaver, pound flat the flaps of lamb that hang from
the sides, then trim off the rough edges of the flaps and tuck them under
the saddle. Score the fat on top of the saddle with crisscrossing diagonal slashes 1 inch apart, cutting almost completely through to the
meat beneath. With white cord, tie the saddle crosswise in at least 3
places to hold it in shape.

Preheat the oven to 425°. Rub the salt and pepper over the top of
the saddle and insert a meat thermometer at least 2 inches into one end
of the lamb. Do not let the tip of the thermometer touch any fat or
bone. Place the lamb, fat side up, on a rack in a roasting pan.

Roast the lamb uncovered and undisturbed in the middle of the oven
for 30 minutes, or until the thermometer registers 120° to 130°. Meanwhile mix the bread crumbs, parsley, shallots and garlic in a bowl. Melt
the ¼ cup of butter. Remove the lamb from the oven, cut off the strings
and raise the heat to 450°. Pat the bread-crumb mixture evenly on top
of the saddle and dribble the butter over it. Roast the lamb for about 10
minutes longer, or until the crumb coating is golden brown (the thermometer should now register 130° to 140°). Then transfer the saddle
to a large heated platter while you make the sauce.

Discard the fat remaining in the roasting pan. Pour in the *fond brun*
and quickly bring it to a boil on top of the stove, stirring constantly
and scraping in the brown bits that cling to the bottom and sides of the
pan. When the stock has been reduced to about 1 cup, strain it through
a fine sieve into a small saucepan. With a bulb baster, collect any juices
that may have accumulated around the lamb and stir them into the sauce.
Taste for seasoning, then stir in the tablespoon of browned butter. Pour
the sauce into a sauceboat.

To serve, arrange the previously prepared garniture *(below)* of green beans, potatoes and artichoke bottoms with tomatoes in a ring around the lamb and present the platter at the dining table. Carve the saddle following the directions on page 41 of the main volume and serve it at once, accompanied by the sauce.

GARNITURE: The beans may be blanched as much as 3 hours beforehand; the potatoes, artichoke bottoms and tomatoes can be shaped hours before serving, but they must be completed at the last minute.

HARICOTS VERTS

1½ pounds fresh green string beans, washed and trimmed evenly to about 3½-inch lengths	Water Salt 2 tablespoons clarified butter *(page 13)*

HARICOTS VERTS (GREEN BEANS): Drop the beans, a handful at a time, into 3 quarts of lightly salted boiling water. Cook the beans briskly, uncovered, for 8 to 10 minutes, or until they are just tender. Immediately drain them in a large sieve, then plunge the sieve into a large pot of cold water for 2 or 3 minutes. Drain the beans, pat them dry with paper towels and set aside. Just before serving, heat 2 tablespoons of clarified butter over moderate heat in a heavy 10- to 12-inch skillet for about 10 seconds. Add the beans and, tossing them about with a spoon, warm them over moderate heat for 3 or 4 minutes. Taste for seasoning.

POMMES COCOTTE

2½ pounds medium-sized boiling potatoes	¼ cup clarified butter *(page 13)* ½ teaspoon salt

POMMES COCOTTE (COCOTTE POTATOES): With a small knife, peel the potatoes and cut them into quarters and then into elongated olivelike shapes about 2 inches long *(photograph, page 22 of the main volume)*. As you shape them, drop the potatoes into cold water to prevent them from discoloring. Before sautéing the potatoes, pat them dry with paper towels. In a heavy 10-inch skillet, heat the clarified butter over high heat for about 10 seconds. Add the potato olives and turn them in the butter to coat them evenly. Then sauté for 8 to 10 minutes, shaking the pan and turning the potatoes from time to time until they are evenly browned and show no resistance when pierced with the point of a small, sharp knife. Sprinkle them with salt and serve at once.

FONDS D'ARTICHAUTS AUX TOMATES

6 medium-sized artichokes, each 3 to 3½ inches in diameter	1 tablespoon plus 1 teaspoon salt 3 medium-sized firm, ripe tomatoes, about 2½ inches in diameter
¼ cup flour	¼ cup clarified butter *(page 13)*
8 cups cold water	½ teaspoon salt
¼ cup fresh lemon juice	Freshly ground white pepper

Continued on next page

FONDS D'ARTICHAUTS AUX TOMATES (ARTICHOKE BOTTOMS WITH TO-
MATOES): Trim the stems and leaves from the artichokes *(Diagrams 1
through 3 below)*. In a heavy 10-inch skillet, whisk the flour and ½ cup of
the cold water together until smooth. Beat in the remaining 7½ cups of
water, the lemon juice and 1 tablespoon of salt. Add the artichoke bottoms, choke side down. Bring to a boil, reduce the heat to low and simmer
covered for 30 minutes, or until the artichokes are tender and show no
resistance when pierced with the point of a sharp knife.

Remove the artichokes from the liquid and wash them under cold running water. With a spoon, carefully scoop out all the chokes. Return
the artichoke bottoms to their poaching liquid and set aside until ready
to use. (They can safely wait at room temperature for 2 or 3 hours.)

Drop the tomatoes into a pan of boiling water and boil briskly for
about 10 seconds. Run cold water over them and peel them with a small,
sharp knife. Cut out the stems, then slice the tomatoes in half lengthwise.
Squeeze the halves gently to remove the seeds and juice. One at a time,
place a tomato half on a kitchen towel. Pull the towel up tightly around
the tomato. Twist the ends of the towel together close to the tomato
and squeeze gently to shape the tomato into a compact ball. Melt the
¼ cup of clarified butter and brush the tomatoes with it. Set them in
a baking dish and lightly salt and pepper them. Cover with foil and set
aside for an hour or so before baking.

To serve, bake the tomatoes for 8 to 10 minutes in a 450° oven, or
until they are tender. Meanwhile, wash the artichoke bottoms and pat
them dry with paper towels. Then heat the ¼ cup of clarified butter
in a heavy 12-inch skillet over moderate heat for 10 seconds. Add the artichoke bottoms, concave side down, and baste them with the hot butter. Sprinkle them with ½ teaspoon salt, reduce the heat to the lowest
possible point, cover and cook for several minutes until they are heated
through. Do not let the artichokes brown. Transfer the artichoke bottoms to a heated platter and place a tomato ball in each one.

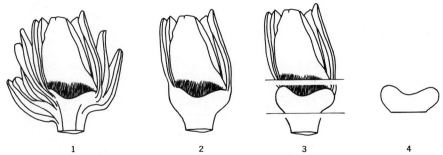

1   2   3   4

One of the most delicate French vegetable garnitures is poached artichoke
bottoms. (1) The bottom is at the base of the heart, below the hairy choke,
shown in the cross-section of a whole artichoke. (2) To separate the bottom
from the whole artichoke, first cut off the outside leaves with a small, sharp
knife, removing as little of the bottom as possible but smoothing the edges.
(3) Then cut off the stem and the remaining cone of leaves above the choke.
(4) Poach the artichoke bottom as described in *selle d'agneau Armenonville*
(page 94). Then scoop out the choke with a spoon to ready it for use.

Selle de veau Orloff

SADDLE OF VEAL WITH SOUBISE, MUSHROOMS, TRUFFLES AND MORNAY SAUCE

To serve 8

SOUBISE
4 tablespoons unsalted butter
2 cups coarsely chopped onions
½ cup uncooked long-grain regular-milled white rice
1 cup *fond blanc de volaille (page 6)*, or substitute 1 cup canned chicken stock, chilled, then degreased

SOUBISE (ONION-AND-RICE MIXTURE) : Preheat the oven to 325°. In a heavy 1½- to 2-quart casserole, melt the 4 tablespoons of butter over moderate heat. When the foam begins to subside, add the chopped onions and, stirring frequently, cook for about 5 minutes until they are soft and translucent but not brown. Watch carefully for any sign of burning and regulate the heat accordingly.

Stir in the rice and stock and bring to a boil over high heat. Cover the casserole tightly and bake in the middle of the oven for 45 minutes, or until the grains are soft and have absorbed all of the liquid. Purée the onion-and-rice mixture through the finest blade of a food mill, or rub it through a fine sieve with the back of a spoon. Set the mixture aside.

PURÉE DE CHAMPIGNONS
1 pound fresh mushrooms
2 tablespoons clarified butter *(page 13)*
1 cup heavy cream
1½ tablespoons strained fresh lemon juice
Beurre manié made from 2 tablespoons unsalted butter, softened and rubbed to a paste with 2 tablespoons flour
½ teaspoon salt
Freshly ground white pepper

PURÉE DE CHAMPIGNONS (MUSHROOM PURÉE) : Wipe the mushrooms with a damp cloth and trim off and discard the base of the stems. Then put them through the finest blade of a food grinder or chop both caps and stems as fine as possible. A handful at a time, place the mushrooms in the corner of a towel or double thickness of cheesecloth and squeeze vigorously to extract as much of their juice as possible.

In a heavy 8- to 10-inch skillet, heat 2 tablespoons of butter over moderate heat for 10 seconds. Add the mushrooms and, stirring constantly, cook over low heat for 3 or 4 minutes. The mushrooms are done when the liquid accumulated in the pan evaporates. Do not let them brown.

Pour in 1 cup of heavy cream and simmer for 5 minutes, stirring occasionally. Then stir in the lemon juice, the butter-and-flour paste *(beurre manié)*, salt and a pinch of white pepper. Continue cooking for 4 or 5 minutes longer, still stirring occasionally until the *beurre manié* has been absorbed. Stir the purée into the onion-and-rice mixture, cool to room temperature, cover with foil or plastic wrap and set aside.

Continued on next page 97

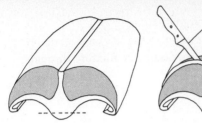

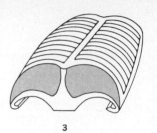

1   2   3

Selle de veau Orloff comes to the table already elegantly carved. (1) Before the saddle is tied up, trim the center bone at the base with a cleaver so that the roast will rest flat on a platter. (2) After it is cooked, separate each loin from the saddle in one piece. First cut along the length of the backbone with a sharp knife, then cut out the loin crosswise about ¼ inch from each end. Finally, free the loin from the base of the saddle. (3) Carve each loin into ¼-inch slices and reassemble the saddle of veal as described in the recipe.

SELLE DE VEAU

A 5½- to 6-pound saddle of veal (a short double loin), with inner fat removed and all but ⅛ inch of fat trimmed from the surface

2 teaspoons salt

½ teaspoon freshly ground black pepper

3 tablespoons butter, softened

1 pound veal bones, sawed into 1-inch lengths

1 large onion, peeled and cut into ¼-inch-thick rounds

½ cup thinly sliced scraped carrots

½ cup thinly sliced celery

1 medium-sized firm, ripe tomato, coarsely chopped

A *bouquet garni* made of ½ cup parsley stems, 1 medium-sized bay leaf and 2 thyme sprigs or ½ teaspoon dried thyme *(see Glossary)*

¼ cup dry white wine

2 tablespoons *glace de viande (page 7)*

2 large black truffles *(see Glossary)*, cut into ⅛-inch-thick rounds

SELLE DE VEAU (SADDLE OF VEAL): Ask the butcher to prepare the veal for roasting in the following fashion, or do it yourself: Trim the bone at the base of the front end of the saddle with a cleaver so that the saddle will lie perfectly flat. Then trim any ragged edges from the flaps. Sprinkle the underside of the veal with 1 teaspoon of salt and ¼ teaspoon of the black pepper. Tuck the flaps under and, with white kitchen cord, tie the saddle crosswise in at least three places.

Preheat the oven to 400°. Sprinkle the top of the saddle evenly with 1 teaspoon of salt and ¼ teaspoon of pepper and rub it with 3 tablespoons of softened butter. Spread the bones as evenly as possible in the bottom of a shallow roasting pan large enough to hold the saddle comfortably and set the saddle, fat side up, on top.

Roast the veal uncovered and undisturbed in the middle of the oven for 30 minutes. Then reduce the oven heat to 350°. Scatter the onion, carrots, celery and tomato around the saddle and add the *bouquet garni*. Cover the pan snugly with heavy foil and braise the veal undisturbed for 30 minutes. Then remove the foil and roast for 30 minutes longer. Transfer the veal to a cutting board and let it cool to room temperature.

With tongs or a slotted spoon remove and discard the bones from the roasting pan and pour in the wine and *glace de viande.* Bring to a boil over high heat, stirring constantly and scraping in the browned particles that cling to the bottom and sides of the pan. Strain the mixture through a fine sieve into a bowl, pressing down on the vegetables with the back of a spoon to extract all their juices before discarding them. Set the strained liquid aside. When it cools, skim all the fat from the surface.

TO ASSEMBLE THE VEAL: Cut off the trussing strings and carve the veal into ¼-inch-thick slices following the diagrams opposite. Keep the slices from each side in separate stacks, and in the order in which you have cut them. Spread a ⅓-inch-thick layer of the onion-and-mushroom mixture over the surface from which the meat was removed. Spread each slice, one at a time, with about a ¼-inch-thick layer of the onion-and-mushroom mixture, place a truffle round in the center of the slice and return the slice to its original place on the saddle.

When the saddle is reassembled, place it on a rack in a roasting pan. With a metal spatula spread the remaining onion-and-mushroom mixture over the surface of the saddle, smoothing and masking it completely.

At this point the saddle, covered with foil, may safely wait at room temperature for 2 to 3 hours. The Mornay sauce also may be made 2 or 3 hours in advance and finished at the last minute. Half an hour before serving preheat the oven to 375°.

SAUCE MORNAY
1½ cups *sauce béchamel (page 9)*
¼ cup heavy cream, plus ¼ cup heavy cream whipped into soft peaks

2 egg yolks
Ground hot red pepper (cayenne)
¼ cup finely grated imported Parmesan combined with ¼ cup finely grated imported Gruyère cheese

SAUCE MORNAY: In a heavy 8- to 10-inch skillet, combine the *sauce béchamel* and ¼ cup of heavy cream. Stirring constantly with a wire whisk, cook over low heat until the sauce is heated through, but do not let it come to a boil. Whisk in the egg yolks, one at a time, add the cayenne, and, stirring constantly, simmer for about a minute longer. Remove the skillet from the heat and stir in half of the grated cheese. At this point the sauce may be dotted with butter to prevent a skin from forming on the top, then covered and kept for 2 or 3 hours before finishing. Just before using fold in the whipped cream.

FINAL COOKING: Spoon the Mornay sauce on top of the saddle of veal, and smooth it evenly with a spatula, again masking it completely. Sprinkle the remaining grated cheese evenly over the sauce. Roast in the middle of the preheated 375° oven for 15 to 20 minutes, or until the topping is a delicate golden brown.

Transfer the saddle to a large heated platter. Arrange the previously prepared garniture of salsify and cucumber-filled tartlets *(following page)* attractively around the veal. Quickly reheat the reserved roasting liquid, spoon some of it onto the platter and pour the remaining liquid into a sauceboat and serve.

Continued on next page

GARNITURE: The fresh salsify may be poached hours in advance and reheated at the last minute; canned salsify needs only to be drained, washed under cold water and patted dry before it is heated for serving. The tartlets may be made a day ahead of time; the cucumbers to fill them can be poached several hours ahead of time but they must be sautéed and sauced at the last minute.

SALSIFIS

¼ cup flour
6 cups cold water
¼ cup fresh lemon juice
1¼ teaspoons salt
2 pounds fresh salsify (or oyster plant), peeled, cut into 1½-inch

lengths and dropped immediately into cold water, or substitute one 15-ounce can imported salsify
2 tablespoons clarified butter *(page 13)*
⅛ teaspoon freshly ground white pepper

SALSIFIS (SALSIFY): Poach the fresh salsify, if you are using it, in the following fashion *(à blanc):* In a heavy 2- to 3-quart saucepan, whisk the flour and ½ cup of the cold water together to make a smooth paste. Beat in the remaining 5½ cups of water, the ¼ cup of lemon juice and 1 teaspoon of the salt. Add the fresh salsify and spoon the liquid over it. Bring to a boil, then reduce the heat to low and simmer for about 20 minutes, or until the salsify is tender and shows only slight resistance when pierced with the point of a small knife. Set the salsify aside to cool to room temperature in its poaching liquid.

Just before serving, drain the fresh salsify or the canned salsify in a sieve or colander, and run cold water over it. Pat the pieces dry with paper towels. In a heavy 8- to 10-inch skillet, warm 2 tablespoons of clarified butter over moderate heat for 10 seconds. Drop in the salsify and, turning it about frequently with a spoon, sauté for about 5 minutes, or until it is heated through. Do not let it brown. Season with ¼ teaspoon salt and ⅛ teaspoon white pepper and serve at once.

TARTELETTES AUX CONCOMBRES

3 medium-sized cucumbers
2 tablespoons clarified butter *(page 13)*
½ cup heavy cream
½ teaspoon salt
⅛ teaspoon freshly ground white

pepper
8 three-inch *pâte brisée* tartlet shells *(page 140)*
1 teaspoon finely cut fresh tarragon or ½ teaspoon crumbled dried tarragon

TARTELETTES AUX CONCOMBRES (CUCUMBERS IN TARTLET SHELLS): With a small, sharp knife, peel the cucumbers and cut them lengthwise into quarters. Scrape out the seeds with a spoon and cut the cucumber strips into olive shapes about 1 to 1¼ inches long and ¾ inches in diameter.

Drop the cucumber-olives into enough lightly salted boiling water to cover them completely. Let the water return to a boil, then reduce the heat to low and simmer uncovered for 5 minutes. Remove from the heat, and pour off all the water. Cover the pan and set the cucumbers aside at room temperature. (They can wait in this state for 2 or 3 hours.)

Just before serving, spread the cucumbers on paper towels and pat them dry. In a heavy 8- to 10-inch skillet, warm 2 tablespoons of clarified butter over moderate heat for 10 seconds. Add the cucumbers and, turning them about constantly with a spoon, cook for 2 or 3 minutes until they are heated through. Do not let the cucumbers brown. Pour in ½ cup of heavy cream and add the ½ teaspoon salt and ⅛ teaspoon white pepper. Stirring all the while, continue cooking for 3 minutes. Taste for seasoning and stir in the tarragon. Immediately spoon the cucumbers and cream into the tartlet shells and serve.

Noisettes d'agneau monégasque

LOIN OF LAMB ROUNDS TOPPED WITH EGGPLANT AND TOMATO FONDUE WITH BLACK OLIVES

To serve 4

FONDUE DE TOMATES
3 large firm, ripe tomatoes (about
    1½ pounds)
3 tablespoons olive oil

1 medium-sized garlic clove, peeled
    and crushed with the side of a
    cleaver or heavy knife
½ teaspoon canned tomato paste
½ teaspoon salt
Freshly ground black pepper

First prepare the fondue in the following fashion: Drop the tomatoes into a pan of boiling water and remove them after 15 seconds. Run them under cold water, and peel them with a small, sharp knife. Cut out the stems, then slice the tomatoes in half crosswise. Squeeze the halves gently to remove the seeds and juice, and chop the tomatoes coarsely.

Combine the chopped tomatoes, 3 tablespoons olive oil, garlic clove, and tomato paste in a heavy 1- to 1½-quart enameled-iron or tin-lined copper saucepan. Stirring constantly, bring to a boil over high heat and cook briskly, still stirring from time to time, until most of the liquid in the pan has evaporated and the mixture is thick enough to hold its shape almost solidly in the spoon. Add the salt and pepper, and taste. Cover and set the fondue aside to keep warm.

8 rounds of fresh eggplant, each
    about ½ inch thick and 2½
    inches in diameter, cut with a
    pastry cutter

Salt
Freshly ground black pepper
½ cup flour
4 to 6 tablespoons olive oil

Continued on next page

Preheat the oven to its lowest setting. Line a large, shallow baking pan with paper towels and place it in the middle of the oven.

Sprinkle the eggplant rounds evenly with a little salt and pepper, dip them in flour lightly to coat both sides and shake off any excess flour. In a 12-inch sauté pan or heavy skillet, heat 4 tablespoons of olive oil until a light haze forms above it. Add the eggplant rounds and, turning them with a slotted spatula, sauté for about 2 to 3 minutes, or until they are golden on both sides. Add up to 2 more tablespoons of olive oil, if necessary. As they brown, transfer the eggplant rounds to the lined baking pan and keep them warm in the oven.

8 *noisettes* of lamb (rib end of loin slices fully trimmed and boned), sliced 1½ inches thick, then tied
4 tablespoons clarified butter *(page 13)*
½ cup dry white wine
1 teaspoon finely cut fresh tarragon leaves, or substitute ½ teaspoon crumbled dried tarragon
½ cup *fond brun de veau (page 4)*
½ teaspoon canned tomato purée
5 tablespoons unsalted butter, chilled and cut into ½-inch bits
12 pitted ripe black olives

Pat the *noisettes* dry with paper towels and season them on both sides with salt and pepper. Wipe the sauté pan with towels and in it warm the clarified butter for about 10 seconds over high heat. Add the *noisettes* and sauté them for 2 to 3 minutes on each side, turning them with a slotted spatula and regulating the heat so that they color richly and evenly without burning. As they are finished, transfer the *noisettes* to the baking pan and keep them warm in the oven while you prepare the sauce.

Pour off the fat remaining in the sauté pan and in its place add the wine. Bring to a boil over high heat, meanwhile scraping in the brown particles clinging to the bottom and sides of the pan, add the tarragon and cook briskly until the liquid is reduced to about ¼ cup. Add the *fond brun de veau* and tomato purée and, stirring with a whisk, simmer for 2 or 3 minutes. Remove the pan from the heat and whisk in the butter bits, a tablespoon at a time. Taste for seasoning.

Eight ½-inch-thick round croutons the size of the *noisettes* and prepared according to the directions in *Tournedos Rossini* *(page 91)* with 4 tablespoons clarified butter

To serve, set each *noisette* on a crouton and arrange them attractively on a heated platter. Place an eggplant round on each one. Scoop up some tomato fondue in a teaspoon and, with another teaspoon, slide it off onto each slice of eggplant in an oval-shaped ball. Spoon the rest of the fondue around the *noisettes* and arrange the black olives attractively in the ring. Serve the sauce separately in a small bowl or sauceboat.

Côtes de veau à la crème aux morilles
SAUTÉED VEAL CHOPS IN CREAM SAUCE WITH MOREL MUSHROOMS

To serve 6

2 ounces dried morels *(see Glossary)*
6 lean loin veal chops, cut about 1½ inches thick and trimmed of excess fat
Salt
Freshly ground black pepper
¾ cup flour
5 tablespoons clarified butter *(page 13)*

2 tablespoons finely chopped shallots
3 tablespoons cognac
1⅓ cups heavy cream
1 teaspoon *glace de viande (page 7)*
½ cup *sauce veloutée (page 8)* made with *fond blanc de veau* or *fond blanc de volaille*
½ teaspoon strained fresh lemon juice

Place the morels in a deep bowl and pour in enough warm water to cover them by at least 2 inches. Soak the morels for about 30 minutes, then wash them 3 or 4 times in warm water, squeezing them gently each time to rid them of any sand. If any of the caps are more than 1 inch in diameter, cut them in half. Set the morels aside.

Preheat the oven to the lowest setting. Season the veal chops on both sides with salt and a few grindings of pepper. Then dip the chops in flour one at a time to coat them evenly, and briskly shake off the excess. In a heavy 12-inch skillet, warm the clarified butter over high heat until a drop of water flicked into it splutters and evaporates instantly. Sauté the chops in the hot butter for 8 to 10 minutes on each side, turning them with tongs or a spatula and regulating the heat so that they color richly and evenly without burning. Transfer the chops to an ovenproof platter and keep them warm in the oven while you prepare the sauce.

Pour off any excess fat from the skillet, then drop in the shallots and, stirring constantly, cook for 2 or 3 minutes. Add the morels and stir for 2 minutes. Carefully pour the cognac into the skillet. It may burst into flame spontaneously; if not, ignite it with a match. Sliding the skillet back and forth gently, cook until the flames die. Then stir in the cream and the *glace de viande.* Pour in the velouté and continue stirring for 2 or 3 minutes until the sauce becomes smooth, thickens and comes to a boil. Add the lemon juice and taste for seasoning. With a bulb baster, transfer any liquid that has accumulated around the chops to the sauce, stirring it once or twice. Then pour the sauce over the chops, masking them completely, and serve at once. *Côtes de veau à la crème aux morilles* is usually accompanied by steamed white rice or wild rice.

Fricadelles de veau Smitane
SAUTÉED VEAL PATTIES WITH ONION SAUCE

To serve 4

¾ pound lean veal loin, very finely chopped or coarsely ground
1 cup heavy cream, chilled, plus 1 cup heavy cream
1½ cups soft fresh crumbs, made from homemade-type white bread, trimmed of all crusts and pulverized in a blender or finely shredded with a fork
A pinch of ground nutmeg, preferably freshly grated
1 teaspoon salt

¼ teaspoon freshly ground white pepper
6 tablespoons clarified butter *(page 13)*
⅓ cup finely chopped onions
1 small bay leaf
¼ cup white wine vinegar
1 tablespoon *sauce béchamel (page 9)*, or substitute *beurre manié* made from 1 teaspoon of softened butter and 1 teaspoon of flour, rubbed together to a smooth paste
2 tablespoons unsalted butter, chilled and cut into ¼-inch bits

Place the veal in a deep mixing bowl, cover with foil or plastic wrap, and refrigerate for at least 1 hour to chill it thoroughly. Preheat the oven to 450°. Set the bowl in a large pot half filled with crushed ice or ice cubes and water and, beating constantly with a wooden spoon, add ⅔ cup of the chilled cream, a tablespoon at a time. Combine the remaining ⅓ cup of chilled cream with ½ cup of the fresh bread crumbs and beat the mixture into the veal by spoonfuls. Beat in the nutmeg, ½ teaspoon of salt and ⅛ teaspoon of the pepper and taste for seasoning.

Divide the veal mixture into 4 equal portions and shape each one into a flat round about 4½ inches in diameter and no more than ½ inch thick. Dip both sides of each veal patty into the remaining cup of bread crumbs to coat it lightly, then score it on both sides with the dull edge of a knife in crisscrossing parallel lines about ½ inch apart. Place the patties, or *fricadelles,* side by side on wax paper and refrigerate them while you prepare the sauce.

In a heavy 1- to 2-quart saucepan, warm 1 tablespoon of the clarified butter over moderate heat for about 10 seconds. Add the onions, the remaining ⅛ teaspoon of pepper and the bay leaf and, stirring constantly, cook for about 5 minutes until the onions are soft and light gold. Watch carefully for any sign of burning and regulate the heat accordingly. Stir in the vinegar and simmer until most of the liquid in the pan has evaporated. Then pour in the remaining cup of cream and, stirring from time to time with a wire whisk, cook over moderate heat until the sauce is reduced to about ⅔ cup. Whisk in the béchamel or *beurre manié* and the remaining ½ teaspoon of salt.

When the sauce thickens lightly, taste for seasoning and strain it through a fine sieve into another small pan, pressing down hard on the onions with the back of a spoon to extract all their juices before discarding them. Swirl in the 2 tablespoons of butter bits, and cover the pan to keep the sauce warm.

In a heavy 10- to 12-inch skillet, warm the remaining 5 tablespoons of clarified butter over high heat. Add the veal *fricadelles* and, turning them with a spatula, sauté for about 3 to 4 minutes on each side, or until they are richly and evenly browned. Then transfer them to a baking sheet and bake in the middle of the oven for 5 minutes.

Serve the *fricadelles* at once, arranged attractively on a heated platter and accompanied by the sauce in a sauceboat.

Côtes de veau en papillote

VEAL CHOPS WITH MUSHROOMS AND HAM BAKED IN PARCHMENT PAPER

To serve 4

1 cup *duxelles (page 114)*	½ cup flour
½ cup heavy cream	2 tablespoons clarified butter *(page 13)*
1¼ teaspoons salt	⅓ cup dry white wine
Four 6- to 8-ounce veal loin chops, each about 1 inch thick, trimmed of excess fat	¾ cup *fond lié (page 10)*
	3 tablespoons softened butter
½ teaspoon freshly ground black pepper	8 thin slices lean uncooked smoked ham such as *jambon de Bayonne* or *prosciutto*

Preheat the oven to 400°. Combine the *duxelles,* cream and ¼ teaspoon of the salt in a small saucepan and, stirring frequently, cook over low heat until the mixture is thick enough to hold its shape almost solidly in a spoon. Set aside off the heat.

Rub the veal chops evenly with the remaining teaspoon of salt and the pepper. Dip them lightly in flour to coat both sides, and shake vigorously to remove the excess flour. In a heavy 12-inch skillet with an ovenproof handle, warm the clarified butter over high heat for about 10 seconds. Add the chops and brown them, turning them frequently with tongs or a spatula and regulating the heat so that they color lightly and evenly on both sides. When the chops are golden brown, place the skillet in the oven and roast the chops for 10 minutes. Then remove the skillet from the oven and transfer the chops to a plate. Turn the oven up to 475°.

Pour the white wine into the skillet and bring to a boil over high heat, meanwhile scraping in the brown bits that cling to the bottom and sides of the pan. Add the *fond lié* and, still stirring, simmer for 2 or 3 minutes. Strain the sauce through a fine sieve into a small pan and, with a bulb baster or spoon, add to it any liquid that may have accumulated around the chops.

With scissors cut 4 large hearts about 11 inches long and 15 inches wide out of parchment paper. Then brush the paper evenly on one side

Continued on next page

with the softened butter. To assemble each *papillote,* place a square of ham on one half of a paper heart and spread 2 teaspoons of the *duxelles* mixture over the ham. Set a chop on top, spread it with another 2 teaspoons of the *duxelles,* and cover it with a second slice of ham. Fold the exposed side of the paper over the chop so the edges of paper meet. Starting at the upper end of the fold, seal the edges by crimping them at about ½-inch intervals. Before crimping the bottom point of the heart, open the seam slightly and blow through the hole to inflate the *papillote.* Then quickly crimp the bottom point closed. Repeat the same procedure until all of the chops are enclosed in their puffed paper hearts.

Arrange the *papillotes* side by side on a baking sheet and bake in the middle of the oven for 10 minutes. The paper should turn a golden brown. Reheat the sauce briefly over low heat. Serve the *papillotes* at once, opening the paper at the table. Present the sauce separately in a bowl or sauceboat.

Ris de veau à la financière en vol-au-vent
SWEETBREADS IN TRUFFLE-FLAVORED MADEIRA SAUCE WITH VEAL MOUSSE DUMPLINGS, GREEN OLIVES, MUSHROOMS AND TRUFFLES IN A PUFF-PASTRY SHELL

To serve 6 to 8

3 pairs calf's sweetbreads (about 2½ pounds)

Soak the sweetbreads in several changes of cold water for 3 hours. Then place them in a 6-quart enameled or stainless-steel pot and pour in 4 quarts of fresh cold water. Bring to a simmer slowly over moderate heat and blanch the sweetbreads by simmering them for 3 minutes. With tongs or a slotted spoon, transfer the sweetbreads to a bowl of cold water and let them rest for 1 or 2 minutes. Pat them dry with paper towels, and gently pull off as much of the outside membrane as possible without tearing the sweetbreads. From each pair of sweetbreads cut the two lobes from the tube between them with a small, sharp knife. Discard the tubes. Arrange the sweetbreads side by side on a large flat platter. Cover them with a kitchen towel and press them flat with an iron casserole or skillet weighing at least 5 pounds. Refrigerate the weighted sweetbreads for at least 2 hours. (They may be kept, weighted, in the refrigerator overnight.)

VOL-AU-VENT
Pâte feuilletée (page 148),
    thoroughly defrosted if frozen

1 egg yolk lightly beaten with 1
    tablespoon cold water

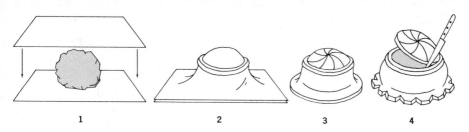

1   2   3   4

To make the *vol-au-vent,* or puff-pastry shell, that will hold the *ris de veau à la financière (drawings above),* roll the dough ⅛ inch thick and cut it into one 11-inch square and one 16-inch square. Crumple aluminum foil into a 4-inch ball. Then (1) place the 11-inch square of dough on a lined jelly-roll pan and set the ball of foil in the center. Drape the 16-inch square of dough over the ball so that the edges of the two squares meet. (2) Shape the top square around the foil and gently press the two layers of dough together as close to the base of the ball as possible without tearing them. Then cut a strip of leftover dough and fit it around the ball like a collar to delineate the lid of the shell. (3) With the tip of a knife, score a pattern on the lid, then trim the base of the pastry and, if you like, scallop or notch the base decoratively. (4) After the *vol-au-vent* has baked, cut the lid free along the top edge of the collar. Let the pastry cool to room temperature before removing the foil ball.

VOL-AU-VENT (PUFF PASTRY SHELL): Preheat the oven to 375°. On a lightly floured surface, roll out the *pâte feuilletée* to make a rough rectangle ⅛ inch thick, about 28 inches long and 17 to 18 inches wide. With a ruler and sharp knife, cut the dough into two squares: one 11 by 11 inches, the other 16 by 16 inches. Reserve the excess rolled-out dough.

Line a 14-by-17-inch jelly-roll pan with a piece of wax paper. Crumple and press enough aluminum foil in your hands to form a ball 4 to 4½ inches in diameter; wrap the ball with a strip of foil to make the outside surface as smooth as possible.

Place the 11-inch square of *pâte feuilletée* in the lined pan and set the foil ball in the center of the dough. Then assemble and decorate the *vol-au-vent,* draping the larger square of dough over the ball, pressing the layers of dough together and then trimming the edges as shown in the diagram above. Gather the scraps and reserved dough into a ball and refrigerate briefly, then roll it out into a long, rough rectangle about 16 inches long, 3 inches wide and ⅛ inch thick. Cut a neat strip of dough ½ inch wide and 16 inches long and place it like a collar around the ball about one third of the distance down from the top to the base, as indicated in the diagram. If you wish, cut out decorative pieces of dough with a small knife, moisten the underside of each piece lightly with water and press it gently against the *vol-au-vent.*

Brush the entire outside surface of the dough with the egg-yolk-and-water mixture. Then bake the *vol-au-vent* in the middle of the oven for 25 to 30 minutes, or until it is puffed and golden brown. Remove the pas-

Continued on next page

try shell from the oven and make the lid by cutting just through to the ball of foil above the collar band with the point of a small knife. Lift off the lid and carefully set it beside the shell on the baking sheet to cool. When the shell has cooled to room temperature, remove the ball of foil.

GODIVEAU

½ pound lean boneless veal, ground twice and chilled
¾ cup heavy cream
½ teaspoon salt
⅛ teaspoon freshly ground white

pepper
3 cups *fond blanc de volaille (page 6)*, or substitute 3 cups canned chicken stock, chilled, then degreased

GODIVEAU (VEAL-MOUSSE DUMPLINGS): Place the chilled ground veal in a deep bowl and, beating constantly with a wooden spoon, add the heavy cream by the tablespoonful. Beat in ½ teaspoon salt and ⅛ teaspoon freshly ground white pepper. Taste for seasoning. Dipping your fingers into cold water frequently, shape the veal mixture into balls about ½ inch in diameter.

In a heavy 10- to 12-inch skillet, bring the chicken stock to a simmer over moderate heat. Gently drop in all the *quenelles* one or two at a time and poach for 3 minutes, turning them carefully about in the liquid from time to time. With a slotted spoon, transfer the *quenelles* to a plate and cover with foil or plastic wrap. (Tightly covered, they may safely be kept in the refrigerator for several hours.)

RIS DE VEAU FINANCIÈRE

1 tablespoon unsalted butter
½ cup finely chopped onions
½ cup finely chopped, scraped carrots
2 medium-sized firm ripe tomatoes, each cut into quarters
4 thin slices fresh side pork, each about 6 inches long, cut into ½-inch squares
1 sprig fresh thyme or ¼ teaspoon

crumbled dried thyme
1 medium-sized bay leaf, crumbled
6 whole black peppercorns, bruised with the side of a cleaver or heavy knife
1 teaspoon salt
½ cup dry Madeira
2 tablespoons truffle juice *(see Glossary)*
3 to 4 cups *fond lié (page 10)*

RIS DE VEAU FINANCIÈRE (SWEETBREADS WITH TRUFFLE-FLAVORED MADEIRA SAUCE): In a heavy 12-inch skillet or sauté pan with an oven-proof handle and a lid, melt the tablespoon of butter over moderate heat. When the foam begins to subside, add the onions, carrots, tomatoes, side pork, thyme, bay leaf, peppercorns and 1 teaspoon salt. Stirring constantly, cook for 3 or 4 minutes.

Pat the sweetbreads dry with paper towels and add them to the vegetable mixture, or *mirepoix*. Turn the sweetbreads about with a spoon to moisten them evenly. Cover them with a piece of buttered wax paper cut to fit snugly into the pan, then set the lid in place. Braise in the middle of the oven for 35 minutes. Remove the lid and the wax-paper cover and baste the sweetbreads with the cooking liquid. Return to the oven uncovered for about 5 minutes longer to glaze the sweetbreads lightly.

With a slotted spoon, transfer the sweetbreads to a plate and drape foil or wax paper over them. Let the braising liquid remaining in the skillet settle for a minute or two, then skim off as much of the surface fat as you can. Stir in the Madeira and truffle juice, and simmer over low heat, stirring until the liquid is reduced to half its original volume.

Pour in 3 cups of *fond lié* and, stirring constantly, bring the sauce to a boil over high heat. Reduce the heat to low and, stirring from time to time, simmer for 20 minutes. Pour the entire contents of the skillet into a fine sieve set over a bowl and let the sauce drain through undisturbed. There should be about 3½ cups; if necessary, add more *fond lié*. Bring to a boil over high heat, skimming off any scum that rises to the surface, then simmer for about 10 minutes, or until the sauce has reduced to 3 cups. Remove the pan from the heat.

GARNITURE

1 cup medium-sized pitted green olives	*turban de sole sauce Nantua, page 31)*
16 firm fresh mushroom caps each about 1½ inches in diameter, fluted and cooked *à blanc (see*	2 large black truffles *(see Glossary),* thinly peeled and cut into ⅛-inch-thick slices

Meanwhile, blanch the olives. Place them in a small saucepan and pour in enough cold water to cover them by 2 inches. Bring to a boil over high heat and cook briskly for a minute or two, then pour the olives into a sieve or colander and run cold water over them. Drain the olives, pat them dry with paper towels and set aside.

FINAL ASSEMBLY: Preheat the oven to 450°. Return the *vol-au-vent* shell and lid on the baking sheet to the oven to reheat for a minute. Then carefully transfer the pastry shell to a large warmed tray or platter. Bring the sauce to a simmer over moderate heat. Then cut the sweetbreads into 1-inch cubes and stir them gently into the simmering sauce. Add the *quenelles* to the sauce together with the blanched olives, fluted mushrooms and sliced truffles. Stirring from time to time, simmer only long enough to heat the ingredients through.

Spoon enough of the sweetbread mixture and its sauce into the *vol-au-vent* shell to fill it completely and partially cover the shell with its lid. Spoon the remaining contents of the skillet around the pastry and serve it immediately.

Vegetables

Pommes sarladaise
POTATO SLICES MOLDED WITH TRUFFLES

To serve 8

½ cup clarified butter *(page 13)*
4½ to 5 pounds baking potatoes

3 black truffles, thinly peeled and
cut into ⅛-inch-thick rounds
(see Glossary)

Preheat the oven to 475°. Brush a tablespoon of the butter over the bottom and sides of a 9-inch cast-iron skillet or a 9-inch round cake pan with a nonstick cooking surface. The pan must be at least 1½ inches deep.

With a swivel-bladed vegetable parer or a small knife, peel and shape the potatoes into neat ovals, dropping them into cold water as you proceed. Then cut the potatoes into ⅛-inch-thick rounds, using a *mandoline* or other vegetable slicer; ideally the thickness of the slices should be as uniform as possible. Rinse the slices as you proceed and then wrap them in a dampened towel. (There should be about 6 cups of potato slices.)

In a heavy 10- to 12-inch skillet, warm ¼ cup of the clarified butter over moderate heat for 10 seconds. Pat a handful of the potatoes completely dry with paper towels and fry them in the butter for 3 or 4 minutes, turning the slices from time to time with a spatula until they are translucent and pale yellow on both sides. Transfer the potatoes to a large platter and proceed with the remaining slices, adding more butter to the skillet when necessary.

Ring the bottom of the 9-inch skillet or cake pan with a row of alternately overlapping potato and truffle rounds. Fill the space in the center with concentric rings of overlapped potato slices and line the sides of the pan with more potato rounds. Then fill the pan completely with the remaining potato and truffle rounds, at random. (The top layer of potatoes may rise slightly above the rim of the pan but the potatoes will settle and shrink as they bake.)

Bake in the middle of the oven for 40 minutes, pressing gently down on the top with a wide spatula every 10 minutes or so. When finished, the potatoes should show no resistance to the point of a sharp knife.

Remove the potatoes from the oven and run a thin metal spatula around the inside edges of the pan. Place a heated serving plate upside down over the pan and, grasping plate and pan together, invert them quickly. The *pommes sarladaise* should slide out in a cake. If any slices stick to the pan, carefully lift them out and return them to their original places.

Pommes Lorette

DEEP-FRIED POTATO PUFFS MADE WITH "PÂTE À CHOUX"

To serve 6

3 pounds firm baking potatoes, all of the same size

PÂTE À CHOUX	1 cup all-purpose flour
1 cup water	4 eggs
6 tablespoons unsalted butter, cut into ½-inch bits	Freshly grated nutmeg
2 teaspoons salt	Vegetable oil or shortening for deep-frying

Preheat the oven to 425° and bake the unpeeled potatoes for 50 to 60 minutes, or until they feel soft when squeezed gently between two fingers. Break the potatoes open and, with a spoon, scoop the potato out of the shells. Discard the shells. Purée the potatoes through a ricer or rub them through a fine sieve with the back of a spoon. (There should be about 4 cups of puréed potatoes.)

PÂTE À CHOUX (PUFF PASTE): Following the directions on page 136, prepare the puff paste with the water, the butter bits, salt, flour, eggs and a few gratings of nutmeg. Beat the puréed potatoes thoroughly into the puff paste and taste for seasoning. At this stage the potato mixture can safely be covered and kept at room temperature for 2 or 3 hours.

Preheat the oven to its lowest setting. Cover a baking sheet with a double thickness of paper towels and set it aside.

Pour oil into a deep fryer or large, heavy saucepan to a depth of at least 3 inches and heat until the oil reaches a temperature of 360°. Fill a pastry bag fitted with a ½-inch star tube about ⅔ full of the potato mixture. Piping the mixture directly into the hot oil, form 4 or 5 strips each about 2 inches long, breaking each one away from the tip with a trussing needle or skewer dipped in the oil from time to time. Fry the *pommes Lorette* for about 3 minutes, turning them gently with a slotted spoon until they are evenly colored and slightly puffed. As they are finished, transfer the *pommes Lorette* to the lined baking sheet and keep them warm in the middle of the oven while you deep-fry the rest. Serve *pommes Lorette* hot, arranged attractively on a platter.

How to Fry Potatoes the Way the French Do

The ubiquitous "French-fry" in the United States is only one version of France's *"pommes frites"*—and not the most interesting one by any means. In France, potatoes are sliced, slivered, ruffled and cut in strips of many sizes before they are fried. For best results, potatoes should be shaped uniformly—and sliced on a French *mandoline* with adjustable blades. Precise frying requires a large, heavy pan that will hold 3 inches of fat when half-full, a wire frying basket, a slotted spoon or skimmer, and a thermometer to keep the fat at the exact temperature required. On these pages are some recipes for authentically French deep-fried potatoes.

INGREDIENTS FOR POTATO RECIPES

To serve 6

3 pounds firm baking potatoes, all of the same size

Vegetable oil or shortening for deep frying
Salt

Pommes gaufrettes
WAFFLED DEEP-FRIED POTATO SLICES

Peel and shape the potatoes into neat ovals, dropping them into cold water as you proceed. With the ruffled blade of a *mandoline* adjusted to make ¼-inch-thick slices, cut one potato at a time crosswise into rounds, turning at right angles after each stroke so that one side of the slice is ruffled horizontally and the other side vertically. Rinse the slices in cold water and wrap them in a dampened towel to prevent discoloring.

Pour oil into a deep-fryer or large, heavy saucepan lined with a basket to a depth of at least 3 inches. Heat until the oil reaches a temperature of 375° on a deep-frying thermometer.

A handful at a time, pat the wafflelike slices completely dry with paper towels. Lift the basket, drop the slices in it and plunge it into the hot oil. Turning the slices frequently with a skimmer or slotted spoon, deep-fry for 2 or 3 minutes until they color lightly and evenly. As they are finished transfer the *pommes gaufrettes* to paper toweling. Sprinkle with salt and serve the *pommes gaufrettes* while they are still warm.

Pommes pailles
STRAW POTATOES

Peel the potatoes, dropping them into cold water as you proceed. Adjust the blade and cross-cutting mechanism of a *mandoline* to produce the thinnest, narrowest strips possible. Rinse in cold water and wrap the strips in a dampened towel to prevent discoloring.

Pour vegetable oil to a depth of at least 3 inches in a deep-fryer or a large, heavy saucepan. Heat until the oil reaches a temperature of 375°

on a deep-frying thermometer. A handful at a time, drop the strips into a frying basket. Plunge it into the hot oil. Turning the strips constantly with a skimmer or spoon, fry them for about 3 minutes until golden. As they brown, transfer them to paper towels to drain. Season with salt and serve the *pommes pailles* while they are still warm.

To make nests, cut the strips as described above. Without rinsing them, wrap in a dampened towel. When the oil reaches 375°, pat half of the potato strips evenly against the bottom and sides of the larger section of a nest-shaped frying basket, letting enough strips extend above the rim of the basket to create a nestlike effect. Set the smaller section of the basket over them and clamp the handles securely together. Plunge the basket into the hot oil and deep-fry the potatoes for about 3 minutes, until they are golden brown. Remove the basket from the oil, and slip out the inside section. Invert the larger section over paper towels and slide out the potato nest. Set aside while you prepare the second nest in the same fashion as the first. Serve the potato nests filled with any of the deep-fried potatoes on these pages.

Pommes allumettes
MATCHSTICK POTATOES

Peel and shape the potatoes into rectangles about 2½ to 3 inches long, dropping them into cold water as you proceed. With an adjustable-blade *mandoline,* cut the rectangles lengthwise into sticks about ¼ inch thick and ¼ inch wide, or cut the potatoes with a sharp knife. Rinse in cold water and wrap the potatoes in a dampened towel to prevent discoloring.

Pour vegetable oil to a depth of at least 3 inches into a deep-fryer or large, heavy saucepan lined with a basket. Heat until the oil reaches a temperature of 330° on a deep-frying thermometer.

A handful at a time, pat the potato strips dry with paper towels. Lift the basket, drop the strips into it, and plunge them into the hot oil. Turning the strips constantly with a skimmer or slotted spoon, fry for about 3 minutes, or until the potatoes are pale gold on all sides. As they are finished, transfer them to paper towels to drain.

Just before serving, heat the oil to 360°. Deep-fry the matchsticks, in the basket by the handful, again, for 1 or 2 minutes, or until lightly browned. Drain on paper towels, add salt to taste and serve at once.

Pommes soufflées
PUFFED DEEP-FRIED POTATO SLICES

Peel and shape the potatoes into smooth ovals about 2 inches in diameter at the widest part, dropping them into cold water as you proceed. With an adjustable-bladed *mandoline* or other slicer, cut the potatoes into ⅜-inch-thick rounds. Wrap the slices in a damp towel to prevent discoloring.

Continued on next page

Pour vegetable oil into two large, heavy saucepans at least 8 inches deep, filling them both to a depth of 3 inches. Heat the oil in one pan until it reaches a temperature of 325° on a deep-frying thermometer, and the oil in the second pan until it reaches 375°.

A handful at a time, pat the slices completely dry with paper towels and drop them one by one into the 325° oil. Sliding the pan gently back and forth on the burner so that the potatoes cook evenly, deep-fry them for 6 minutes. Transfer the slices to the 375° oil with a skimmer. They should puff up almost immediately. As they puff, place them on a linen towel to drain. (Set the potatoes which have not puffed aside separately to serve as plain *pommes frites;* there may be a few in each batch.) Proceed in similar fashion with the remaining slices. At this point, the potatoes can wait for several hours before final cooking.

Just before serving, heat one pan of oil to 385°. Drop in the potatoes a few at a time and deep-fry for 1 minute or until they puff up again and are golden. Remove them from the oil with a skimmer, drain briefly on paper towels, salt to taste and serve.

Pommes pont-neuf
POTATO STICK "BRIDGES"

Peel and cut the potatoes into bricklike rectangles about 2½ to 3 inches long, dropping them into cold water as you proceed. With an adjustable-bladed *mandoline,* cut the rectangles lengthwise into sticks about ½ inch thick and ½ inch wide. Lacking a *mandoline,* cut the potatoes into strips with a vegetable slicer or a sharp knife. Rinse in cold water and then wrap the potatoes in a dampened towel to prevent discoloring.

Pour vegetable oil to a depth of at least 3 inches in a deep-fryer or large, heavy saucepan equipped with a frying basket. Heat until the oil reaches a temperature of 350°. A handful or two at a time pat the potatoes dry with paper towels. Drop them into the basket and plunge it into the oil for 5 minutes. Transfer the potatoes to paper towels to drain. Just before serving, reheat the oil to 375° and return the potato sticks to the oil for 1 to 2 minutes longer until they are golden brown on all sides. Drain briefly again on paper towels and sprinkle with salt. *Pommes pont neuf* are traditionally arranged in three-layered "bridges" with 2 or 3 potato strips to a layer and with the middle layer laid at right angles to the sticks above and below it *(see photograph, pages 188-189 in the main volume).*

Duxelles
CHOPPED MUSHROOMS SAUTÉED WITH SHALLOTS AND ONIONS

To make about 2 cups	
	⅓ cup finely chopped onions
	2 tablespoons strained fresh lemon
1 pound fresh mushrooms	juice
⅓ cup clarified butter *(page 13)*	Salt
⅓ cup finely chopped shallots	Freshly ground white pepper

Wipe the mushrooms with a damp cloth and trim off the base of the stems. Then chop both caps and stems finely. A handful at a time, place the chopped mushrooms in the corner of a kitchen towel and squeeze vigorously to extract as much juice as possible.

In a heavy 10- to 12-inch skillet, melt the butter over moderate heat. As the foam begins to subside, add the shallots and onions and stir for 1 to 2 minutes. When the shallots and onions are soft but not brown, add the mushrooms and lemon juice. Stirring frequently, cook for 10 to 15 minutes longer. The mushrooms are done when any liquid that may have accumulated in the pan has completely evaporated. Do not let the mushrooms turn at all brown.

If you plan to use the *duxelles* at once, season it to taste with salt and white pepper. If you wish to refrigerate or freeze it for future use, do not season; let the *duxelles* cool to room temperature, then transfer it to a container with a tight cover and refrigerate.

Endives braisées
BRAISED ENDIVE

To serve 4

8 medium-sized firm endives with tightly closed unblemished leaves
6 tablespoons water
2 tablespoons strained fresh lemon juice
2 tablespoons unsalted butter, cut into ¼-inch bits, plus 2 tablespoons clarified butter *(page 13)*
½ teaspoon sugar
½ teaspoon salt
¼ cup *fond lié (page 10)*, warmed to serving temperature over low heat
2 tablespoons finely chopped fresh parsley

With a small, sharp knife trim the base of the endives and remove and discard any bruised or discolored leaves. Wash the endives thoroughly under cold running water.

Combine the water, lemon juice, 2 tablespoons of butter bits, sugar and salt in a heavy enameled or stainless-steel skillet just large enough to hold the endives in one layer, and stir well. Add the endives and cover them with a buttered piece of wax paper cut to just fit the pan.

Bring to a simmer over moderate heat, then reduce the heat to the lowest possible setting and braise the endives for about 20 minutes, or until they are tender and their bases show only the slightest resistance when pierced with the point of a small skewer or knife. With a slotted spoon transfer the endives to a plate.

Discard the cooking liquid, dry the skillet, and in it warm the clarified butter over moderate heat for 10 seconds. Add the endives and turn them over and over in the hot butter until they glisten, but do not let them brown. Arrange the endives attractively on a heated serving plate, pour the *fond lié* over them, and spoon the butter remaining in the pan on top. Sprinkle with parsley and serve at once.

Desserts & Pastry

Riz à l'impératrice

MOLDED VANILLA BAVARIAN CREAM WITH RICE AND GLACÉED FRUITS

To serve 8 to 10

½ cup finely diced mixed glacéed
    fruit
¼ cup imported kirsch
1 envelope plus 1 teaspoon
    unflavored gelatin
¼ cup water
Vegetable oil
½ cup uncooked long-grain white
    rice (not the converted variety)

2½ cups milk
1 cup sugar
2 tablespoons unsalted butter
1 vanilla bean *(see Glossary)*
5 egg yolks
¼ cup apricot jam, rubbed through
    a fine sieve
2 cups heavy cream
Angelica and assorted thinly sliced
    candied fruits

Combine the glacéed fruit and the kirsch in a small bowl, stir well and marinate at room temperature for at least 45 minutes. Sprinkle the gelatin over ¼ cup of water and set it aside to soften. Brush the inside of a 2-quart charlotte mold with vegetable oil, then rub it with paper towels to remove the excess.

In a heavy 2- to 3-quart saucepan, bring 1 quart of water to a boil over high heat, drop in the rice and cook briskly for 5 minutes. Pour the rice into a sieve, rinse it under cold water and drain.

Pour 1 cup of the milk into the top of a double boiler, add ¼ cup of the sugar, the butter and vanilla bean. Stirring occasionally, cook over moderate heat until the sugar and butter are dissolved and small bubbles appear around the edge of the pan. Set the pan above simmering (not boiling) water and stir the rice into the mixture. Cover tightly and cook for 25 to 30 minutes, or until the rice is soft. Check from time to time and if the milk seems to be evaporating too rapidly, add a few spoonfuls more. When the rice is finished, however, the milk should be absorbed. To remove any excess moisture, drain the rice in a fine sieve. Remove and discard the vanilla bean.

In a 2- to 3-quart enameled or stainless-steel saucepan, heat the remaining 1½ cups of milk over moderate heat until bubbles form around the edge of the pan. Set aside off the heat and cover.

With a wire whisk or a rotary or electric beater, beat the egg yolks and the remaining ¾ cup of sugar together in a deep bowl for 3 or 4 minutes, or until the yolks form a slowly dissolving ribbon when the beater is lifted from the bowl. Whisking constantly, pour in the milk in a slow, thin stream. When thoroughly blended, return the mixture to the saucepan. Cook over low heat, stirring constantly, until the custard is as thick as heavy cream. Do not let the custard come near a boil or it will curdle. Mix in the softened gelatin and continue to mix until it is dissolved.

Strain the custard through a fine sieve set over a bowl. Stir in the glacéed fruits, kirsch and the apricot jam, then gently mix in the rice.

With a wire whisk, rotary or electric beater, whip the cream in a large chilled bowl until it forms soft peaks. Set aside. Place the bowl of custard in a pot filled with crushed ice or ice cubes and water, and stir for 4 or 5 minutes, or until the custard is cool and begins to thicken very slightly.

Remove the bowl from the ice and scoop the whipped cream over the custard. With a rubber spatula, fold the custard and cream gently together, using an over-under cutting motion rather than a stirring motion until no trace of white remains. Ladle the mixture into the mold, cover with foil, and refrigerate for 6 hours until it is completely firm.

To unmold the *riz à l'impératrice,* run a sharp knife around the sides of the mold and dip the bottom in hot water for a few seconds. Then wipe the mold dry, place a chilled serving platter upside down over the mold and, grasping plate and mold firmly, invert them. Rap the platter on a table and the *riz à l'impératrice* should slide out of the mold.

Decorate this dessert as fancifully as you like with the angelica and candied fruit, pressing the slices gently in place. Refrigerate the *riz à l'impératrice* until ready to serve. Before serving pour some of the raspberry sauce around the edge of the platter, and present the rest in a small bowl.

SAUCE DE FRAMBOISES	frozen whole raspberries
2 cups fresh raspberries, or	¾ cup sugar
substitute four 10-ounce packages	¼ cup imported kirsch

SAUCE DE FRAMBOISES: Wash the raspberries quickly under a spray of cold water, remove the hulls, and discard any badly bruised or discolored berries. (Frozen raspberries need only to be thoroughly defrosted and well drained in a sieve.)

Combine the raspberries, sugar and kirsch in the jar of an electric blender and blend at high speed for 10 seconds. Turn off the machine, scrape down the sides of the jar with a rubber spatula, and blend again for a minute. Then, with the back of a spoon, rub the purée through a fine sieve set over a small bowl. Cover tightly with foil or plastic wrap and refrigerate until ready to use. (The sauce may be kept for 3 to 4 days.)

Bavarois Clermont

VANILLA-FLAVORED BAVARIAN CREAM WITH GLACÉED CHESTNUTS

To serve 10 to 12

BAVAROIS
Vegetable oil
2 envelopes unflavored gelatin
⅓ cup water
3 cups milk

1 vanilla bean
5 egg yolks
1½ cups sugar
3 cups heavy cream, chilled
1 cup finely chopped *marrons glacés*
    (glacéed chestnuts, not the
    chestnuts packed in syrup)

BAVAROIS (BAVARIAN CREAM) : Brush the inside of a 2½-quart decorative mold with oil and remove the excess with a paper towel. Sprinkle the gelatin into ⅓ cup of water in a heatproof cup. When the gelatin has softened for 2 or 3 minutes, set the cup in a skillet of simmering water and stir over low heat until the gelatin dissolves. Remove from the heat but leave the cup of gelatin in the water to keep warm. In a heavy 3-quart enameled-iron or copper saucepan, bring 3 cups of milk and the vanilla bean to a boil over moderate heat. Cover and set aside.

With a wire whisk or a rotary or electric beater, beat the 5 egg yolks and 1½ cups of sugar together in a deep bowl for 3 or 4 minutes, or until the yolks fall in a slowly dissolving ribbon when the beater is lifted from the bowl. Remove the vanilla bean from the milk and reserve it. Whisking constantly, pour the milk into the egg yolks in a slow thin stream. When thoroughly blended, return the mixture to the saucepan. Stir over low heat until the custard thickens enough to coat a spoon evenly or reaches 180° on a candy thermometer. Do not let it come to a boil or the custard will curdle. Add the gelatin and stir until it is completely absorbed. Strain the custard through a fine sieve into a stainless-steel bowl.

With a wire whisk or a rotary or electric beater, whip the cream in a chilled bowl until it forms almost firm peaks. Then set the bowl of custard into a larger bowl filled with crushed ice or ice cubes and water and stir until the custard is just cool. Do not let it chill enough to become the least bit lumpy.

Remove the bowl of custard from the ice and scoop the whipped cream over it. With a rubber spatula, fold the two quickly but gently and thoroughly together, using an over-under cutting motion rather than a stirring motion, until no trace of white remains. Fold in the chestnuts, then pour the mixture into the oiled mold and smooth the top with the spatula. Cover with foil or plastic wrap and refrigerate for at least 6 hours, or preferably overnight until the Bavarian cream is firm.

CRÈME ANGLAISE
2 cups milk
1 vanilla bean (re-use the bean above)

4 egg yolks
½ cup sugar

CRÈME ANGLAISE (ENGLISH CUSTARD) : Combine 2 cups of milk and the reserved vanilla bean in a 3-quart enameled saucepan. Bring to a boil and immediately remove the milk from the heat. Cover and set aside.

Beat the 4 egg yolks and ½ cup of sugar together with a wire whisk or a rotary or electric beater until they are thick enough to form a slowly dissolving ribbon when the beater is lifted. Remove the vanilla bean and pour the hot milk gradually into the yolks, whisking all the while. Return the mixture to the saucepan and stir over low heat until the *crème anglaise* thickens lightly. (Do not let it come near a boil or it will curdle.) Pour the *crème anglaise* into a bowl, and cool to room temperature. Cover tightly and refrigerate until ready to serve.

MARRONS CARAMÉLISÉS

2 cups sugar
2 cups water
2 tablespoons unsweetened
   imported cocoa

7 whole *marrons glacés* (glacéed chestnuts), 6 cut in half and rounded with a knife and one reserved

MARRONS CARAMÉLISÉS (CARAMELIZED CHESTNUTS): In a heavy 2- to 3-quart saucepan, bring 2 cups of sugar, 2 cups of water and the cocoa to a boil over high heat, stirring until the sugar dissolves. Bring the syrup to a boil, then reduce the heat to low and simmer the syrup for 25 to 30 minutes until it reaches 300° on a candy thermometer. As soon as the syrup reaches the proper state, remove the pan from the heat and place it in a pot half-filled with hot water to keep the caramel fluid and warm.

To make each caramelized chestnut, impale one chestnut half on a thin long skewer. Holding the skewer vertically, submerge the chestnut in the hot syrup and twirl it around until it is heavily coated with caramel. Lift the chestnut and, holding the skewer horizontally over wax paper, let the excess caramel drip off. The caramel will form a thin iciclelike thread as it drips. With scissors, keep this thread to a length of about 6 inches, cutting it repeatedly until the caramel stops dripping and becomes firm.

Place the chestnut on a sheet of buttered aluminum foil and carefully pull out the skewer. Repeat the entire procedure with all of the remaining chestnut halves. Set the caramelized nuts aside.

FINAL ASSEMBLY: To unmold the *bavarois,* run a thin knife or spatula carefully around the inside rim of the mold and briefly dip the bottom of the mold into hot water. Wipe the mold dry, place a chilled serving plate upside down over the top and, grasping the mold and plate securely together, quickly invert them. The *bavarois* should slide out easily.

Spoon the chilled *crème anglaise* around the base of the *bavarois* and arrange the caramelized chestnuts in a ring surrounding it. If you like you may decorate the *bavarois* or outline the details of its form by piping melted semisweet chocolate onto it with a pastry tube fitted with a very small plain pastry tip. A few spoons of chopped *marrons glacés* may be stirred into the *crème anglaise*. Place the remaining whole glacéed chestnut decoratively on the top of the *bavarois* and serve.

Abricots Condé

BAVARIAN CREAM WITH RICE GARNISHED WITH POACHED APRICOTS AND
APRICOT SAUCE

To serve 6

1 tablespoon vegetable oil
1 cup uncooked long-grain white
    rice (not the converted variety)
½ cup plus 1⅓ cups sugar
3 tablespoons unsalted butter
A vanilla bean, broken in half *(see
    Glossary)*

3 cups milk
2 cups water
1 pound fresh young apricots,
    peeled, halved and pitted
2 tablespoons imported kirsch
6 egg yolks, lightly beaten
2 teaspoons finely grated fresh
    lemon peel

Preheat the oven to 325°. Brush the inside of a 4-cup ring mold with the vegetable oil and, with a paper towel, wipe out the excess oil.

Blanch the rice by combining it with 1 quart of cold water in a small saucepan and bringing the water to a boil over high heat. Drain the rice in a sieve and run cold water over it to remove the excess starch. Place the rice in a heavy 1½- to 2-quart casserole and add ½ cup sugar, the butter, half of the vanilla bean and the milk. Bring to a boil over high heat, stirring until the sugar dissolves and the butter melts. Cover tightly and bake in the middle of the oven for 30 minutes, or until the rice is soft. Remove the vanilla bean.

Meanwhile, in a heavy 2- to 3-quart enameled or stainless-steel saucepan, bring 1 cup of sugar, 2 cups of water and the remaining half of the vanilla bean to a boil over high heat, stirring until the sugar dissolves. Reduce the heat to low and add the apricots to the syrup. Turning the fruit about occasionally with a slotted spoon, poach for about 10 minutes, or until the apricots show only the slightest resistance when pierced deeply with the point of a small skewer. Transfer 12 of the apricot halves to a plate, cover with plastic wrap and refrigerate. Then stir ⅓ cup of sugar into the remaining apricots and, stirring almost constantly, simmer until most of the liquid has evaporated and the fruit has become a thick purée. Rub the purée through the medium disc of a food mill and stir in the kirsch. The sauce may be served hot or cold. Set it aside to reheat before serving or, if you prefer, pour it into a bowl and refrigerate until you are ready to serve the *abricots Condé.*

Add the beaten eggs and lemon peel to the hot cooked rice and stir vigorously with a wooden spoon to mix them well. Immediately spoon the rice mixture into the ring mold and pack it down firmly with the back of the spoon. Refrigerate for 4 to 5 hours, or until thoroughly chilled. To serve, run a small knife around the edge of the mold. Then dip the bottom of the mold briefly in hot water. Place an inverted serving plate on top of the mold and, grasping plate and mold together firmly, turn them over. The rice ring should slide out easily. Arrange the reserved apricot halves side by side on top of the ring and pour the hot or cold sauce over the fruit and rice. Serve at once.

Soufflé glacé au Grand Marnier
FROZEN GRAND MARNIER SOUFFLÉ

To serve 6 to 8

8 ladyfingers, each about 3 inches long and 1 inch wide, split in half horizontally	1 tablespoon finely grated fresh orange peel
6 tablespoons Grand Marnier	⅓ cup water
6 egg yolks	2½ cups heavy cream, chilled
1 cup sugar	1 tablespoon unsweetened imported cocoa

Fold a 24-inch-long piece of wax paper in half lengthwise. Wrap the paper strip around the outside of a 1-quart soufflé dish to make a collar extending 2 to 3 inches above the top edge of the dish. Tie the paper in place with string, then chill the dish in the freezer until you are ready to fill it with the soufflé.

Spread the ladyfinger halves, cut side up, in one layer in a shallow baking dish or platter. Sprinkle them evenly with 3 tablespoons of Grand Marnier and set them aside at room temperature while you prepare the soufflé mixture.

Beat the egg yolks in a large bowl with a whisk or a rotary or electric beater until they are thick and lemon-colored. In a small saucepan, combine the sugar, orange peel and water and bring to a boil over moderate heat, stirring until the sugar dissolves. Boil briskly without stirring until the syrup thickens and reaches a temperature of 230° on a candy thermometer, or until a few drops spooned into ice water immediately form coarse threads.

Immediately pour the hot syrup in a thin stream into the egg yolks, beating constantly. Continue beating for 10 to 15 minutes longer until the mixture becomes a thick, smooth cream. Beat in the remaining 3 tablespoons of Grand Marnier.

In a chilled bowl, beat the cream with a whisk or a rotary or electric beater until it is firm enough to form soft peaks on the beater when it is lifted from the bowl. With a rubber spatula, gently fold the egg-yolk mixture and whipped cream together until no trace of white shows.

Spoon enough of the soufflé mixture into the chilled dish to fill it to a depth of about 1½ inches. Arrange half of the ladyfingers evenly over the top trimming them to fit smoothly. Cover the ladyfingers with another inch of the soufflé, add the rest of the ladyfingers and then spoon in enough of the soufflé mixture to fill the dish to the rim. Place the dish in the freezer and chill for about 20 minutes. Meanwhile, refrigerate the remaining soufflé mixture. Then fill the collar with the soufflé mixture smoothing the top with a rubber spatula.

Freeze for at least 6 hours or overnight. About 15 minutes before serving, transfer the soufflé to the refrigerator to let it soften slightly. Sift powdered cocoa on top to simulate the browned surface of a baked soufflé and gently remove the paper collar. Serve at once.

Pêches Ninon

POACHED FRESH PEACHES WITH MOLDED VANILLA-FLAVORED PUDDING AND
APRICOT GLAZE

To serve 8

GÂTEAU DE SEMOULE
Vegetable oil
2 cups milk
1 vanilla bean
1 teaspoon finely grated fresh lemon
   peel

¼ cup farina or cream of rice
5 egg yolks
½ cup sugar
1 envelope plus 1 teaspoon
   unflavored gelatin
1½ cups heavy cream
2 tablespoons confectioners' sugar

Brush the inside of a 6-cup shallow ring mold with vegetable oil. Then rub it with paper towels to remove the excess.

In a 2- to 3-quart enameled-iron or copper saucepan, bring the milk, vanilla bean and grated lemon peel to a boil over moderate heat. Remove the pan from the heat and let the flavorings steep for 10 or 15 minutes. Strain the milk through a fine sieve and return it to the pan. Wash off the vanilla bean and set it aside. Then bring the milk to a simmer over moderate heat and, stirring constantly, pour in the farina or cream of rice in a slow, thin stream. Reduce the heat to low and, still stirring to prevent any lumps from forming, cook for about 5 minutes, or until the mixture thickens enough to coat a spoon. Set aside off the heat.

In a deep bowl, beat the egg yolks, the ½ cup of sugar and the gelatin together with a wire whisk or a rotary or electric beater for 3 or 4 minutes, or until the mixture forms a slowly dissolving ribbon when the beater is lifted from the bowl. Slowly pour the beaten eggs into the farina mixture, stirring continuously until no streaks of yellow show. Still stirring, bring to a simmer over low heat and cook slowly for 1 or 2 minutes. Do not let the mixture come anywhere near the boiling point. Remove the pan from the heat to cool.

With a whisk or a rotary or electric beater whip the cream in a chilled mixing bowl until it forms soft peaks. Beat in 2 tablespoons of confectioners' sugar. Set the farina mixture into a pot filled with crushed ice or ice cubes and water, and stir for 4 or 5 minutes, or until it is cool but still fairly fluid. Beat with a whisk to be sure it is perfectly smooth.

With a rubber spatula scoop the whipped cream over the farina mixture and fold them together gently but thoroughly. Pour the entire contents of the bowl into the oiled mold, smoothing the top with the spatula. Cover with foil or plastic wrap and refrigerate for at least 6 hours, or until very firm.

PÊCHES POCHÉES
2 cups sugar
The yellow peel of 2 lemons, cut in

long strips
8 firm ripe peaches, each about
   2½ inches in diameter

PÊCHES POCHÉES: Meanwhile, combine 2 quarts of water, 2 cups of sugar, the strips of lemon peel and the reserved vanilla bean in a heavy 3- to 4-quart saucepan. Bring to a boil over high heat, stirring until the sugar dissolves. Reduce the heat to low and simmer for about 10 minutes. Place the peaches in the syrup, cover the pan partially and poach the peaches for 10 to 15 minutes, or until they are barely tender and show only slight resistance when pierced deeply with the tip of a small skewer. Let the peaches cool completely in the syrup. Then peel and return them to the syrup. Covered with foil or plastic wrap, they can be kept at room temperature for several hours or in the refrigerator for a day or more.

About half an hour before serving, unmold the pudding ring. Run a knife around the sides of the mold to a depth of about 1½ inches and dip the bottom in hot water for a few seconds. Place a serving plate upside down over it and, grasping plate and mold together, invert them. Rap the plate on a table; the pudding ring should slide out easily. Drain the peaches and arrange them around the pudding.

CRÈME CHANTILLY
1½ cups chilled heavy cream

3 tablespoons confectioners' sugar
1 crystallized violet (*see Glossary*)

CRÈME CHANTILLY (CHANTILLY CREAM): In a chilled bowl whip 1½ cups of chilled heavy cream with a whisk or a rotary or electric beater until it begins to thicken. Add 3 tablespoons of confectioners' sugar and continue beating until the cream is firm enough to form stiff, unwavering peaks on the beater when it is lifted from the bowl. Using a pastry bag with a decorative tip, pipe decorative rosettes or spirals of whipped cream into the center of the pudding ring. Center the candied violet on top of the cream. (Lacking a pastry bag, spoon the cream into the center of the ring and create fanciful swirls on its surface with a small spatula.)

SAUCE D'ABRICOTS
1½ cups apricot jam
⅓ cup sugar

¼ cup water
3 tablespoons imported kirsch

SAUCE D'ABRICOTS (APRICOT SAUCE): Bring the apricot jam, ⅓ cup sugar and ¼ cup water to a boil over moderate heat, stirring until the sugar dissolves. Reduce the heat to low and, stirring from time to time, simmer for 5 minutes, or until the sauce clears. With the back of a spoon, rub the sauce through a fine sieve set over a bowl. Stir the kirsch into the warm apricot sauce and pour it around the ring. Serve at once.

Like many other elegant French desserts, *pêches Ninon* may be garnished as fancifully as you like. The peaches may be topped by sugar leaves, or leaflike shapes cut from angelica. The pudding ring may be festooned with chocolate leaves and flowers made of semisweet chocolate melted in a double boiler and piped through a wax paper cone of your own fashioning. The flowers may be tinted with apricot glaze.

Bombe Coppelia
MOLDED COFFEE ICE CREAM WITH PRALINE FILLING

To serve 8 to 10

2 quarts coffee-flavored brick ice cream

If the ice cream is solidly frozen, place it in the refrigerator and let it soften slightly; do not let it begin to melt. Cut the ice cream into ½-inch-thick slices and one at a time quickly press them firmly against the bottom and sides of a decorative 2-quart mold. Make sure the ice cream fills all the contours of the mold. With a spatula, smooth the ice cream to create a shell ½ inch thick. (Freeze the remaining ice cream for later use.) Place the mold in the freezer for one hour or until the ice cream shell is completely firm. Meanwhile, prepare the praline filling.

PRALINE

1 tablespoon vegetable oil	2 tablespoons water
¼ cup sugar	¼ cup whole blanched almonds

PRALINE: With a pastry brush, spread the vegetable oil over a 1-foot-square section of a marble slab or over a large baking sheet. In a small saucepan, bring ¼ cup of sugar and 2 tablespoons of water to a boil over moderately low heat, stirring until the sugar dissolves. Cook uncovered and undisturbed until the syrup reaches a temperature of 236° on a candy thermometer, or until a few drops spooned into cold water immediately form a soft ball. Add the almonds and, stirring constantly, cook until the syrup caramelizes and becomes a rich tealike brown. At once pour the praline mixture onto the oiled marble or baking sheet and spread it out evenly with a spatula. Cool until firm. Then break the praline into small pieces with a mallet and pulverize it in the jar of an electric blender, or place the praline between two sheets of wax paper and pound it as fine as possible with the mallet, a rolling pin or the side of a cleaver. There should be about ½ cup of pulverized praline.

APPAREIL À BOMBE

8 egg yolks	⅓ cup water
⅔ cup sugar	½ cup heavy cream, chilled

APPAREIL À BOMBE: (BOMBE MIXTURE) Beat the egg yolks in a large bowl with a whisk or a rotary or electric beater until they are thick and lemon-colored. Combine the ⅔ cup sugar and ⅓ cup water in a small saucepan and, stirring constantly, bring to a boil over moderate heat. When the sugar has dissolved, boil briskly uncovered and undisturbed until the syrup reaches a temperature of 236° on a candy thermometer, or until a few drops spooned into ice water immediately form a soft ball.

Beating constantly, pour the hot syrup in a slow thin stream into the egg yolks. Continue beating for 10 to 15 minutes longer, until the mixture becomes thick and smooth, and reaches room temperature. Then beat in the pulverized praline.

With a wire whisk or a rotary or electric beater, whip the heavy cream in a chilled bowl until it is stiff enough to stand in firm unwavering peaks on the beater when it is lifted from the bowl. Fold the whipped cream into the praline mixture with a rubber spatula, using an over-under cutting motion rather than a stirring motion and folding until no trace of white remains.

FINAL ASSEMBLY: Pour the *bombe* mixture into the center of the mold and return the mold to the freezer for 2 or 3 hours until the filling is firm. Then slightly soften the remaining ice cream in the refrigerator, cut several more ½-inch-thick slices and place them over the filling to cover the mold completely. Smooth the top with a spatula. Cover with foil and freeze the *bombe* for at least 6 hours, or until it is firm and set.

To unmold and serve the *bombe,* dip the mold briefly into hot water. Place a chilled serving plate upside down over the mold and, grasping plate and mold firmly together, invert them, rapping them sharply on the table. The *bombe* should slide out easily. Serve immediately or return to the freezer until ready to serve.

Fraises Romanoff
FRESH STRAWBERRIES IN ORANGE-FLAVORED LIQUEUR WITH CHANTILLY CREAM

To serve 4 to 6

1 quart ripe strawberries	Cointreau
½ cup Grand Marnier, Curaçao or	½ cup strained fresh orange juice

Pick over the berries carefully, discarding any that are bruised. Wash the berries quickly under cold water, pat them gently dry with paper towels and remove their stems and hulls. Place the berries in a deep bowl and pour the liqueur and orange juice over them. Cover the bowl with foil or plastic wrap and refrigerate the berries for at least 3 hours, turning them over gently from time to time.

CRÈME CHANTILLY	2 tablespoons confectioners' sugar, sifted
1 cup heavy cream, chilled	½ teaspoon vanilla extract

CRÈME CHANTILLY (CHANTILLY CREAM): Just before serving, whip the cream in a large chilled bowl with a wire whisk or a rotary or electric beater. When it begins to thicken add the confectioners' sugar and vanilla and continue to beat until the cream forms unwavering peaks on the beater when it is lifted from the bowl.

Crystallized violets *(see Glossary)*

Transfer the strawberries and all their juices to a serving bowl. Then, using a pastry bag with a decorative tip, pipe the cream over the berries in as fanciful a manner as you like, or ladle the cream over the berries and create decorative swirls and peaks on its surface with a spatula. Garnish the top with crystallized violets and serve at once.

Mousse aux framboises

RASPBERRY MOUSSE WITH RASPBERRY SAUCE

To serve 8

MOUSSE
Vegetable oil
1 envelope plus 1 teaspoon
   unflavored gelatin
½ cup water
4 egg yolks

¾ cup sugar
2 cups fresh raspberries, rubbed
   through a fine sieve with the back
   of a spoon
¼ cup *eau de vie de framboise,* or
   substitute imported kirsch
2 cups heavy cream, chilled

MOUSSE: Brush the inside of a 2-quart melon or other decorative mold with a film of vegetable oil, then rub it thoroughly with a paper towel to remove the excess.

Sprinkle the gelatin into a heatproof measuring cup or small bowl filled with ¼ cup of cold water. When the gelatin has softened for 2 or 3 minutes, set the cup in a small skillet of simmering water and stir over low heat until the gelatin dissolves completely. Remove the skillet from the heat but leave the cup in the water to keep the gelatin fluid.

With a wire whisk or a rotary or electric beater, beat the egg yolks in a deep bowl until they form a slowly dissolving ribbon when the beater is lifted from the bowl. Set aside.

Combine the sugar and the remaining ¼ cup of water in a small saucepan and bring to a boil over high heat, stirring until the sugar dissolves. Cook briskly, uncovered and undisturbed, until the syrup reaches a temperature of 230° on a candy thermometer or a few drops spooned into cold water immediately form a coarse thread.

Remove the pan from the heat at once and, beating constantly, pour the syrup into the egg yolks in a very slow, thin stream. Continue to beat until the mixture thickens and cools. Add the gelatin and beat until it is completely absorbed. Then stir in the 2 cups of sieved raspberries and the ¼ cup of liqueur.

In a chilled bowl, beat the cream with a whisk or a rotary or electric beater until it is stiff enough to form soft peaks when the beater is lifted from the bowl. Stir a large spoonful of the cream into the raspberry mixture; then with a rubber spatula fold in the remaining cream until no traces of white remain. Pour the mousse into the oiled mold and smooth the top with the spatula. Cover tightly with foil or plastic wrap and refrigerate for at least 6 hours, or until the mousse is firm to the touch.

SAUCE
2 cups fresh raspberries, rubbed
   through a fine sieve with the back
   of a spoon

1½ cups superfine sugar
¼ cup *eau de vie de framboise,* or
   substitute imported kirsch

SAUCE: In a deep bowl, combine 2 cups of sieved raspberries with the superfine sugar. Stir until the sugar dissolves completely, then add the ¼ cup of liqueur. Cover and chill until ready to serve.

Crème Chantilly (see gâteau Saint-Honoré, page 136), optional

FINAL ASSEMBLY: To unmold the mousse, run a thin spatula or knife around the inside edges of the mold, then dip the bottom briefly in hot water. Place an inverted serving plate over the mold and, grasping plate and mold together firmly, turn them over. The mousse should slide out easily. Spoon some of the sauce around the base of the mousse and present the rest separately in a sauceboat. If you like, you may decorate the mousse with Chantilly cream piped through a pastry tube and additional whole raspberries. Serve at once.

Savarin au rhum
YEAST CAKE RING WITH RUM SYRUP AND CHANTILLY CREAM

To make one 9-inch cake ring

½ cup lukewarm milk (110° to 115°)
1 package active dry yeast
3 tablespoons plus 1 cup sugar
2 cups flour
½ teaspoon salt
4 eggs, lightly beaten

2 tablespoons butter, softened, plus 12 tablespoons (1½ sticks) unsalted butter, softened and cut into ½-inch bits
2 cups water
½ cup dark rum
Crème Chantilly (see fraises Romanoff, page 125)

Pour the milk into a small, shallow bowl and sprinkle it with the yeast and 1 tablespoon of the sugar. Let the mixture stand for 2 or 3 minutes, then stir it well. Set the bowl in a warm, draft-free place, such as an unlighted oven, for about 8 to 10 minutes, or until the yeast bubbles up and the mixture almost doubles in volume.

Sift the flour, 2 tablespoons of sugar and the salt into a deep mixing bowl and make a well in the center. Pour in the yeast mixture and eggs and, with a wooden spoon, gradually incorporate the flour into the center ingredients. Beat until the whole is a smooth, soft, slightly sticky dough. Then beat the dough with your hands for about 2 minutes by slapping and pulling it up out of the bowl and letting it fall back in thick strands. Drape the bowl loosely with wax paper and set aside in the warm place for about 45 minutes, or until the dough has doubled in volume.

With a pastry brush, spread the 2 tablespoons of softened butter evenly over the bottom and sides of a 4-cup savarin mold.

Stir the dough vigorously for a minute or so with a wooden spoon, then beat in the 12 tablespoons of butter bits, a few pieces at a time. Beat the dough with your hands—slapping, lifting and letting it fall—for 4 or 5 minutes. Then spread the dough all around the bottom of the buttered mold, smoothing the top gently with the back of a spoon. The dough should fill the mold halfway. Set aside in the warm place again until the dough rises to the top of the mold.

Continued on next page

Preheat the oven to 450°. Bake the savarin in the middle of the oven for 10 minutes, reduce the heat to 350° and continue baking for 30 minutes longer, or until the top is golden brown. Prick the savarin in 3 or 4 places to deflate it slightly, then turn it out on a deep plate to cool.

Meanwhile, combine the water and the remaining 1 cup of sugar in a small enameled or stainless-steel saucepan. Bring to a boil over high heat, stirring until the sugar dissolves. Remove the pan from the heat and let the syrup cool to lukewarm, then stir in the rum. Drip about one third of the syrup slowly around the top of the savarin. Allow the savarin to rest for about 15 minutes, then pour half of the remaining syrup over the cake as before. Fifteen minutes later pour the rest of the syrup evenly over the savarin.

To serve, transfer the savarin to a serving plate and fill the center of the ring with *crème Chantilly,* piping the cream through a pastry bag or spooning it into the center and swirling the top attractively with a spatula.

Soufflé Rothschild
HOT DESSERT SOUFFLÉ WITH GLACÉED FRUIT

To serve 6 to 8

4 tablespoons unsalted butter, softened
2 tablespoons plus ½ cup sugar
⅓ cup finely chopped mixed glacéed fruits
¼ cup gold-flecked *eau de vie de Dantzig* or *Goldwasser,* or

substitute imported kirsch
3 tablespoons flour
¾ cup cold milk
1 teaspoon vanilla extract
4 egg yolks
6 egg whites
12 firm ripe strawberries, washed and with hulls removed
¼ cup superfine sugar

Preheat the oven to 400° and place a large baking sheet on the middle shelf. With a pastry brush, spread 1 tablespoon of the softened butter over the bottom and sides of a 2-quart soufflé dish. Sprinkle the butter with 2 tablespoons of the sugar and tip the dish from side to side to spread it evenly. Invert the dish and rap it gently on a table to remove the excess sugar. Refrigerate the dish until ready to use. Combine the glacéed fruits and liqueur in a small, shallow bowl, turn the pieces of fruit about with a spoon, then set aside to marinate at room temperature while you make the soufflé base.

In a heavy 2½- to 3-quart enameled saucepan, stir the flour and ¼ cup of the milk together with a wire whisk until the flour has completely absorbed the milk, then beat in the remaining ½ cup of milk and ½ cup of sugar. Whisking constantly, cook over moderate heat until the sauce comes to a boil. Lower the heat, and cook for 2 to 3 minutes until it thickens heavily. Remove the pan from the heat and beat in the remaining 3 tablespoons of butter. Let the mixture cool for 5 to 10 minutes.

Drain the marinated fruits into a bowl through a fine sieve, whisk the liquid into the sauce, and reserve the fruit. Beating constantly, add the vanilla and then the egg yolks, one at a time.

With a wire whisk or a rotary or electric beater, beat the egg whites until they are stiff enough to stand in firm, unwavering peaks on the beater when it is lifted from the bowl. Stir 2 large spoonfuls of the egg whites into the sauce; then pour the sauce over the rest of the egg whites and, with a spatula, fold them together gently but thoroughly with an over-under cutting rather than a stirring motion. Fold in the reserved marinated fruits and pour the soufflé into the chilled dish, smoothing the top with a rubber spatula.

Place the dish in the oven on top of the hot baking sheet and immediately turn the heat down to 375°. Bake for 25 minutes, or until the soufflé is golden brown and puffed above the dish.

Meanwhile, roll the strawberries in the superfine sugar to coat them on all sides. When the soufflé has baked its allotted time, without removing the dish from the oven, quickly but carefully arrange the sugared berries in a ring around the top of the soufflé. Bake about 5 minutes more, or until the berries are lightly glazed. Serve at once.

Mont Blanc aux marrons
CHESTNUT PURÉE ON MERINGUE WITH WHIPPED CHANTILLY CREAM

To serve 8

2 pounds fresh chestnuts
2½ cups water
2 cups milk
A 1½-inch piece of vanilla bean
  (see Glossary)
⅔ cup sugar
1 tablespoon unsalted butter, softened

1 to 2 tablespoons heavy cream
  (optional)
A 7-inch meringue round made with
  3 egg whites, 6 tablespoons of
  sugar and 1½ teaspoons cornstarch
  (see Dacquoise, page 144)
Crème Chantilly (see fraises
  Romanoff, page 125)

Preheat the oven to 450°. With a small, sharp knife, cut a deep crisscross on the top of each chestnut. Spread the nuts out in a single layer in a shallow baking pan and pour in about ¼ cup of water—just enough to fill the bottom of the pan. Roast the chestnuts for 10 minutes, or until they pop open. Turn off the oven and remove half the nuts from the pan. While the chestnuts are still hot, remove their shells and inner brown membranes with a small, sharp knife. Then peel the remaining hot chestnuts in the same fashion.

In a heavy 3- to 4-quart saucepan, combine 2 cups of water, the milk and vanilla bean, and bring to a simmer over moderate heat. Drop in the chestnuts. The liquid should cover them by about 2 inches; if not, add

Continued on next page

more water and milk in equal proportions. Reduce the heat to low, and simmer the chestnuts partially covered for about 30 minutes, or until they are tender enough to crumble when mashed against the side of the pan. Drain the chestnuts in a sieve and purée them through the medium disc of a food mill or through a ricer into a deep bowl.

Dissolve the sugar and the remaining ¼ cup of water in a small saucepan and, stirring constantly, bring to a boil over moderate heat. Boil briskly, uncovered and undisturbed, until the syrup reaches a temperature of 236° on a candy thermometer, or until a few drops spooned into cold water immediately form a soft ball.

Pour the syrup in a slow, thin stream into the puréed chestnuts, beating vigorously with a large spoon or an electric mixer. When the syrup has all been absorbed and the mixture is a smooth, thick paste, beat in the butter. If the chestnut mixture seems too dense to put through a ricer easily, beat in a little heavy cream, adding it 1 teaspoon at a time.

Force the purée, ½ cup at a time, through a ricer into a shallow 7-inch ring mold set on a piece of wax paper, moving the ricer around the pan to distribute the strands evenly. When all of the chestnut mixture has been put through the ricer, scrape up any strands of chestnut from the wax paper, and again force them through the ricer into the mold. Do not pat or pack the chestnut strands into the mold. Cover the mold with foil or plastic wrap and refrigerate until thoroughly chilled.

To unmold and serve the *Mont Blanc aux marrons,* place the meringue round gently over the mold and invert a flat serving plate on top of the meringue. Grasping the plate and mold carefully together, turn them over. The *Mont Blanc aux marrons* should slide out easily. Fill the center of the ring with *crème Chantilly,* piping it through a pastry bag fitted with a decorative tip or spooning it into place and swirling the top attractively with a spatula. Serve at once.

Bombe Marinette
MOLDED VANILLA ICE CREAM WITH STRAWBERRY MOUSSE FILLING

To serve 10 to 12

2 quarts vanilla-flavored brick ice cream

If the ice cream is solidly frozen, place it in the refrigerator and let it soften slightly; do not, however, allow it to reach the point of melting. Cut the ice cream into ½-inch-thick slices and quickly press them, firmly against the bottom and sides of a decorative 2-quart hollow mold until the entire surface is covered. Make sure the ice cream fills all the contours of the mold, then with a spatula, smooth the ice cream to create a shell ½ inch thick. (Freeze the remaining slices for use later.) Place the mold in the freezer for one hour, or until the ice-cream shell is completely firm. Meanwhile, prepare the strawberry mousse.

5 cups fresh ripe strawberries, hulled and wiped with a damp cloth

6 egg yolks

¾ cup plus 2 tablespoons sugar

2 tablespoons water

2 tablespoons imported kirsch

1 tablespoon strained fresh lemon juice

1 cup heavy cream, chilled

MOUSSE DE FRAISES (STRAWBERRY MOUSSE) : Select the 8 most perfect berries, cover with foil or plastic wrap, and refrigerate to use as garnish for the finished *bombe*. With a sharp knife, cut 1 cup of the strawberries into ⅛-inch-thick slices; set aside. Purée the remaining berries through the fine disc of a food mill, or rub them through a fine sieve with the back of a spoon.

With a wire whisk or a rotary or electric beater, beat the egg yolks in a deep bowl for 3 or 4 minutes, or until the yolks form a slowly dissolving ribbon when the beater is lifted from the bowl.

In a heavy 2- to 3-quart enameled or stainless-steel saucepan, combine the sugar and water, and stir over moderate heat. When the sugar dissolves, add the strawberry purée. Stirring constantly, cook until the strawberry syrup reaches a temperature of 230° on a candy thermometer, or until a few drops spooned into cold water immediately separate into coarse threads.

Beating constantly, pour the hot syrup into the egg yolks in a slow thin stream and continue to beat until the mixture cools to room temperature. Beat in the kirsch and lemon juice.

In a chilled bowl, whip the cream with a whisk or a rotary or electric beater until it is stiff enough to stand in soft peaks on the beater when it is lifted from the bowl. Scoop the cream over the strawberry mixture and, with a rubber spatula, fold them together gently but thoroughly, using an over-under cutting motion rather than a stirring motion. Carefully fold in the reserved cup of strawberry slices.

FINAL ASSEMBLY: Pour the strawberry mousse mixture into the center of the mold and return the mold to the freezer for 2 or 3 hours until the mousse is firm. Then slightly soften the remaining ice cream slices in the refrigerator and place enough of them over the mousse to cover the mold completely. (Freeze any remaining ice cream for another use.) Smooth and flatten the top with a spatula. Cover with foil or plastic wrap and freeze the *bombe* for at least 6 hours, or until it is firm and set.

To unmold and serve the *bombe,* dip the mold briefly into hot water. Place a chilled serving plate upside down over the mold and, grasping plate and mold firmly together, invert them, rapping them sharply on the table. The *bombe* should slide out easily. Arrange the reserved whole strawberries attractively in a ring on top of the ice cream and serve the *bombe* immediately.

Mille-feuille
NAPOLEON

To make one 12-by-5-inch cake

Pâte feuilletée (page 148)

Preheat the oven to 375°. On a lightly floured surface, roll the chilled *pâte feuilletée* dough into a rectangle 17 inches long, 14 inches wide and ⅛ inch thick. Lift the dough and turn it at right angles after each rolling, sprinkling a little flour over and under it to prevent it from sticking. With your hands transfer the dough to a baking sheet lined with wax paper. Gather any scraps of remaining dough into a ball and freeze it or refrigerate it for another use *(see fleurons, page 144)*.

With a ruler and sharp knife, trim the dough on the baking sheet into a rectangle exactly 15 inches long and 13 inches wide. Pierce the dough in 9 places, 3 in a row, with a table fork, pressing the tines completely through it. Bake in the middle of the oven for 15 to 20 minutes until the "thousand-leaf" pastry has puffed and is golden brown. Remove the pastry from the oven and let it cool on the baking sheet.

CRÈME PÂTISSIÈRE

4 cups milk	¾ cup sugar
½ cup cornstarch	4 teaspoons vanilla
6 large eggs	1 cup heavy cream, chilled

CRÈME PÂTISSIÈRE (PASTRY CREAM): In a large bowl beat ½ cup of the milk and the cornstarch to a paste with a whisk, then beat in the eggs one at a time. In a heavy 1½- to 2-quart enameled saucepan, combine the remaining 3½ cups of milk with the sugar and bring it to a boil over moderate heat. Whisking the milk vigorously, pour in the egg mixture in a very slow thin stream. Continue to whisk until the mixture comes to a boil and thickens heavily. Lower the heat and continue to beat for 2 or 3 minutes until any lumps disappear and the mixture is perfectly smooth. Remove the pan from the heat, stir in the vanilla and set aside to cool to room temperature.

Just before you assemble the Napoleon, pour the heavy cream into a large chilled bowl. Beat with a wire whisk or a rotary or electric beater until the cream is thick enough to stand in firm unwavering peaks on the beater when it is lifted from the bowl. Stir 2 generous spoons of the cream into the egg mixture, then pour the egg mixture over the remaining cream. With a rubber spatula, fold the two together gently but thoroughly. Set aside.

GLACE ROYALE

1 large egg white	sugar
1½ cups sifted confectioners'	1 teaspoon strained fresh lemon juice

GLACE ROYALE (ROYAL ICING): With a wire whisk or a rotary or electric beater, beat the egg white and ½ cup of the confectioners' sugar together in a deep bowl until they begin to thicken. Beating constantly, gradually add the remaining cup of confectioners' sugar. Add the lemon juice and continue to beat until the icing is thick enough to form unwavering peaks on the beater when it is lifted from the bowl.

1 ounce semisweet chocolate

FINAL ASSEMBLY: With a long, sharp knife, carefully slice the sheet of pastry crosswise into thirds, forming three rectangles 13 inches long and 5 inches wide. Set one layer, right side up, on a platter large enough to work on. Spread half of the pastry cream smoothly over the pastry. Cover the pastry cream with a second layer of pastry, right side down, pressing it gently to anchor it in place. Cover the pastry with the remaining pastry cream, then put the top layer in place, right side down, and press it gently to secure it and make it level. If necessary trim the sides of the cake so that they are even.

Ice the top of the *mille-feuille* with the *glace royale,* spreading it evenly with a metal spatula. You may then decorate the icing with melted chocolate as shown in the diagram below, piping it through a pastry tube with a very fine plain tip or through a wax paper cone of your own fashioning and then lightly running a knife across the liner. Carefully transfer the cake to a serving platter with a large, metal spatula.

Mille-feuille should be served as soon as possible after assembling; the pastry becomes soggy as it sits. If it has to wait at all refrigerate the cake to keep the cream firm. To serve, cut the cake crosswise at about 2-inch intervals into 6 rectangular pieces.

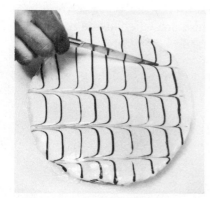

After a *mille-feuille* or Napoleon cake is baked, filled and glazed *(recipe opposite)*, it can be decorated with the feathery chevronlike pattern shown at right above. First stripe the top of the cake by piping delicate parallel lines of melted chocolate about 1½ inches apart over the glaze. To create the chevron design, first draw the dull edge of a knife blade lightly across the stripes from the right side of the cake to the left at 2-inch intervals *(left)*, barely cutting through the surface of the glaze. Then draw the knife across the stripes in the opposite direction *(right)*, midway between the first cuts.

Gâteau moka

GENOESE LAYER CAKE WITH MOCHA-FLAVORED BUTTER CREAM

To make one 9-inch cake

GÉNOISE
3 tablespoons butter, melted

2 tablespoons, plus ½ cup flour
½ cup cornstarch
6 eggs at room temperature
1 cup sugar

GÉNOISE (GENOESE CAKE): Preheat the oven to 375°. With a pastry brush, spread 1 tablespoon of the melted butter over the bottom and sides of two 9-inch-round cake pans. Sprinkle 1 tablespoon of flour into each pan, tipping the pan from side to side to spread it evenly. Invert the pans and rap them sharply on a table to remove the excess flour. Sift the remaining ½ cup of flour and the cornstarch together onto a long strip of wax paper and set aside.

Place a large heatproof mixing bowl over a pan of hot water off the heat. Add the eggs and 1 cup of sugar to the bowl and, with a wire whisk or a rotary or electric beater, beat them vigorously until they are thick and foamy and are lukewarm. Remove the bowl from the pan and continue to beat until the egg mixture has almost tripled in volume. It should be thick enough to stand in peaks when the beater is lifted from the bowl. (This will take about 15 minutes with an electric beater, and may require as much as 30 minutes of continuous beating by hand.)

With a rubber spatula, gently and gradually fold in the flour-and-cornstarch mixture, making sure each addition is completely incorporated before adding more. Stir in the remaining 2 tablespoons of melted butter, 1 teaspoon at a time.

Pour the batter into the buttered and floured pans, spreading it evenly and smoothing the top with the spatula. Bake in the middle of the oven for 10 minutes, then reduce the heat to 350° and continue baking for 30 minutes longer, or until the cakes have puffed and their sides have begun to come away from the sides of the pans.

Remove the cakes from the oven and let them cool in the pans for 3 or 4 minutes. Turn the cakes out on wire racks to cool completely.

CRÈME AU BEURRE MOKA
4 egg yolks
1 cup unsalted butter, softened
1½ cups sugar
2 tablespoons light corn syrup
½ cup water
3 tablespoons instant *espresso* coffee

3 tablespoons sugar
2 tablespoons instant *espresso* coffee
3 tablespoons water
1 cup sliced almonds, toasted *(see poires Bourdaloue, page 146)*

CRÈME AU BEURRE MOKA (MOCHA BUTTER CREAM): In a large bowl, beat the 4 egg yolks with a wire whisk or a rotary or electric beater for 2 or 3 minutes. Then cream the cup of softened butter in another bowl by mashing and beating it against the sides of the bowl with a large spoon until it is light and fluffy. Place the butter in the refrigerator until ready to use; it should still be soft but not oily at that point.

Combine the 1½ cups sugar, corn syrup, ½ cup water and 3 tablespoons of instant coffee in a small saucepan, and, stirring constantly, bring to a boil over moderate heat. Boil briskly without stirring until the syrup reaches a temperature of 236° on a candy thermometer, or until a few drops spooned into ice water immediately form a soft ball.

At once pour the hot syrup in a thin stream into the egg yolks, beating constantly. Continue beating for 10 to 15 minutes, until the mixture becomes a thick, smooth cream and has cooled completely. Then beat in the creamed butter, a tablespoon or so at a time. Cover the bowl and refrigerate for at least 30 minutes; before using, the cream should be firm enough to spread easily.

FINAL ASSEMBLY: Slice each of the cakes in half horizontally with a large, sharp, preferably a serrated knife, to make four 9-inch layers. Dissolve the 3 tablespoons of sugar and 2 tablespoons of instant coffee in 3 tablespoons of water. Invert a 9-inch cake pan on a flat surface and spread 1 teaspoon of the chilled butter cream over the middle of the pan. Place one layer of cake, cut side up, on top of the pan; the butter cream will act as an adhesive to hold it in place. Brush 1 tablespoon of the instant-coffee mixture evenly over the cake, then spread it with a ¼-inch layer of the butter cream. Repeat this layering twice, brushing the cake layers with the instant-coffee mixture, spreading them with butter cream each time.

Set the last layer of cake over the butter cream cut side down, so that the flatter and firmer side is on top. Spread the top and sides of the cake with butter cream. If you like, set aside about ½ cup of the butter cream for decorating the top of the cake. Spoon the butter cream into a pastry bag with a decorative tip and pipe a design around the top edge of the cake. With a small, plain tip you can also pipe lattice strips over the top. If at any time during the assembly the butter cream becomes too soft, refrigerate it and the cake until both are firm enough to handle easily. When the cake is completely assembled, hold it in one hand on the cake pan and with the other hand press the toasted almonds gently against the sides. Loosen the bottom of the cake from the inverted pan with a long, thin knife and carefully transfer the cake to a serving plate with a large spatula. Refrigerate the cake until 15 minutes before serving.

Gâteau moka can be decorated with mocha coffee beans made with almond paste. If you would like to present the cake in this fashion, combine 2 tablespoons of water, 1 tablespoon of sugar and 1 tablespoon of instant coffee. Mix well, then add 1 tablespoon of almond paste and enough confectioners' sugar to make a firm ball. Roll the ball into a pencillike cylinder about ¼ inch in diameter and cut it into ½-inch lengths. Then shape each piece into an oval "coffee bean" and make an indentation along the center of each with the dull edge of a knife. Arrange the "beans" at equal intervals in a ring around the top edge of the cake.

Gâteau Saint-Honoré
CREAM PUFF AND PASTRY CREAM CAKE

To serve 10

PÂTE SUCRÉE
1 cup plus 2 tablespoons all-purpose
    flour
1 tablespoon sugar
¼ teaspoon salt

6 tablespoons unsalted butter,
    chilled and cut into ½-inch bits
    plus 1 tablespoon butter, softened
2 tablespoons vegetable shortening,
    chilled and cut into ½-inch bits
3 to 4 tablespoons ice water

PÂTE SUCRÉE (SWEET PASTRY): In a large mixing bowl combine 1 cup of flour, 1 tablespoon of sugar, ¼ teaspoon of salt, the 6 tablespoons of butter bits and the vegetable shortening. With your fingertips rub the flour and fat together until they look like flakes of coarse meal. Do not over-blend or let the mixture become oily.

Pour 3 tablespoons of ice water over the mixture all at once, toss together lightly and gather the dough into a ball. If the dough crumbles, add up to 1 tablespoon more ice water by drops until the particles adhere. Dust the pastry dough with a little flour and wrap it in wax paper. Refrigerate for at least 30 minutes before using.

With a pastry brush, spread the tablespoon of softened butter over a large baking sheet. Sprinkle 2 tablespoons of flour over the butter, tipping the sheet to coat it evenly. Then invert the sheet and rap it sharply to remove the excess flour.

On a lightly floured surface, pat the dough into a rough circle about 1 inch thick. Dust a little flour over and under it and roll it out, from the center to within an inch of the far edge of the pastry. Lift the dough and turn it clockwise about 2 inches; roll again from the center to within an inch or so of the far edge. Repeat—lifting, turning, rolling—until you have created a rough circle about 10 to 11 inches in diameter and no more than ¼ inch thick.

Roll the dough loosely over the rolling pin, lift it and unroll it carefully on the buttered baking sheet. With a pastry wheel or sharp knife, and using a pie tin or plate as a guide, cut the dough into a 9-inch round. Remove and discard the excess dough, then prick the pastry all over with the tines of a table fork, but do not pierce through it completely. Refrigerate the pastry while you make the *pâte à choux*.

PÂTE À CHOUX
6 eggs
1½ cups water
12 tablespoons unsalted butter, cut
    into ½-inch bits plus 1

tablespoon butter, softened
1 tablespoon sugar
¼ teaspoon salt
1½ cups plus 2 tablespoons all-
    purpose flour

PÂTE À CHOUX (PUFF PASTE): Break one egg into a small bowl, beat lightly with a fork and set aside. In a heavy 2-quart saucepan, bring 1½ cups of water, 12 tablespoons of butter bits, 1 tablespoon of sugar and ¼ teaspoon of salt to a boil over high heat, stirring occasionally. As soon as the butter has completely melted, pour in the 1½ cups of flour all at once, remove the pan from the heat, and beat vigorously with a wooden spoon for 2 or 3 minutes until the paste moves freely with the spoon and pulls away from the bottom and sides of the pan in a mass.

Use the spoon to make a well in the center of the paste. Break an egg into the well and beat it into the paste. When this egg has been completely absorbed, add the 4 remaining eggs, one at a time—beating well after each egg is added. The finished paste should be smooth, shiny and just thick enough to fall slowly from the spoon in a thick strand when it is lifted out of the pan. To achieve this consistency, add as much of the reserved beaten egg as necessary, beating it in by the tablespoonful. (The paste, covered with plastic wrap, may be safely kept at room temperature for several hours before baking if you like.)

When you are ready to bake the *pâte à choux,* preheat the oven to 425°. Brush a large baking sheet with the tablespoon of softened butter. Sprinkle 2 tablespoons of flour over the sheet, invert and rap the sheet sharply to remove the excess flour.

Spoon the *pâte à choux* into a pastry bag fitted with a ½-inch plain tip and pipe the paste onto the *pâte sucrée* base, creating a ring about ½ inch wide and ¼ inch or so from the outside edges of the base. Pipe the remaining *pâte à choux* onto the buttered baking sheet into puffs about 1½ inches in diameter and 1 inch high, spacing them approximately 2 inches apart. (There should be about 15.)

Place the baking sheets side by side on the middle shelf of the oven if it is wide enough to accommodate them. If the oven is too narrow, bake the *pâte sucrée* base first, then bake the individual cream puffs later. Keep the puffs at room temperature while waiting. In either case use the following sequence of oven temperatures. Bake at 425° for 8 minutes, reduce the heat to 350° and, with the point of a small knife, prick the bubbles that have formed in the *pâte sucrée.* Continue baking for 15 to 20 minutes longer, or until the crust base is golden brown and the ring and puffs are firm and dry to the touch. Turn off the oven and let the pastry rest for 15 minutes to allow it to become dry and crisp. With a wide metal spatula, carefully slide the crust base and the individual puffs onto wire cake racks to cool to room temperature.

CARAMEL	½ cup water
2 cups sugar	⅛ teaspoon cream of tartar

CARAMEL: When the base and puffs have cooled completely, prepare the caramel. In a 1- to 1½-quart enameled cast-iron or copper saucepan, bring the 2 cups of sugar, ½ cup of water and cream of tartar to a boil over moderate heat, stirring until the sugar dissolves. Boil the syrup briskly until it turns a rich golden tealike color. This may take 10 minutes or more. Watch carefully and do not let the sugar burn; it colors very quickly. (As the syrup bubbles up around the sides of the pan, brush the sugar

Continued on next page

crystals back down with a hair bristled [not nylon] pastry brush that has been dipped into cold water.)

As soon as the syrup reaches the proper color, remove the pan from the heat and place it in a wide pot half filled with hot water. This will keep the caramel fluid and warm.

Working quickly but carefully, pick up one puff at a time with tongs and submerge the top in the caramel. Hold the puff in place over the ring on the pastry crust and let the excess caramel drip off the puff onto the ring. When the caramel stops flowing freely, carefully set it glazed side up over the drops of caramel on the ring. (The whole procedure is somewhat like anchoring a candle in hot wax.) Place the glazed puffs side by side completely around the ring. There should be several puffs left over; glaze one of the extra puffs to decorate the center of the cake and set it aside on a plate. The cake may now be kept at room temperature for 3 or 4 hours.

CRÈME SAINT-HONORÉ

2 cups milk	6 egg whites
1 whole vanilla bean, or substitute	¼ cup Grand Marnier or other
2 teaspoons vanilla extract	orange-flavored liqueur
6 egg yolks	1 envelope unflavored gelatin
½ cup sugar	⅓ cup water
⅓ cup flour	1½ cups heavy cream, chilled
A pinch of salt	½ cup confectioners' sugar

CRÈME SAINT-HONORÉ (SAINT-HONORÉ PASTRY CREAM): In a 2- to 3-quart enameled cast-iron or copper saucepan, heat the milk and vanilla bean over moderate heat until small bubbles appear around the edge of the pan. Remove the pan from the heat and cover to keep the milk warm.

With a wire whisk or a rotary or electric beater, beat the egg yolks and ½ cup of sugar together until the yolks are thick enough to fall in a ribbon when the beater is lifted from the bowl. Beating constantly, gradually sift in ⅓ cup of flour. When the flour is absorbed, remove the vanilla bean from the milk and pour in the warm milk in a thin stream, beating all the while. Immediately pour the mixture back into the saucepan.

Stirring deeply along the sides and into the bottom of the pan with a whisk or a wooden spoon, bring to a simmer over moderate heat. Do not let the pastry cream come near a boil at any point, but simmer it long enough to remove any taste of raw flour, about 5 minutes. Remove the pan from the heat and strain the hot pastry cream into a large bowl.

Then, working quickly, add a pinch of salt to the egg whites in another bowl and, with a wire whisk or a rotary or electric beater, beat until they are just stiff enough to form unwavering peaks on the beater when it is lifted from the bowl. Scoop about ¼ of the egg whites at a time over the hot pastry cream, stirring after each addition until no trace of white shows. Stir in the Grand Marnier and set the pastry cream aside to cool to room temperature.

Complete the pastry cream no more than an hour before you plan to serve the cake. Sprinkle the gelatin into a heatproof measuring cup or small bowl filled with ⅓ cup of cold water. When the gelatin has softened for 2 or 3 minutes, set the cup or bowl in a small pan of simmering water and, stirring constantly, cook over low heat until the gelatin dissolves completely. Remove the pan from the heat but leave the cup or bowl of gelatin in the water to keep it fluid.

With a wire whisk or a rotary or electric beater, whip 1½ cups of chilled heavy cream until it begins to thicken. Sprinkle in the ½ cup of confectioners' sugar and continue beating until the cream is stiff enough to form soft peaks on the beater when it is lifted from the bowl. Beat in the dissolved gelatin.

Scoop the whipped-cream mixture over the pastry cream and, with a rubber spatula, fold them together gently but thoroughly, using an over-under cutting motion rather than stirring. Taste for flavoring and refrigerate for at least 30 minutes.

CRÈME CHANTILLY | 1 tablespoon confectioners' sugar
½ cup heavy cream, chilled | ½ teaspoon vanilla extract

CRÈME CHANTILLY (CHANTILLY CREAM): In a large chilled bowl, beat ½ cup of chilled heavy cream with a wire whisk or a rotary or electric beater until it begins to thicken. Sprinkle the top with 1 tablespoon of confectioners' sugar and ½ teaspoon of vanilla extract, and continue beating until the cream is very stiff and stands in firm peaks on the beater when it is lifted from the bowl. Refrigerate until ready to use.

FINAL ASSEMBLY: Carefully slide the puff-topped cake onto a serving plate with a large metal spatula.

With the point of a skewer gently make a hole near the base of each individual cream puff from the inside edge of the ring. Spoon one third of the pastry cream into a pastry bag fitted with a ¼-inch plain tip and carefully fill each puff with a little of the cream. To prevent the puffs from crushing or loosening at this stage, hold each one lightly with one hand while filling it with the other. (Fill the reserved glazed cream puff with crème Saint-Honoré and set it aside.)

Fill the center of the cake with the remaining crème Saint-Honoré, smoothing it evenly with a spatula and mounding the center slightly.

Decorate the top of the cake as fancifully as you like with the crème Chantilly piped through a pastry bag fitted with a star tip. Set the reserved cream puff in the center. If you like, surround the edge of the cake with spun sugar (page 141). (To serve gâteau Saint-Honoré as a birthday cake, insert a small candle in the center of each cream puff.)

Pâte brisée et pâte sucrée

SHORT-CRUST PASTRY AND SWEET SHORT-CRUST PASTRY

To make one 9-inch tart shell or
    eight to ten 2- to 3-inch tartlet shells

1½ cups all-purpose flour	plus 1 tablespoon butter, softened
¼ teaspoon salt	2 tablespoons vegetable shortening,
6 tablespoons unsalted butter,	chilled and cut into ¼-inch bits
chilled and cut into ¼-inch bits,	3 to 4 tablespoons ice water

PÂTE BRISÉE: In a large chilled bowl, combine the flour, salt, 6 table-spoons butter bits and vegetable shortening. With your fingertips rub the flour and fat together until they look like flakes of coarse meal. Do not let the mixture become oily.

Pour 3 tablespoons of ice water over the mixture all at once, toss to-gether lightly and gather the dough into a ball. If the dough crumbles, add up to 1 tablespoon more ice water by drops until the particles adhere. Dust the dough with a little flour and wrap it in wax paper. Refrigerate for at least 1 hour before using.

To prepare a baked but unfilled, or "blind," pie shell, spread 1 table-spoon of softened butter over the bottom and sides of a 9-inch fluted false-bottomed quiche pan 1 inch deep.

On a lightly floured surface, pat the dough into a rough circle about 1 inch thick. Dust a little flour over and under it and roll it out, from the center to within an inch of the far edge of the pastry. Lift the dough and turn it clockwise about 2 inches; roll again from the center to within an inch or so of the far edge. Repeat—lifting, turning, rolling—until the circle is about ⅛ inch thick and 12 inches in diameter. If the dough sticks to the surface, lift it with a metal spatula and sprinkle a little flour under it.

Roll the dough loosely over the rolling pin, lift it up and unroll it slackly over the buttered pan. Gently press the dough into the bottom and against the sides of the pan. Roll the pin over the rim of the pan, pressing down hard to trim off the excess dough. Chill for 1 hour.

Preheat the oven to 400°. Spread a sheet of buttered heavy-duty alu-minum foil across the tin and press it gently into the edges to support the sides of the pastry as it bakes. Bake on the middle shelf of the oven for 10 minutes, then remove the foil. Prick the bubbles that have puffed up in the pastry with the point of a skewer or small knife, then return it to the oven for about 10 minutes, or until it begins to brown. Remove the pastry from the oven and let it cool on a wire rack.

To bake tartlet shells, spread 1 tablespoon of softened butter over the bottom and sides of 8 to 10 tartlet tins each measuring 2 to 3½ inches across the top and about ½ inch deep.

Roll the dough out into a rough circle about ⅛ inch thick as de-scribed above and, with a 3- to 4-inch round fluted pastry cutter, cut the dough into rounds. Gently press each round of dough into the bottom and against the sides of a buttered tin. To support the sides of the pastry as it bakes, line each tartlet with a paper baking cup or a circle of buttered wax paper, and then fill the liner with uncooked rice almost to the top of the tin.

Place the tartlet tins side by side on a large baking sheet or jelly-roll pan and bake in the middle of the oven for 10 minutes. Discard the rice and remove the lining papers, then bake the tartlets about 5 minutes longer, or until golden. Gently turn the tartlets onto a wire rack to cool.

ADDITIONAL INGREDIENT FOR PÂTE SUCRÉE   4 teaspoons sugar

PÂTE SUCRÉE: To prepare a sweet pastry dough, simply add 4 teaspoons of sugar to the flour-and-fat mixture before adding the water. Proceed with the rest of the recipe exactly as described above.

Sucre filé
SPUN SUGAR

1 cup sugar   A pinch of cream of tartar
½ cup water

Before making the syrup, prepare a place in your kitchen to spin it. Place two wooden spoons at least 12 inches long parallel to one another and 18 to 24 inches apart on top of wax paper, with the bowls of the spoons weighted down on a counter or table and the handles projecting from the edge of the surface by 8 or more inches. (If you have no long wooden spoons, use long metal skewers instead.) Cover all the nearby floor and counter space with wax paper or newspapers to catch any drippings of syrup when you spin the sugar.

In a heavy 1- to 1½-quart saucepan, bring the sugar and water to a boil over moderate heat, stirring until the sugar dissolves. Cook briskly, uncovered and undisturbed, until the syrup reaches a temperature of 290° on a candy thermometer, or a few drops spooned into ice water immediately separate into flexible, but not brittle, threads. The syrup should remain absolutely clear. Remove the pan from the heat immediately.

Working quickly, grasp two table forks in one hand so the tines form a fairly straight row. Dip the tines of the fork into the hot syrup and let the excess drip off into the pan. Then, using a figure-eight motion, swirl the syrup over the protruding handles of the spoons. The syrup will quickly harden into glossy threads and cling to the handles. Let the threads accumulate on the handles to the desired thickness, and then sweep them up with both hands and lay them on a plate. Repeat the entire procedure until you have spun all of the syrup into threads. Spun sugar is used as nests for desserts or to veil them.

NOTE: To produce even longer strands of spun sugar, place the spoon handles farther apart—or instead of spoons use thin 3-foot long wooden poles. Rather than using two forks to spin the sugar, you may make a shaker by cutting the loops from a sauce whisk, leaving a cluster of straight wires 3 or 4 inches in length. Many professional confectioners prefer a shaker of wood studded with nails (see page 93 of the main volume).

Crêpes Suzette
DESSERT CRÊPES WITH GRAND MARNIER-FLAVORED SAUCE

To serve 8

CRÊPES
1¼ cups all-purpose flour
3 tablespoons sugar
4 eggs
1¾ cups milk

¼ cup Grand Marnier, Cointreau
or other orange-flavored liqueur
2 tablespoons unsalted butter,
melted and cooled, plus 6
tablespoons melted clarified
butter *(page 13)*

CRÊPES: To make the batter with an electric blender, combine the flour, 3 tablespoons sugar, eggs, milk, ¼ cup Grand Marnier and 2 tablespoons melted, cooled butter in the blender jar. Blend at high speed for a few seconds. Turn off the machine, scrape down the sides of the jar with a rubber spatula and then blend again for about 30 or 40 seconds. Pour the batter into a deep mixing bowl.

To make the crêpe batter by hand, stir the flour, sugar and eggs together in a mixing bowl and gradually stir in the milk and Grand Marnier. Beat with a wire whisk or a rotary or electric beater until the flour lumps disappear, then rub through a fine sieve into another bowl and stir in the melted, cooled butter.

Cover and refrigerate the batter for at least two hours before using it. To fry the crêpes, warm a 4- to 5-inch crêpe pan or skillet over high heat until a drop of water flicked into it splutters and evaporates instantly. With a hair bristled (not nylon) pastry brush, lightly grease the bottom and sides of the heated pan with a little of the melted clarified butter.

Stir the crêpe batter lightly with a wire whisk or a spoon; then, using a small ladle, pour about 2 tablespoons of the batter into the pan. Tip the pan from side to side so that the batter quickly covers the bottom; the batter will cling to the pan and begin to firm up almost immediately. At once tilt the pan over the bowl and pour off any excess batter; the finished crêpe should be paper-thin.

Cook the crêpe for a minute or so until a rim of brown shows around the edge. Turn it over with a spatula and cook the other side for a minute longer. Slide the crêpe onto a plate. Brush clarified butter on the pan again and make the remaining crêpes similarly. As the crêpes are finished, stack them one upon the other. The crêpes may be made hours ahead of time and kept, covered with plastic wrap, at room temperature.

SAUCE SUZETTE	¼ pound unsalted butter, softened
6 large sugar cubes	1 tablespoon sugar
1 large lemon	¼ cup Grand Marnier
1 or 2 large juice oranges	2 tablespoons dark rum

SAUCE SUZETTE: One at a time, infuse 3 of the sugar cubes with lemon oil by pressing and rubbing them into the surface of the lemon, turning each cube about to coat it on all sides. Similarly, infuse 3 sugar cubes with orange oil by rubbing them into the orange. Set the lemon aside for another use, but squeeze the orange. Strain the juice into a measuring cup; there should be ½ cup, if necessary squeeze another orange. Drop the 6 flavored sugar cubes into the orange juice and mash and stir until they dissolve completely. Set aside at room temperature.

In a deep bowl, cream the ¼ pound of softened butter with 1 tablespoon of sugar, beating and mashing them together against the sides of the bowl with the back of a large spoon until the mixture is light and smooth. Cover the bowl tightly with plastic wrap and refrigerate until it is ready to use.

FINAL ASSEMBLY: When you are ready to serve the crêpes suzette, complete them at the dinner table. Light an alcohol burner or table-top stove and set a 12-inch copper crêpe suzette or flambé pan over the flame. Place the plate of crêpes, the remaining ¼ cup of Grand Marnier and the dark rum conveniently beside the pan. (You may also measure the liqueur and rum ahead of time and combine them in a pitcher or cruet.)

Warm the creamed butter and sugar in the crêpe pan, stirring from time to time so that the mixture melts evenly without burning. Add the orange juice mixture and, stirring frequently, cook briskly until the sauce has been reduced to ½ cup.

With a serving fork in one hand, and a serving spoon in the other, lift up a crêpe and lay it in the sauce. Quickly turn the crêpe over and when both sides are moistened with sauce, fold it in half and then in half again to make a triangular shape. Push the finished crêpe to the side of the pan and repeat the procedure with the remaining crêpes, arranging them attractively in overlapping rows as they are sauced.

When you have folded as many of the crêpes as you plan to serve, carefully pour the Grand Marnier and rum into the sauce remaining in the pan. It may burst into flame spontaneously. If not, ignite the sauce with a match. Gently slide the pan back and forth over the heat until the flames die. Then spoon the sauce over the crêpes and serve at once. (Any extra unsauced crêpes may be wrapped tightly in foil and frozen. Defrost thoroughly and let them come completely to room temperature before separating and using them.)

Fleurons
PUFF PASTRY DECORATIONS

¼ to ½ recipe *pâte feuilletée*   *pâte feuilletée,* thoroughly
  (page 148) or scraps of unbaked   defrosted if frozen

Preheat the oven to 400°. On a lightly floured surface, roll the *pâte feuil-letée* into a rough rectangle about ⅛ inch thick, lifting and turning the dough at right angles after each roll.

"*Fleuron*" literally means any kind of flowerlike decorative ornament made of puff pastry. *Fleurons* are used to decorate the tops of *pâtés en croûte,* but they are usually associated with small crescent-shaped pastries. You may cut out any shape you like with a pastry cutter or small, sharp knife.

To shape crescents, cut a half circle of dough from the bottom edge of the rectangle with a 2- to 3-inch round, fluted pastry cutter. Set the half circle of dough aside. Place the cookie cutter ½ to 1 inch above the outline of the missing half circle, and cut out a crescent of dough. Place the crescent on a baking sheet lined with wax paper.

Repeat the process, cutting each crescent similarly about ½ to 1 inch above the outline of the last. Arrange the crescents about an inch apart on the baking sheet as you proceed. Then cut out another half circle from the bottom edge of the remaining rectangle of dough and set aside. Cut out as many more crescents as you like, following the identical procedure as before. Gather the scraps of dough together into a ball and refrigerate or freeze them for future use.

Refrigerate the crescents for about 30 minutes. Then bake in the middle of the oven for 8 to 10 minutes, or until they are puffed and golden brown. Serve at once, or let cool and serve at room temperature.

Dacquoise
MERINGUE LAYERS WITH ALMONDS AND MOCHA BUTTER CREAM FILLING

To make one 10-inch round cake   pulverized in a blender or with a
                                   nut grinder

6 egg whites   1 tablespoon cornstarch
12 tablespoons sugar   *Crème au beurre moka (opposite)*
¾ cup blanched almonds,   2 tablespoons confectioners' sugar

MERINGUES: Preheat the oven to 250°. Cover two large baking sheets with parchment baking paper and set them aside. (Or brush each sheet with 1 tablespoon of softened butter, sprinkle it with 2 tablespoons of flour and rap sharply to remove any excess flour.)

In a deep bowl, preferably of unlined copper, beat the egg whites with a wire whisk or a rotary or electric beater until they just begin to form soft peaks on the beater when it is lifted from the bowl. Beating constantly, slowly pour in 10 tablespoons of the sugar, and continue to beat for at least 5 minutes, or until the meringue is glossy and thick enough to form firm, unwavering peaks when the beater is lifted from the bowl. Combine the almonds, cornstarch and the remaining 2 tablespoons of sugar and, with a rubber spatula, fold them gently, but thoroughly into the meringue.

Spoon half of the meringue onto the center of a baking sheet and, with a spatula or knife, spread and smooth it into a circle about 10 inches in diameter and ½ inch thick. Make an identical circle of the remaining meringue mixture on the second baking sheet. Bake the meringues in the middle of the oven for 45 minutes, or until they are firm and dry but not brown. Remove them from the oven and let the meringues cool to room temperature. Then gently ease them off the paper or baking sheets with a wide spatula and transfer them to separate flat plates.

FINAL ASSEMBLY: Place one meringue round on a serving plate and, with a spatula or knife, spread two thirds of the *crème au beurre moka* smoothly over the surface of the meringue to within ½ inch of the edge. Put the remaining butter cream into a pastry bag fitted with a star tube and pipe a decorative border around the outside of the butter-cream layer. Gently place the second meringue layer on top, sprinkle with the confectioners' sugar and serve at once or refrigerate. The *Dacquoise* should not be refrigerated for more than 2 hours lest the meringue soften.

Crème au beurre moka
MOCHA BUTTER CREAM

To make about 2½ cups

5 egg yolks
16 tablespoons (2 quarter-pound sticks) unsalted butter, softened

⅔ cup sugar
⅛ teaspoon cream of tartar
⅓ cup water
1 tablespoon instant powdered coffee, preferably *espresso*

Beat the egg yolks for 2 to 3 minutes in a large bowl with a whisk or a rotary or electric beater. Then cream the softened butter in another bowl by mashing and beating it against the sides of the bowl with a large spoon until it is light and fluffy. Place the butter in the refrigerator until ready to use; it should still be soft but not oily at that point.

Combine the sugar, cream of tartar, water and coffee in a small saucepan and, stirring constantly, bring to a boil over moderate heat. Boil briskly without stirring until the syrup thickens and reaches a temperature of 236° on a candy thermometer, or until a drop spooned into ice water immediately forms a soft ball.

Immediately pour the hot syrup in a thin stream into the egg yolks, beating constantly. Continue beating for 10 to 15 minutes, until the mixture becomes a thick, smooth cream and has cooled completely. Then beat in the creamed butter, a tablespoon or so at a time. Cover the bowl and refrigerate for at least 30 minutes; before using, the cream should be firm enough to spread easily. The mocha butter cream is used as a filling for dessert pastries such as *Dacquoise (opposite)*.

Poires Bourdaloue

PEAR AND FRANGIPANE TART

To make one 9-inch tart

POIRES

4 cups cold water
2 cups sugar
A 2-inch piece of vanilla bean, split in half lengthwise

2 one-by-two-inch strips of lemon peel
2 tablespoons strained fresh lemon juice
3 large firm ripe pears, preferably Bosc pears

POIRES (PEARS): In a 3-quart enameled casserole, bring the water, 2 cups of sugar, vanilla bean, lemon peel and lemon juice to a boil over high heat, stirring until the sugar dissolves. Remove from the heat.

One at a time, peel the pears, cut them in half lengthwise and remove the stems and cores, dropping each pear into the syrup as you proceed. Shape one of the halves into a peachlike round by cutting off the stem end. The syrup should cover the pears completely; if necessary add a little water. Bring to a simmer over moderate heat, reduce to low, and poach partially covered for 10 to 15 minutes, or until the pears show only slight resistance when pierced deeply with the point of a small knife. Remove the pan from the heat and let the pears cool in the syrup. With a slotted spoon arrange the pears, cored side down, on a wire rack to drain.

FRANGIPANE

½ cup whole blanched almonds
2 cups milk
A 2-inch piece of vanilla bean, split in half lengthwise
2 eggs
2 egg yolks
¾ cup sugar
1 cup flour
6 tablespoons unsalted butter, cut into ½-inch bits
½ cup dry or stale macaroons

(about 6 macaroons), pulverized in a blender or with a rolling pin
½ cup imported kirsch
1½ cup apricot jam
¼ cup imported kirsch
A 9-inch *pâte brisée* pastry shell *(page 140)* baked in a fluted quiche pan
3 tablespoons finely chopped fresh blanched pistachios
1 dry or stale macaroon, finely crushed with a rolling pin

To toast the blanched almonds preheat the oven to 350°. Spread the nuts in a shallow roasting pan and toast them in the middle of the oven for about 5 minutes, or until golden brown, turning them occasionally. Pulverize the nuts in an electric blender or with a nut grinder or a mortar and pestle.

In a heavy 2- to 3-quart enameled-iron or copper saucepan, heat the milk and the vanilla bean over moderate heat until small bubbles appear around the edge of the pan. Remove the pan from the heat and cover.

With a wire whisk or a rotary or electric beater, beat the eggs and egg yolks together in a large bowl for a minute or two. Slowly add the sugar and continue to beat until the eggs are thick enough to fall in a ribbon when the beater is lifted from the bowl. Add the flour ¼ cup at a time.

When all the flour is absorbed, remove the vanilla bean from the milk and add the hot milk to the bowl in a thin stream, beating all the while. Immediately strain the mixture back into the saucepan.

Stirring deeply into the sides and bottom of the pan with a whisk or a wooden spoon, simmer over moderate heat for 3 to 5 minutes until the mixture thickens into a smooth heavy cream. Do not let the cream boil at any point but simmer it long enough to remove any taste of raw flour.

Pour the mixture into a bowl and stir in the 6 tablespoons of butter bits. Stir in the pulverized almonds and macaroons and the ½ cup of kirsch and let the frangipane cool to room temperature, stirring it every now and then to prevent a skin from forming on top. Then refrigerate it for 3 or 4 hours until thoroughly chilled.

Just before assembling the tart, rub the apricot jam through a fine sieve into a small saucepan with the back of a spoon. Add ¼ cup of kirsch and, stirring constantly, heat the mixture until it clears.

To assemble the tart, spread a thin layer of the apricot glaze in the bottom of the pastry shell with a pastry brush. Spoon in the frangipane cream, spreading and smoothing it out with a spatula. Set the pear round in the center of the cream and around it place the pear halves, arranging them in such a way that their stem ends face the central pear round and radiate from it like the spokes of a wheel. Press the pears gently into the cream. Brush the glaze over the pears and cream. Mix the pistachios and the crushed macaroon and sprinkle them over the pears. Refrigerate again. Remove the tart from the refrigerator about 15 minutes before serving.

Sabayon
EGG DESSERT SAUCE WITH WINE AND KIRSCH

To make about 1½ cups	½ cup sugar
	½ cup dry white wine
4 large egg yolks	1 tablespoon imported kirsch

Combine the egg yolks and sugar in the top of a double boiler above simmering water or in a deep heatproof bowl set in a shallow pan of barely simmering water. Beat with a wire whisk or a rotary or electric beater until the mixture is thick and fluffy. Beating constantly, pour the wine into the egg-yolk mixture in a slow, thin stream, and continue beating until the mixture almost triples in volume and thickens enough to hold its shape lightly in a spoon. This may take 10 minutes or more. Do not let the mixture come anywhere near a boil at any time; if necessary, lift the pan or bowl from the heat for a minute or so to cool it.

Remove the pan from the heat, beat in the kirsch and taste for flavoring. Serve the sauce at once or, if it is to be served chilled, refrigerate it for at least 30 minutes before serving. *Sabayon* can be served warm or cold over soufflés, puddings, Bavarian creams or ladyfingers.

Pâte feuilletée

"THOUSAND-LEAF" OR PUFF PASTRY

4 cups sifted all-purpose flour
1 teaspoon salt
¼ teaspoon strained fresh lemon
   juice
1 to 1¼ cups ice water
4 tablespoons unsalted butter,
   softened, plus 3 quarter-pound
   sticks unsalted butter, slightly
   softened

Sift the flour and salt together into a deep mixing bowl and make a well in the center. Pour in the lemon juice and 1 cup of the ice water, add the 4 tablespoons of softened butter and, with a wooden spoon or your hands, gradually incorporate the flour. Continue to stir or knead the dough for 5 minutes, or until it can be gathered into a ball. If the dough crumbles, add up to ¼ cup more ice water, stirring it in 1 tablespoon at a time and using only enough to make the particles adhere.

Shape the dough into a ball. With a large, sharp knife, slash a cross in the middle of the ball, cutting about an inch deep into the dough. One at a time, push each quarter segment out and away from the center as if you were making a flower. Then, with your hands pat and shape the dough into a perfect 7-inch square about ½ inch thick. Wrap the dough in a dampened towel, then refrigerate it for about 30 minutes.

Meanwhile, beat the remaining 3 quarter-pound sticks of slightly softened butter together with a wooden spoon, just long enough to combine them. Turn the butter out on a sheet of wax paper. With your hands, shape the butter into a rough square about 1 inch thick. Then roll and shape the butter into a perfect 7-inch square. Flour the surface of the butter thoroughly and then wrap the butter in the wax paper and refrigerate for about 30 minutes, or until the dough and the butter feel equally firm when pressed gently with your fingers. Do not now, or at any other time in the preparation of the puff pastry, allow the dough or the butter to harden or become too soft. It should be just malleable.

On a lightly floured surface, roll the dough into a 14-inch square. Pat and shape the edges smooth with your fingertips. Center the square of butter diagonally on the dough so that the corners of the butter square bisect the sides of the dough square. Fold one corner of the dough at a time over the butter, thus enclosing it completely and creating a neat packet about 8 inches square.

Turn the packet over (seam side down) on the lightly floured surface. Then roll it out into a rectangle about 20 inches long and 12 inches wide. Starting at either of the narrow ends, fold the dough into thirds to form a 3-layered rectangular packet, reducing its dimensions to 6 by 12 inches. With a dry pastry brush, dust off any flour clinging to the outside surfaces of the pastry as you are making the folds so that no loose flour is rolled into the dough. Wrap the packet in a dampened towel and refrigerate for about 30 minutes.

Place the chilled packet of dough on the lightly floured surface and turn it so that one of the open ends faces you; roll it out once more to a 20-by-12-inch strip. Fold it into thirds as before, brushing the dough carefully as you fold it. Wrap and refrigerate the dough for 30 minutes.

To achieve a multilayered effect repeat this entire process three more times (for a total of five rollings), ending with the pastry folded into a 6-by-12-inch packet. (After each rolling, make light indentations along the edge of the packet with your thumb to indicate the number of times you have repeated the procedure.)

The pastry may be used at once or tightly covered with plastic wrap and kept in the refrigerator for 2 or 3 days or in the freezer for several months. If you freeze the pastry, let it soften in the refrigerator until it is pliable enough to retain the light imprint of your finger.

NOTE: If at any time during the rolling or folding, bits of butter break through the surface of the dough, sprinkle enough flour over the exposed butter to cover it. Generally, however, try to use as little flour as possible to coat the rolling surface. And brush away as much surface flour from the finished packets as you can to ensure a light, tender pastry. "Thousand-leaf" pastry is used to make *vol-au-vents (see ris de veau à la financière en vol-au-vent, page 106),* dessert pastry *(see mille-feuille, page 132)* and to make decorations for main dishes *(see fleurons, page 144).*

Crème anglaise
ENGLISH CUSTARD SAUCE

To make about 2 cups

2 cups milk

1 vanilla bean *(see Glossary)*
4 egg yolks
½ cup sugar

Combine the milk and vanilla bean in a heavy 2- to 3-quart enameled-iron or copper saucepan. Bring to a boil and immediately remove from the heat. Cover and set aside.

Beat the egg yolks and sugar together with a wire whisk or a rotary or electric beater until they are thick enough to form a slowly dissolving ribbon when the beater is lifted from the bowl. Remove the vanilla bean from the pan and gradually pour the hot milk into the yolks, whisking all the while. Pour the mixture into the saucepan and stir over low heat until the *crème anglaise* thickens lightly. (Do not let it come anywhere near a boil or it will curdle.)

The sauce may be served warm, at room temperature or chilled. *Crème anglaise* is served with cold Bavarian creams and puddings.

Recipe Index: English

NOTE: Size, weight and material are specified for pans in the recipes because they affect cooking results. A pan should be just large enough to hold its contents comfortably. Heavy pans heat slowly and cook food at a constant rate. Aluminum and cast iron conduct heat well but may discolor foods containing egg yolks, wine, vinegar or lemon. Enamelware is a fairly poor conductor of heat. Many recipes therefore recommend tin-lined copper or enameled cast iron, which do not have these faults.

Stocks and Sauces

Soups

Fish

Photographs on pages 44 and 133 by Mark Kauffman.
Drawings on pages 31, 64 and 96 by Matt Greene;
drawings on pages 53, 58, 70, 71, and 81 by Otto
van Eersel; drawings on pages 98 and 107 by Gloria
duBouchet.

Recipe Index: French

Stocks and Sauces

Soups

Fish

Fowl and Eggs

Meats

Vegetables

Desserts and Pastry

Printed in U.S.